Relational and Body Practices for Healing

Lifting the Burdens of the Past

Sharon Stanley

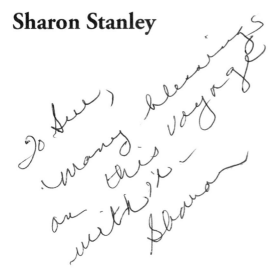

To Sue,
many blessings
on this voyage
with it —
Sharon

Routledge
Taylor & Francis Group

NEW YORK AND LONDON

First published 2016
by Routledge
711 Third Avenue, New York, NY 10017

and by Routledge
2 Park Square, Milton Park, Abingdon, Oxon, OX14 4RN

*Routledge is an imprint of the Taylor & Francis Group,
an informa business*

Library of Congress Cataloging-in-Publication Data
Stanley, Sharon, author.
    Relational and body-centered practices for healing trauma : lifting
the burdens of the past / by Sharon Stanley.
        pages cm.
    Includes bibliographical references and index.
    ISBN 978-1-138-90595-5 (hardback : alk. paper) —
    ISBN 978-1-138-90596-2 (pbk. : alk. paper) —
    ISBN 978-1-315-69236-4 (ebook)
    1. Stress Disorders, Traumatic—therapy.   2. Mind-Body Relations,
Metaphysical.   3. Psychotherapy—methods.   I. Title.
    RC552.T7
    616.85′210651—dc23
    2015032542

ISBN: 978-1-138-90595-5 (hbk)
ISBN: 978-1-138-90596-2 (pbk)
ISBN: 978-1-315-69236-4 (ebk)

Typeset in Garamond
by Apex CoVantage, LLC

Relational and Body-Centered Practices for Healing Trauma

Relational and Body-Centered Practices for Healing Trauma provides psychotherapists and other helping professionals with a new bodily-based clinical model for the treatment of trauma. This model synthesizes emerging neurobiological and attachment research with somatic, embodied healing practices. Tested with hundreds of practitioners in courses for more than a decade, the principles and practices presented here empower helping professionals to effectively treat people with trauma while experiencing a sense of mutuality and personal growth themselves.

Sharon Stanley, PhD, is an educator and psychotherapist in private practice on Bainbridge Island, Washington, where she also develops and facilitates courses on Somatic Transformation, a two-year curriculum for healing trauma.

Dedicated to the memory of Eileen Stanley

Contents

Preface

I can trace the roots of Somatic Transformation back to 1978, when my father called and asked me to come home and help care for my younger sister Eileen. A nineteen-year-old college student, Eileen was lifeguarding at a beach in Bellevue, Washington, when she was severely assaulted. Although the visible wounds healed in time, the impact of this trauma changed our lives. Despite her suffering, Eileen lived with joy and love. A gifted physical therapist, she became known as a "physical therapy whisperer," teaching colleagues to attend to the person rather than the trauma. Eileen not only showed me how to deeply and patiently connect with others, gently calling out the life force hidden in immobilized states, but she became the primary medical contributor and first coordinator of Somatic Transformation.

A number of other experiences have shaped the principles and practices of Somatic Transformation, including my work with the prevention of youth suicide in Tacoma and the discovery of phenomenology and its somatic, embodied approach at the University of Victoria. Following the completion of research that focused on the development of empathy in educators working with traumatized youth, I was invited to teach principles of neuroscience and somatic practices for healing trauma to Indigenous communities in Canada. As we worked together, the significance of their ancient ways of knowing and healing trauma began to take root with me over a number of years, and I recognized the power of nonverbal communication, participation in ceremony, the lived experience of traditional community, and a spirituality that valued interconnectivity with all. The teachings they offered to me led me to explore other ancient practices for healing trauma. A traditional Afro-Brazilian community invited me to learn and participate in their ceremonies, embodied practices of expression, love, and sensuality that were sustained through four hundred years of slavery. Participation in a Seattle study group for ten years with Allan Schore has grounded my interest in the phenomenology of traditional and Indigenous cultures with the emerging neuroscience of human attachment and regulation of intense emotions. Much of the emerging neurobiological information about trauma has been well known for centuries in the "teachings" of Indigenous Nations and in the stories, myths, and ceremonies of traditional and ancient cultures throughout the world.

As I have attempted to integrate my own lived experience and enrich my clinical and educational practice in healing trauma, I have tried to discern the essence of healthy human development, the life-changing interruptions to optimal development and culturally appropriate ways to heal those wounds. The curriculum of Somatic Transformation, a small-group educational process, presents emerging principles of neuroscience and fosters the development of relational somatic practices for healing trauma that are based on the wisdom known to human beings for centuries. I have taught Somatic Transformation to hundreds of mental health practitioners over the last ten years and synthesized the essential themes, concepts, and practices into this book.

Three primary interdependent themes are interwoven throughout this book:

Subjectivity. We must pay attention to, have respect for, and understand the profound significance of the bodily-based subjective knowledge of individuals. The effect of their lived experience is written in the functions of muscles, glands, bones, and the nervous system, and the structures of the developing brain. The human body holds the record of all that has been lived, including all encounters with others—stories of love and connection combine with moments of pain, anguish, and loss that the mind often "forgets" in order to survive. If we wish to know and heal the trauma of others, we need to know their ongoing subjective experience of their bodies.

Embodied Intersubjectivity. Embodied intersubjectivity, interpersonal sharing of specific subjective experience in the moment, requires practitioners to develop new ways of knowing by attending to fixed and changing perceptions; seeing, hearing, and feeling the ways the body communicates its truth. To assist another in processing trauma and resuming the interrupted growth and development from trauma, a sense of safety and interconnection is essential. Relationships that value authentic embodied intersubjective communications are at the core of healthy parenting, couples, families, friendship, and professional support.

Community. The support of the larger community and culture is essential to nurture and support the most wounded among us in the context of healing relationships. The actual interpersonal contributions of professional organizations, churches, schools, governments, and geographical communities can be distinguished from each other when we see their actions through the eyes and feelings of suffering human beings. Respect for the embodied subjective experience of individuals despite the disturbing effects of their trauma is at the heart of healing communities.

Each of these themes appears in this book in four distinct bodies of knowledge, each with its own language and forms of communication. The first is the changing language of the dominant culture, neuroscience, and its emerging interest and discovery in the less obvious, implicit ways of knowing. The second is the respect and incorporation for the rich and diverse language of Indigenous people and traditional ancient societies, spoken now by people of those traditions in the global re-vitalization of less dominant cultures, voices that reveal a commitment to phenomeno-logical ways of knowing through tradition-based, direct embodied experi-ence. The third language is the intimate communication of bodily-based lived experience that is first shared in the mother-infant attachment process and remains a fundamental need for all human beings, a form of contin-gent, collaborative communication that includes eye gaze, vocal prosody, gesture, and touch, women's ways of knowing that are now validated by science, but lie at the root of my own family and cultural traditions. The fourth voice is the language of Somatic Transformation, my attempt to synthesize essential human wisdom for professionals into somatic practices to consider as they assist people recover from trauma. I am humbled in this attempt as I recognize all that I do not know and have not included in this book.

The Bhagavad Gita—a seven-hundred-year-old Hindu scripture—advocates an inner way of knowing that differentiates between an uncon-scious experience of the body and the ability to witness autonomic changes in the body, an expansion of perception that promises freedom (Swami 1983). A primary theme of this book is the value and use of right-hemispheric ways of knowing and communicating with people who are suffering from relational and shock trauma and helping them restore the fluid, natural healing of optimal human growth and development that comes through embodied intersubjective relationships.

Reference

Bhaktivedanta Swami Prabhupada, A. C. 1983. *Bhagavad Gita As It Is*. Los Angeles: The Bhaktivedanta Book Trust.

Acknowledgments

I am deeply grateful for the contributions of my teachers, mentors, and colleagues, whose insight has helped shape Somatic Transformation and the friends and family who have supported me in the writing of this book. Delores Biblarz supported my vision to research the development of empathy in teachers working with traumatized youth. I give thanks to Don Knowles who invited me to conduct research in the doctoral program at the University of Victoria, Vance Peavy who opened the doors of phenomenology, and Lon McElroy and Nora Trace who guided the application of somatic phenomenology to lived experience. Peter Levine expanded my knowledge of somatic practices and Allan Schore leads the Seattle Study Group where I learned the theories of developmental neuroscience that guide relational somatic practices. I also hold profound gratitude for the generosity of First Nation sponsors who invited me to lead trauma trainings.

Eileen Stanley, Lisa Mortimore, Stacy Jenson, Penny Holland, Julie Kilpatrick, Kathy Haskin, and Erika Dorsey graciously helped coordinate live courses in Somatic Transformation, whose participants and facilitators significantly influenced the development of the concepts and practices in this book. Insights into the relational somatic practices presented here have been refined in interactions with clients for over forty years. I offer each person heartfelt thanks.

This book would not have come into existence without the midwifery of my dear friend and colleague, Trip Quillman. The manuscript has been patiently edited by my writing coach, Meredith Bailey. The illustrations were created in collaboration with Debbie and Brian Hulbert, Rose Goodman, and David Baker. Maria Stella and Susan Sweetwater assisted in assembling references. Su Russell has offered an unusual depth of friendship and support for this work for twenty-five years. Many thanks for patient friends on Bainbridge Island and Seattle. I am also grateful for Anna Moore, senior editor of Routledge, who has guided the book toward publication.

And finally, my amazing family, a tribe of fifty, including siblings and their families, my four children, their spouses, and eight grandchildren have given unbounded love, encouragement, and gracious forgiveness for my distraction. Many thanks to Jack Verharen who regularly offers inspiration and Connor Verharen who approved my description of our encounters following his medical trauma. I appreciate the honesty of Sam Verharen, the subtle humor of Coulter Quinn Verharen, the curiosity of Dane Verharen, the courage of William Kurtz, the intuition of Hatch McNabb, the fierce loving strength of Genoa Verharen, and the parents of these amazing grandchildren, Arthur and Lucy Cooke Verharen, Timothy and Juli Reynvaan Verharen, Tab and Sarah Verharen McNabb, and Michael and Jennifer Carstairs Verharen. And heartfelt gratitude to my own parents, Alice and Charles Stanley, and my aunts, uncles, and cousins that continue to inspire and guide me with their own vital and spirited lives.

Introduction

Somatic Transformation was developed through the collaboration of hundreds of scholar-practitioners interested in creating somatic healing practices inspired in part by the emerging research of the "new paradigm"—the neuroscience of relational human development (Schore 2012). Informed by extensive research describing the effect of traumatic experience on the development of the brain and the nervous system, this "new paradigm" offers the possibility of unifying the field of psychology with overarching theories and bodily-based practices that attend to people's perceptions of lived experience—aspects of our lives that have not yet come into conscious awareness.

With overarching evidence-based theories of human development, we can perceive human life through a multidimensional lens that can help us transcend vast cultural differences in our efforts to enter into authentic interpersonal relationships in helping professions—to suffer with another in a felt sense and to transform that suffering into wisdom. The principles of evidence-based theories of human development foster the creation of embodied practices from ancient, traditional cultures, current strategies of phenomenological methodology, and interventions drawn from the wisdom of contemporary bodywork.

Allan Schore, a prolific leader in the emerging field of interpersonal neurobiology, encourages helping professionals to move from an exclusive reliance on left-hemispheric ways of knowing and helping others to explore and develop clinical expertise in implicit, relational ways of knowing that are favored by the right hemisphere of the brain. The right hemisphere knows through contact with the direct phenomena of lived experience and is interested in the sensations, movements, emotions, and images that spontaneously emerge when we process internal and external events. Schore (2012, 12) writes, "Psychotherapy involves changes not in the cognitions of the patient's mind-brain machine but in the affective embodied experiences of his or her brain/mind/body." Affective embodied experiences are emotional experiences that are shared in relationships where people are observant of bodily-based cues to discern the meaning of lived experience.

Affective embodied experiences open us to an aspect of consciousness that transcends our habitual limited perceptions. We are moved, changed, and transformed as we surrender our abstract, logical, and sequential ways of knowing to the bodily-centered, emotional, and imaginal dynamics of our lived experience. An affective embodied experience of the brain, mind, and body in relationship opens us to direct, experiential, bodily-based changes that restore interrupted processes of growth and development. An affective embodied experience has the power to spontaneously shift trauma-based neurological states and stimulate an intrinsic vitality to transform the brain/mind/body patterns that formed with traumatic experience. Throughout this book we will explore how professional healers can expand and refine their ability to provide creative and engaging "affective embodied experiences" (Schore 2012) in the reconsolidation of traumatic memories.

The initial chapters of this book focus on neurological-based theories of human development and ways of thinking about trauma as interruptions of growth and development. The chapters that follow offer embodied somatic healing practices that link the emotional, symbolic, imaginal, reflective elements of right-hemispheric processing to uncouple the neural bonds of trauma and stimulate new creative interconnections within the brain and in interpersonal relationships, as well as a sense of presence within the environment. Throughout this book, case examples demonstrate theories and practices, and exercises offer opportunities to apply knowledge. Because many of the exercises are intended to be done with partners or small groups, it can be helpful to maintain a professional learning community to practice somatic techniques. I would suggest reading this book with a small group and stopping at regular intervals to engage in a dialogue regarding the concepts and taking time together to practice the exercises. More experienced groups can include experiential practice with the very real trauma that emerges in participants as they study dynamics of trauma.

Somatic Transformation is based on a two-person psychology (Schore 2012; Bromberg 2011; Delgado 2015), an embodied intersubjective relationship where each person's subjective lived experience influences the other. In a two-person psychology, a healing professional's dissociated trauma can strongly affect the outcome of a therapeutic encounter. It is critical for helping professionals to create authentic, supportive collegial relationships in which they can explore their own unacknowledged trauma and distorted perceptions and receive the support and encouragement to process their own intense, yet disembodied, emotions. Though Somatic Transformation is a two-person psychology, it can be expanded easily into triads and into enduring committed communities of small groups of people searching for authentic, meaningful, and embodied support for their own development—particularly those aspects that have been unconsciously limited by trauma. In the era of a multi-person relational and contingent change dynamic, we cannot rely on self-help strategies to resolve trauma that occurred in and through relationships. Personal disciplines, such as meditation, exercise, and nutrition prepare one for transformation of trauma; only intersubjective relationships can heal relational wounds.

References

Bromberg, P. M. 2011. *The Shadow of the Tsunami: and the Growth of the Relational Mind.* New York: Routledge.

Delgado, S., J. R. Strawn, and E. Pedapati. 2015. "Key Pioneers of Two Person Relational Psychology." In *Contemporary Psychodynamic Psychotherapy for Children and Adolescents: Integrating Intersubjectivity and Neuroscience,* 63–75. Heidelberg: Springer.

Schore, A. N. 2012. *The Science of the Art of Psychotherapy.* New York: Norton.

1 Trauma and Embodied Relational Therapy

> What is necessary is not that the initiated should learn something, but a transformation should come about in them, which makes them capable of receiving the teaching.
>
> (Simone Weil 1952, 83)

The Healer Within

"What do you think actually helps people heal from trauma?"

The question came from an insightful woman named Karolyn during a community dialogue on Somatic Transformation.

In response, I described a somatic—bodily—form of empathy that can emerge in interpersonal relationships that fosters transformation from one state of being to another. Somatic empathy communicates to people suffering from trauma that they are seen, felt, and understood just as they are, allowing them to *feel felt*. With somatic empathy the practitioner is receptive to another's suffering while offering containment, aliveness, and vitality in the moment, despite darkness and confusion. In an authentic relationship based on a somatic sense of empathy, practitioners are committed to *knowing the other in the other's own internal terms.*

"So interactions can become healing experiences for both," I concluded.

"Then we are all healers!" Karolyn replied, a smile on her face.

She is right: We each hold the human capacity to offer healing through our interactions. Yet without intentional empathy and mindful attention to the bodily-based cues that reveal our own subjectivity and that of other people, our innate power to heal others remains underdeveloped. We miss ordinary moments of possible restoration. An essential aspect of adult maturity, somatic empathy is achieved through a personal and communal struggle with the internal dynamics from trauma that threaten to separate and isolate us. Somatic ways of knowing and relating have formed the epistemology of diverse, flourishing cultures around the world and have been used to restore connection, vitality, and innate growth processes to trauma victims throughout history (Berman 1989).

What Is Somatic Transformation?

Soma is a Greek word that describes a unity of the body and mind. Somatic Transformation is a healing modality that incorporates bodily ways of knowing—our own as well as that of others—into consciousness, an ancient path for changing the imprint of trauma. The professional expertise necessary for somatic practice includes a left-hemispheric knowledge of neurobiology and a right-hemispheric development of embodiment, empathy, and intuition. Schore (2005) writes, "It is certainly true that the clinician's left brain conscious mind is an important contributor to the treatment process" and that current treatment is "now focusing intensely on implicit nonverbal communications, bodily-based affective states, and interactive regulation as essential change mechanisms within the therapeutic relationship" (25–27). As we explore the development of embodiment, empathy, and intuition, we will focus on the development of helping relationships where people can communicate with their bodies as well as words, resolve the emotional reaction of past trauma, and regulate current experiences of adversity, pain, sorrow, and joy.

The principles and practices of Somatic Transformation draw from a number of areas including the neuroscience of human development; interpersonal neurobiology (Cozolino 2014; Schore 2003a, 2003b, 2012; Siegel 1999, 2010; Kalsched 2013); phenomenological philosophy and methodology (Merleau-Ponty 1962); and somatic healing practices from traditional societies (Diamond 2012; Atleo 2004, 2011).

An emergent model, Somatic Transformation practices expand clinical expertise in six areas: embodiment, somatic awareness, somatic empathy, somatic inquiry, somatic intervention, and somatic reflection. These therapeutic practices engage mindful awareness of subtle changes in the inner worlds of clinicians as well as clients. Our inner world is shaped by our own subjective lived experience and coming to know the inner subjective world of another opens new ways of perceiving for both. Somatic practices attend to the suffering that endures from trauma and provides creative ways to resolve the conscious and hidden memories that can overwhelm one's inner subjective world.

The foundation for helping people suffering from trauma lies in the development of an empathic embodied relationship, a connection that provides the intuitive wisdom to respond to the person *in the moment* with resonance and contingency. Research in interpersonal neurobiology has revealed that injuries from trauma lie in the brain and body, not just the mind. We now know what traditional societies have always known: the brain changes through empathic relational experiences between individuals within caring communities and, particularly, in the repair of breaches in those relationships. Numerous studies confirm the value of empathic relationships in healing even the most difficult trauma (The Boston Change Process Study Group 2010).

The goal of Somatic Transformation is to create relationships of unusual safety, attunement, resonance, and coherence that can identify and creatively resolve the obstacles to right-hemispheric processing of lived experience that come with trauma. Mindful attention to the shifting, sensory-based inner world in the context of a trusted relationship initiates the transformation of trauma. Before we take a closer look at what trauma is, take a moment to explore your own somatic experience in Exercise 1.1: Embodiment—Sensory-Motor Awareness and Regulation on page 199 of the appendix. This exercise will give you a felt sense of the concepts discussed in this book.

What Is Trauma?

Since the Vietnam War, the word *trauma* has been used to describe a variety of adversities, overwhelming experiences with long-term, destructive effects on individuals and communities. People who have experienced war, terrorism, disaster, assault, poverty, and other forms of violence often communicate their distress through confusing behavior. Some may withdraw when it seems they should engage, or engage aggressively when it seems that a gentle approach would suffice. Posttraumatic behavior seems disconnected from present day reality, and it is. Time does not move on for people with unresolved trauma; they remain locked in the moment of impact and injury when development was interrupted. Traumatic memories remain active, even if they are not conscious, and live on in the body as implicit memories even if the mind has forgotten or intentionally forgiven the event.

Traumatic events fall into two overlapping categories: *Shocking adversities events* include abuse, assault, injury, disaster, and massive loss. The subtler, yet profoundly debilitating, losses in human connection are known as *relational-developmental trauma*. This type of trauma refers to the emotional neglect an infant or young child experiences in interpersonal interactions with caregivers, as well as the failures in human connection and attachment throughout the life span. Incidences of relational-developmental trauma are far more profound than is obvious, and as Philip Bromberg (2011) claims, we all carry relational trauma deep within our inner worlds. We have all suffered emotional neglect in significant relationships from the absence of attunement, resonance, and *feeling felt*, some more devastating than others that may be traced back several generations. Symptoms of relational-developmental trauma can be similar to those suffering from adversities events and can include stress, anxiety, anger, aggression, dissociation, depression, addiction, and medical illness.

When relational-developmental trauma and adversities events occur simultaneously or in accumulative experiences that link together in dysfunctional neural patterns, *complex trauma* is the result. As a way of protecting the inner self, people who have experienced complex trauma tend to be either chronically highly vigilant or drop into flaccid, collapsed defenses.

These defenses are unconscious and remain impervious to attempts of logical reasoning, willpower, and other cognitive strategies to effect permanent change until the underlying dysfunctional neural patterns have been shifted. In other words, the disruptions from trauma result in disturbing bodily-based symptoms and endless suffering. Unable to end the suffering or find it meaningful or redemptive, people who have experienced complex trauma develop survival strategies, including personality adaptations and addictions to avoid their inner anguish.

Dan Siegel synthesizes the concept of trauma: "When the negative impacts of a life-threatening or mind-disabling experience are long lasting, when the psychological wounds of such an experience persist and do not heal well, we call this unresolved trauma" (2012, 39–1). The psychological wounds of trauma result in the inability to emotionally self-regulate, particularly in stressful situations. Allan Schore writes that relational trauma leaves an enduring imprint with "an impaired capacity to regulate stressful affect and an overreliance on the affect-deadening defense of pathological dissociation. . . . Highs and lows are too extreme, too prolonged, or too rapidly cycle and are unpredictable" (2012, 164).

Stressful affect, the emotional remnant of complex trauma, can involve very high-energy reactions such as terror, anger, rage, and aggression, as well as very low-energy reactions such as despair, depression, and dissociation—each exhibiting a lack of embodied awareness of the present moment. People who have experienced trauma can cycle up and down between these states of "aggressive terror," known as *hyperarousal*, and "frozen terror," known as *hypoarousal*, in ways that are difficult to predict (Schore, personal communication). People suffering from these dysregulated nervous system patterns commonly experience disembodiment and disassociation—survival defenses that can leave them vulnerable to a lifetime of further trauma.

Trauma Survival Defenses: Disembodiment and Disassociation

We know ourselves fundamentally and most vividly through relational bodily-based experiences (Damasio 2011). Disembodiment and dissociation cause us to miss out on these experiences—cutting off our connection to our essential self and the essential self of others. Perpetuating the long-lasting symptoms of trauma, *disembodiment* involves a loss of connection with bodily-based sensations, movements, and primitive emotions. The innate feelings that arise in response to danger and life threat, *primitive emotions arise from disrupted neural perceptions* and are held in the body after an overwhelming experience, becoming disruptive emotions and physical symptoms throughout the life span (Panksepp and Biven 2011). The neural perception of danger can fuel primitive emotions of rage, while the neural perception of safety opens one to care for another. The neural perception of life threat results in a profound sense of powerlessness (Porges 2011).

While disembodiment acts as a protective device, numbing unbearable sensory information from terrifying neural states and primitive emotions in the moment of trauma, people who are disembodied lack authentic vitality and a sense of aliveness. Disembodiment can lead to dissociation of the mind and altered mental states. To *dissociate*, people unconsciously dull their ability to perceive and respond to their own bodies' sensory cues. As attention is withdrawn from bodily-based processes, awareness of the present moment is diverted. A person who dissociates loses track of sensations in his body and unconsciously alters awareness to avoid sensory or emotional reminders of trauma. In dissociated left-hemispheric dominant states, people can ruminate on their "issues," confabulate stories and alternative realities that provide protection and escape from suffering, rather than endure the intense feelings and meaning of the actual lived experience.

The spiritual effect of dissociation in traumatic moments is intriguing. The Jungian psychoanalyst Donald Kalsched (2013) describes how a radical disconnection of the mind from the body during a traumatic event becomes an opening, a breaking through, which allows spiritual energy to enter the internal world for protection and solace. Kalsched (2013) describes the spiritual forces available to people who have entered into dissociated states as both numinous—bringing help, protection, wonder, and beauty—and demonic—bringing dark, frightening, and chaotic energies. For Kalsched, people who experience trauma have access to spiritual powers that both protect and persecute the soul.

These overwhelming neural states, intense emotions, and spiritual energy from traumatic events can emerge in authentic helping relationships—and are then accessible for healing. Helping professionals need to create containment and safety for the overwhelming sensations and feelings that come from dissociated memories. In the processes of disembodiment and dissociation, we lose connection with the truth of our lived experience and the actual environment as it exists in the present moment; however, the truth of the lived experience continues to exist hidden in our bodies and can be met, known, and integrated in relationship with an empathic other. When people suffering from trauma are able to stay embodied and regulate their affective states, they can tolerate small doses of suffering and pain while processing traumatic memories. In the following section, we'll explore some of the effects of trauma that extend beyond dissociation and disembodiment.

Pervasiveness, Risk Factors, and the Toll of Trauma

The psychological effects of trauma are emotional, physical, behavioral, social, and spiritual with a wide variety of symptoms, and recent studies indicate that far more people are suffering from trauma than has been previously acknowledged. An ongoing epidemiological study of early childhood trauma, the National Comorbidity Survey (NCS), was first conducted in the United States in 1990. It was replicated with new participants between 2000 and 2004 in an attempt to predict mental health and substance abuse disorders. In an analysis of the data from a national probability sample, Koenen et al. (2010) found that 40 percent of the U.S. population has experienced at least one event of trauma before the age of thirteen, children of color have more violence in the home than Caucasians, and malnutrition is implicated in 50 percent of deaths of children under the age of five, findings that are far more extensive than previously known. The study was conducted through self-reports of adolescents and adults. Self-reports of early traumatic experiences can be affected by amnesia and dissociation, so the incidence of trauma may actually be far more pervasive than currently documented.

In addition to the high prevalence of trauma, the study revealed important information about risk factors associated with experiencing traumatic events. Children growing up in poverty are particularly at risk for parent-child aggression. Lower socioeconomic status is also associated with a higher incidence of mental health disorders in the home, such as depression, anxiety, and substance abuse—also risk factors for trauma. Koenen et al. (2010) theorized that parents need social support to reduce risk factors for parental aggression. Protective factors include maintaining healthy nutrition, having good friends, and having high intelligence. The researchers concluded that childhood trauma before the age of thirteen is highly prevalent internationally. Similarly, Raghaven says, "Several longitudinal studies have found that childhood mental health problems predict subsequent traumatic events" (quoted in Koenen et al. 2010, 20).

According to Felitti and Anda (2010), early adversities experiences are also associated with developing physical and mental illnesses later in life. The Adverse Childhood Experiences (ACE) study, a joint project of Kaiser Permanente and the Centers for Disease Control and Prevention, was launched when a previous study they conducted uncovered a surprising link between sexual trauma and obesity: mainly that weight loss was threatening to individuals who had experienced sexual trauma, and obesity was an unconscious compensatory behavior from the earliest years. Researchers began the ACE to study the lives of volunteers enrolled in Kaiser Permanente, connecting the data of early trauma with later medical and psychological illnesses. With a population that was 80 percent white and 74 percent college graduates, the ACE study indicated a high prevalence of trauma in middle-class populations, similar to the results of the NCS.

The results of the ACE research indicate a "profound relationship between adverse childhood experiences and important categories of emotional state, health risks, disease burden, sexual behavior, disability, and health care costs decades later" (Felitti and Anda 2010, 79). ACE scores, the number of categories of trauma that a person reports through childhood up to the age of eighteen, directly correlate with the occurrence of medical diseases including liver disease, chronic obstructive pulmonary disease, coronary artery disease, and autoimmune diseases. Heart disease was linked to emotional abuse and neglect, physical neglect, physical abuse, sexual abuse, domestic violence, substance abuse, mental illness, and a criminal living in the household.

The work of Felitti and Anda (2010) and Koenen et al. (2010) indicate what a severe toll trauma can take on a person's physical and emotional well-being. Traumatic experiences, such as abuse, family dysfunction, and neglect, during one's formative years are risk factors for impaired quality of life, addictive behaviors, and mental and physical illnesses. Somatic Transformation provides a way for helping professionals to restore the well-being of people who have experienced trauma, complex trauma in particular. In the following section, we'll take a closer look at a case of complex trauma and its root: the neglect of intense emotions.

Case 1.1: Jeanie

Jeanie, an energetic woman in her sixties, had been seeing me for several years when she recalled an event that was linked with relational-developmental trauma. Jeanie and I had established an affectionate and caring bond as we struggled to make sense of her intimate relationships that often ended in feelings of terror and collapse. We reestablished a sense of trust and safety through consistent attunement and presence and by regulating moments of terror that emerged in our relationship. Perhaps most significantly, we reestablished her ability to maintain a sense of embodiment, vitality, and aliveness when she felt the "black velvet" of collapse and dissociation descend upon her. Her collapses were a fall into the darkness that felt like death. This darkness held aggressive terrors that interfered with her sleep and her relationships with men, caused food addictions and digestive issues, and led to spiritual bypasses of her embodied self.

In the spontaneous return of a dissociated memory during one of our sessions, Jeanie recalled that at the age of three, she had been balancing on logs in a small pond behind her home when she slipped and fell into the water. A log rolled on top of her. Unable to move, her face pushed into the mud, she began to drown. She described a feeling of black velvet softly coming over her as she gave up her struggle to extricate herself. Holding her in the black velvet was a loving and beautiful woman. Suddenly, she felt her father roughly pull her out. His rage was more terrifying than the fall or her struggle to breathe. She remembered that his eyes were "hard and bulging out." For many years after the event, she felt a sense of panic and then dissociation whenever her father expressed anger or rage.

As we explored the memory of her father's anger, Jeanie felt the sensations of falling, the log pushing her under the water and into the mud, and the struggle to breathe as mud was sucked into her nostrils and mouth. She remembered her father carrying her into the house, her mother's attempt to remove the mud, and the rage in her father's voice as he described how he had found her. Although Jeanie survived physically, she felt emotionally alone with her terror, horror, and shame.

The immobility of the near-death experience had been fused with the terror of her father's rage. This coupling of neural states, one from a perception of life threat, the other from a perception of intense fear, needed to be healed in the context of an authentic intersubjective relationship. An *intersubjective relationship* involves two people who each bring their own subjectivity and legitimize the other's unique subjectivity into a shared connection. For several sessions following Jeanie's recall, we differentiated small neural and emotional aspects of this trauma until the memory had reconsolidated.

People who have experienced complex trauma suffer from insecure and disorganized attachment patterns. Insecure attachment relationships result in patterns of ambivalence and avoidance in intimate connections, while disorganized attachment relationships are often managed by dissociation. (I will address more about attachment patterns in Chapter 3.) Attachment-based trauma needs repair of the interpersonal relationship, not necessarily the mobilization of sympathetic arousal, such as energy to fight or flee. Mobilizing sympathetic arousal in people with relational trauma can further alienate them from others—a frightening prospect. A more helpful approach is to mobilize the "innate vitality affects" (Stern 2010, 41), the diminished life force that has been thwarted with trauma, an activation that occurs with somatic empathy and other somatic practices.

The term *vitality affects* refers to experiences of a mother matching the form of vitality in her infant and communicating understanding in another modality (Stern 2010). For example, a baby's face "opens up" in wonder. His mother's face also opens, and then she communicates understanding through her own modality, perhaps through sound. There is a "match of internal feeling states, not overt behaviors" that communicates a mutual understanding (Stern 2010, 41) and the sense of feeling felt. Vitality affects used in therapeutic alliances allow the intersubjective field to grow beyond imitation and mirroring and into the realm of interconnection, "earned secure" attachment, and development. The *intersubjective field* is the space that is created between people that includes both unformulated and known experiences of each. With Jeanie, vitality affects melted her immobility and restored her ability to authentically meet the anger that came from fear in her relationships.

People who have experienced complex trauma are in need of embodied intersubjective relationships, where the intense dissociated emotions from "forgotten" traumatic memories can be met, felt, and incorporated into the relational field. Feeling with another allows us to slowly and gently incorporate our disembodied trauma-related immobility into the body's way of knowing and the intersubjective field. Treatments for less interpersonal trauma, like falls or motor vehicle accidents, are not always interchangeable with treatments for relational-developmental trauma; a committed relationship over time is *essential* for healing complex trauma. Bromberg describes how complicated it is to relate to the dissociative aspects of the self and "affect driven voices from parts of the self that were disconfirmed relationally" (2011, 58). When a child's emotions are consistently ignored and dismissed, affect becomes severed from a sense of self, yet continues to exist deeply within the body and mind. With this internal split, a person's sense of self excludes emotions that were neglected as a child, a fundamental separation that underlies mental, physical, and social difficulties.

Jeanie experienced this internal split, which could only be healed in the context of an intersubjective relationship. As we differentiated the felt sense of her memories of near drowning from her father's rage with phenomenological methods, she no longer collapsed into the "black velvet" when she perceived rage in other men.

Perception and Trauma

As a body-mind approach to complex trauma, Somatic Transformation is particularly interested in unconscious perceptions through the eyes, ears, face, throat, larynx, pharynx, skin, muscles, and other parts of the body. These unconscious perceptions, called *neuroceptions* by Porges (2003), stimulate reactions of safety, danger, and life threat that then affect sensations, movement, emotions, images, and thoughts.

A perception of danger brings contraction to the muscles of the face, eyes, ears, neck, throat, and viscera while the perception of life threat can bring flaccid, still reactions to the same muscles (Porges 2011). Here we see the beginning of a rapid cycling between very high and very low neurological states described by Schore. Using Porges's (2011) theories of neuroception of danger and life threat, we can track the neurological shifts within the specific phenomena of a traumatic event. For example, when Jeanie slipped and felt the log roll over her, her eyes would likely have been wide open with the whites very visible and the muscles of her face contracted in horror. This state of hyperarousal would not have lasted long; with the perception of life threat that came when she couldn't breathe, Jeanie shifted quickly into a state of hypoarousal and dissociation, where she was comforted by the deep black smooth feelings of immobility as well as an image of an embracing spiritual feminine figure. A state of immobilization is a natural, neurological preparation for death (Porges 2011) that comes from the perception of life threat. In this immobilized state, Jeanie could have died in peace, having surrendered the fight to breathe. It was in this state that her father found her and interrupted her near-death experience. Her father's anger precipitated an immediate shift into a perception of danger, causing Jeanie to then feel both immobilized and frightened. She had no opportunity to shift from the hypoaroused state of immobility before she perceived her father's anger. This dissociated memory remained alive for her. Although she had consciously forgotten the evening she nearly drowned, she re-experienced it when she perceived that men were angry with her—or could become angry in any moment. Until this memory surfaced in our embodied inter-subjective relationship, the source of her perceptions in her ordinary life was unconscious and confusing.

Bromberg speaks about the role of perception in trauma: "We are all either explicitly or implicitly attempting clinically to facilitate a patient's access to the broadest possible range of consciousness through enhancing perception. Perception is where the action is—and always has been" (2011, 159). Perceptions are the interpretation of sensory impressions, an action that is learned and usually unconscious, unless we practice attention to sensory impressions and delay our conditioned interpretation. For example, Jeanie unconsciously interpreted other people's anger, particularly that of men, through her neural imprint in the moment of trauma and emotional lens as terror, horror, immobility, and shame. Because of unconscious, neurological survival reactions, traumatic experiences result in impaired perceptions and distorted interpretations of lived experience. These impaired perceptions and interpretations form the bodily-based experience and the inner subjective world of people suffering from trauma.

Restoring Perception through Somatic Transformation

Bromberg (2011) challenges helping professionals to consider how we can help people suffering from trauma clarify perceptual awareness of their inner world as well as the larger environment. Rodolfo Llinas (2001) describes the fixed-action patterns in the perceptual systems of the eyes, ears, skin, and internal kinesthetic sensory systems of the viscera. *Fixed-action patterns* involve the distortions of perceptual, sensory, motor, emotional, imaginal, and mental behavior that develop as a defense against stress and trauma (Llinas 2001). Examples include patterns of perceptual errors that blind a person to reality, such as disembodiment; emotional-based prejudices; behaviors such as enactment, withdrawal, collapse, and contraction; and bodily-based defenses using the hands, legs, facial grimaces, glares, snarls, or growls (Llinas 2001). (Enactment refers to dynamics in relationship where people experience a kind of blindness regarding their own unconscious emotional communication, a phenomenon I discuss further in Chapter 7.)

Even the most accomplished and conscious people have embedded errors in perception with fixed-action patterns of interpretation due to implicit, unconscious effects of dissociated trauma. People literally cannot see, hear, and feel specific aspects of the present moment when they are in the grip of unconscious implicit memories. The muscular doors of perception unconsciously shut down, forming dissociated physical and mental states. Following a traumatic experience, the small muscles in the eyes can become locked in fixed-actions patterns of hyperarousal and hypoarousal and the small muscles in the ears, the stapedius and tensor tympani, can also be held in states of intense arousal or collapse (Porges 2011). The internal viscera, lungs, heart, and guts can hold fixed-action patterns of intense trauma (Tucker 2007) that lead to emotional, mental, and physical illnesses including depression, dissociation, and respiratory, digestive, and circulatory disorders.

Somatic Transformation practices are designed to shift the fixed-action patterns of perception through embodiment, awareness, empathy, inquiry, interventions, and reflection. Somatic interventions for the expansion and restoration of perceptual systems involve both voluntary and involuntary sensory-based movements of the face, eyes, ears, throat, and neck. These practices restore the capacity to play with images through imaginal and spiritual experience. Bodily-based images emerge when we somatically attend to sensory and motor dynamics, and in our conversations, day-dreams, night dreams, and reflections on our lived experiences. Bodily-based images are distinct from the images that come with fantasy and hallucinations.

An important part of clarifying and restoring perceptual systems is developing a sense of personal embodiment with somatic awareness—the practice of mindful, focused, and embodied consciousness. Somatic awareness involves the intention and attention to bodily-based lived experience and opens a way of knowing that is distinct from mental forms of knowledge. With an embodied consciousness, fresh and stimulating perceptions about the self, others, and the world can break through the fixed-action patterns that limit awareness (Llinas 2001). These new ways of seeing, hearing, and feeling can pierce the fog of dissociation to reveal surprising new resources of physical vitality and meaning. An embodied consciousness is necessary for practicing somatic ways of knowing one's own inner world and witnessing the subjective experience of others, activities that invite spirit back into the body.

Because the wounds of trauma become deeply imprinted in the soul, the imagination, the brain, the nervous system, the visceral organs, and the muscular structures of the body, healing is a complex process that goes far beyond a "talking cure." An interdisciplinary paradigm shift where "theory and research are changing from left brain conscious cognitions to right brain unconscious affect" (Schore 2012, 3) offers opportunities to explore bodily-based practices for healing. In the chapters that follow, you will learn how to tap into unconscious affect to help clients transform unresolved trauma into a sense of vitality.

References

Atleo, E. R. 2004. *Tsawalk: A Nuu-chah-nulth Worldview*. Vancouver: University of British Columbia Press.

Atleo, E. R. 2011. *Principles of Tsawalk: An Indigenous Approach to Global Crisis*. Vancouver: University of British Columbia Press.

Berman, M. 1989. *Coming to Our Senses: Body and Spirit in the Hidden History of the West.* New York: Simon & Schuster.

The Boston Change Process Study Group. 2010. *Change in Psychotherapy: A Unifying Paradigm.* New York: Norton.

Bromberg, P. M. 2011. *The Shadow of the Tsunami: and the Growth of the Relational Mind.* New York: Routledge.

Cozolino, L. 2014. "Attachment-Based Teaching: Enhancing Learning through Human Connection." Presented at the Annual Interpersonal Neurobiology Conference, Los Angeles, CA, March 15. Retrieved from http://lifespanlearn.org/index.php/conferences/handouts/syllabus-2014/lou-cozolino/6-cozolino-slides-attachment/file

Damasio, A. 2011. *Self Comes to Mind: Constructing the Conscious Brain*. New York: Pantheon.

Diamond, J. 2012. *The World Until Yesterday: What Can We Learn from Traditional Societies?* New York: Penguin.

Felitti, V. J., and R. F. Anda. 2010. "The Relationship of Adverse Childhood Experiences to Adult Health, Well-being, Social Function, and Healthcare." In *The Hidden Epidemic: The Impact of Early Life Trauma on Health and Disease,* edited by R. Lanius, E. Vermetten, and C. Pain, 77–87. Cambridge: Cambridge University Press.

Kalsched, D. 2013. *Trauma and the Soul: A Psycho-spiritual Approach to Human Development and Its Interruption*. London: Routledge.

Koenen, K. C., A. Roberts, D. Stone, and E. Dunn. 2010. "The Epidemiology of Early Childhood Trauma." In *The Hidden Epidemic: The Impact of Early Life Trauma on Health and Disease,* edited by R. Lanius, E. Vermetten, and C. Pain, 13–24. Cambridge: University Press.

Llinás, R. R. 2001. *I of the vortex: From Neurons to Self.* Cambridge: MIT Press.

Merleau-Ponty, M. 1962. *Phenomenology of Perception*. Translated by Donald Landes. New York: Routledge.

Panksepp, J., and L. Biven. 2011. *The Archaeology of Mind: Neuroevolutionary Origins of Human Emotions*. New York: Norton.

Porges, S. W. 2003. "The Polyvagal Theory: Phylogenetic Contributions to Social Behavior." *Physiology and Behavior* 79: 503–513.

Porges, S. W. 2011. *The Polyvagal Theory: Neurophysiological Foundations of Emotions Attachment, Communication, and Self-Regulation*. New York: Norton.

Schore, A. N. 2003a. *Affect Dysregulation and Disorders of the Self.* New York: Norton.

Schore, A. N. 2003b. *Affect Regulation and the Repair of the Self.* New York: Norton.

Schore, A. N. 2005. "A Neuropsychoanalytic Viewpoint: Commentary on Paper by Steven H. Knoblauch." *Psychoanalytic Dialogues* 15(6): 829–854.

Schore, A. N. 2012. *The Science of the Art of Psychotherapy*. New York: Norton.

Siegel, D. J. 1999. *The Developing Mind: Toward a Neurobiology of Interpersonal Experience*. New York: Guilford.

Siegel, D. J. 2010. *Mindsight: The New Science of Personal Transformation*. New York: Bantam.

Siegel, D. J. 2012. *Pocket Guide to Interpersonal Neurobiology: An Integrative Handbook of the Mind*. New York: Norton.

Stern, D. N. 2010. *Forms of Vitality: Exploring Dynamic Experience in Psychology, the Arts, Psychotherapy, and Development*. Oxford: Oxford University Press.

Tucker, D. 2007. *Mind from Body: Experience from Neural Structure*. Oxford: Oxford University Press.

Weil, S. 1952. *Gravity and Grace*. Translated by Emma Crawford and Mario von der Ruhr. London: Routledge & Kegan Paul.

2 Structures and Functions of the Brain and Polyvagal Theory of Autonomic Functioning

> Our culture honored our warriors right after they returned and listened to each and every warrior tell their war stories. This fact along with the survival reasons we fought and killed assisted in eliminating any PTSD.
>
> (Tick 2014–2015, 71)

The Lateral Structure of the Brain

A path to healing the effects of trauma is through implicit recall of dissociated memories in the form of neural-emotional states, processing them with somatic practices, and then embodying these experiences in the context of nurturing relationships. In the context of an embodied, caring, and skilled relationship, fear from trauma dissipates and the restoration of the life force and its innate vitality stimulate the internal organization of disorganized patterns. In addition, resolved memories and embodied dream life accelerate repair to the developmental interruptions created by traumatic experience. Advances in neuroscience are guiding helping professionals in the creation of affective embodied experiences, mutual interactions that offer radical transformation of disruptive states. To effectively engage in these practices, practitioners need to understand how the structures and functions of the brain can be used to rewire neural networks of maladaptive neural-emotional states and restore healthy functioning.

A primary function of the brain is to help us connect with other humans, animals, the external environment, and our own inner lived experiences in order to adapt to present moment reality. Each hemisphere of the brain specializes in what is most useful for predicting, surviving, and flourishing. The left hemisphere develops with the formation of verbal language between eighteen and thirty-six months of age and is most interested in abstract language, categories, sequencing of experience, and analysis based on logic. Conversely, the right hemisphere develops what are called implicit memories even before birth in the prenatal experience shared with the mother; an intense intimacy captured by the term *prenate* (Thompson 2007). Implicit memories from lived experience are recalled in the body as sensory emotional fragments.

The brain's right hemisphere is the locus of affect—the various ways emotion is expressed. The right hemisphere discerns individuals and makes meaning of emotion when it recognizes familiar sensations (McGilchrist 2010). Hecht (2014) describes the need for affiliation, empathy, ethics, and other prosocial attitudes as dependent on the right hemisphere. The right hemisphere deals directly with life experience, explores context, and seeks to understand the relationship between things, a concept clearly expressed in First Nations culture as the "right relation." The right relation refers to the respect that must be given in a spirit of humility to all human, nonhuman, and divine life forms (Atleo 2004).

To be in the right relation with one another, the two hemispheres of the brain must collaborate to allow the other to function in its most effective manner, an activity that is supported by the corpus callosum (Hecht 2014). This band of neural tissue connects the right and left hemispheres at the base of the brain. The main purpose of the corpus callosum is to inhibit one hemisphere from interfering with a task being carried out by the other hemisphere (McGilchrist 2010). For example, if a person is engaged in a meditation on sensory-based experience, the corpus collosum will attempt to inhibit left-hemispheric analysis, allowing for integrative right-hemispheric processing. How can helping professionals strengthen the right relation between the left and right hemisphere through interactions? To answer this question, we must understand how the two hemispheres of the brain work together.

Iain McGilchrist (2010) offers an overview of the interweaving functions of the right and left hemispheres of the brain. In order to make sense of the vast stimuli in the world, we first pay attention. The left hemisphere focuses on what is most interesting, that which we value. The left hemisphere is concerned with what it already knows and is drawn by its expectations. Personal and generational trauma can severely distort perceptions on a sensory-motor level and form into left-hemispheric dominance, which results in the need for power and is associated with anger, hostility, aggression, and jealousy. Control and exploitation of others in social situations is associated with a bias to the left hemisphere (Hecht 2014).

Unlike the left hemisphere, the right hemisphere is open to what is new and novel and perceives stimuli before they are accessible to the left hemisphere. We perceive stimuli with our eyes, ears, nose, and mouth and feel overall kinesthetic somatic shifts. Consequently, emotional assessments based on distorted perceptions (as a result of trauma) are made in the memory system of the right hippocampus—not the left, leading to intense emotional reactions that can seem disproportionate in the moment.

The distinctions between the right and left hemisphere extend to problem solving as well. The right hemisphere is able to consider a variety of solutions while exploring alternatives. It can hold opposites and tolerate paradox in a dialectical oscillation, generating new creative, complex forms of knowing—the core of somatic practices for healing trauma. The left hemisphere, on the other hand, applies solutions it is already familiar with, a strategy that is useful when things are not changing. Holding one theory at a time, the left hemisphere searches for information to support its strongest belief and likes to avoid discrepancies while the right hemisphere revels in them (McGilchrist 2009).

Discrepancies stimulate the right hemisphere to move beyond a present dilemma and enter into a more expansive perspective. This difference in approaches to problem solving is in part due to the fact that the right hemisphere is more densely myelinated (McGilchrist 2009). *Myelination* refers to the fatty coating on the axon of a nerve cell that speeds the flow of information and energy between subcortical and cortical processes of the brain. See Figure 2.1. As a result of increased myelination, the right hemisphere is better able to alter and integrate the different sensory perceptions of vision, hearing, and touch in the vestibular system—the system that organizes incoming sensory information from the body—and coordinate those perceptions with the movement of small muscles in the face, eyes, and ears. The right hemisphere brings together the vast diversity of lived experience to create the fabric of a rich, complex, and coherent world in a fast-moving synthesis. Right-hemispheric processing excels in differentiating the specific phenomena of a lived experience and then linking them in new relationships, an activity that forms new neural connections and creative adaptation.

McGilchrist (2009) points out that bodily-based synthesis gleaned from right-hemispheric processing must go to the left hemisphere to form knowledge that is accessible through logic, sequence, and abstract language. The left hemisphere is adept at containing, organizing, and expressing truths that have been discerned through right-hemispheric processing, a mental file cabinet that contains factual information organized into logical patterns. This type of knowledge is unlike affective experience, which is transformational, continually shifting and taking new forms. Right-hemispheric reflection, where a person creates a synthesis of embodied affective experiences, provides the material for new logical structures for the left hemisphere. People experiencing trauma often dissociate from right-hemispheric processing when they encounter intense emotions, dissociating to left-hemispheric dominance, logic, sequence, and abstract knowing to organize their inner worlds. This shift can intensify worry, preoccupation, rumination, and even obsessions due to the left hemisphere's limitations in creative processing. When the left hemisphere doesn't keep up with the dynamic processing of the right hemisphere and the changing environment, the left-hemispheric authoritarian concepts of truth and accuracy do not change over time, causing fixed-action patterns in thinking and

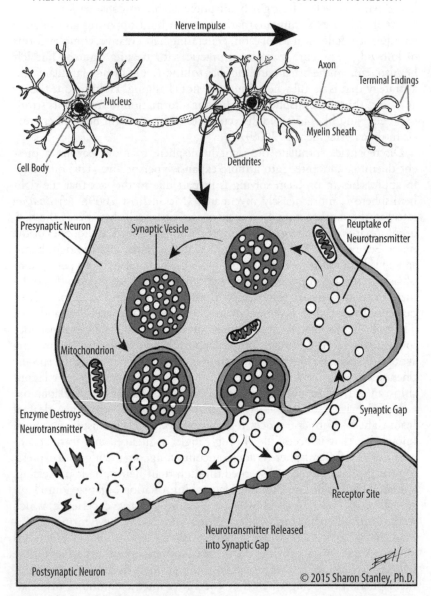

Figure 2.1 Pre- and Postsynaptic Neuron

The synaptic gap between neurons allows for rapid change, especially in the myelinated neurons connecting the brain, face, ears, eyes, throat, lungs, and heart.

behavior. While the right and left hemisphere offer a lateral understanding of the human brain, to fully discern the effects of trauma we must also explore the vertical structure of the brain.

The Vertical Structure of the Brain

The human brain evolved in a vertical piecemeal fashion, creating a structure that makes recovery from trauma very difficult in the absence of an attuned relationship with another. Trauma interrupts and severs the neural connections between the most primitive parts of the brain and the neural connections to the more complex and recently evolved parts of the brain. On the bottom of the brain's three-tiered structure (MacLean 1990) is the brain stem, which transports messages from the spinal cord and other parts of the body to the brain. The most primitive part of the brain, the brain stem is responsible for basic functions of life, such as digestion, respiration, circulation, management of the immune system, and regulation of the autonomic nervous system. The brain stem unconsciously perceives safety, danger, and life threat. These neuroceptions (Porges 2011) prompt us to engage socially, defend with aggression, or withdraw into terror, dissociation, and immobility through unconscious arousal. See Figure 2.2.

The next structure to evolve was the limbic brain, which organizes the sensory-motor stimulation of the brain stem into emotion. Panksepp and Biven (2011) describe how circuits of the limbic brain—which include seeking, fear, grief, lust, play, and care—carry perceptual neural stimulation to the higher cortical parts of the brain. The limbic brain also houses the amygdala and cingulate and interacts with the orbitofrontal cortex. This threefold internal perceptual system forms one's core sense of self and is linked to higher cortical processes such as empathy, compassion, and wisdom (Schore and Newton 2013).

The most recent addition to the brain is the very thin outer layer known as the cerebral cortex (also called the neocortex), which features the more distinctly human parts of our brain (MacLean 1990). The cerebral cortex observes, participates, and guides the less conscious, subcortical areas of the brain—including the limbic system and the brain stem—when they are optimally connected. A mature cerebral cortex is able to plan complex strategies that include the wisdom of the body, make executive decisions based on innate ways of knowing, and authentically feel compassion and empathy for oneself and others. The practice of witnessing the moment-to-moment activity of the body from the vantage of the cerebral cortex is called somatic awareness—a consciousness that makes it possible to see through the visible to discover the invisible, to reveal dynamics that have long been considered unconscious, dissociated, and unavailable for observation, participation, and modification. Let's take a closer look at how affective emotionally based messages travel between the brain stem, the limbic brain, and the cerebral cortex.

VERTICAL CROSS SECTION OF THE BRAIN

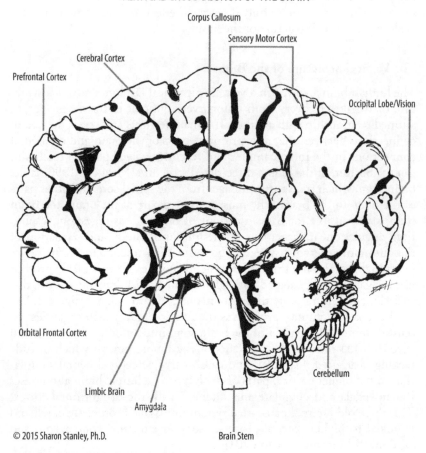

© 2015 Sharon Stanley, Ph.D.

Figure 2.2 Cross Section of the Brain

Trauma disrupts the connectivity between the primordial brain stem, the emotional limbic brain, and the more recently evolved human cerebral cortex.

Affective Communication from the Brain Stem to the Limbic Brain

Messages from the brain stem on the right hemisphere of the brain transform from perceptions, to neural arousal with sensation, then into primitive emotions as the arousal moves through the limbic brain along emotional brain circuits (Panksepp and Biven 2011). Neuroceptions of danger and life threat from the brain stem and amygdala may be processed into a variety of different emotions such as seeking, grief, rage, play, lust, care, or fear. Perceptions of safety may be processed as caring, seeking, lust, or even grief. The intensity of emotions is fueled by the degree of neural arousal in the brain stem and alarm sent by the amygdala. From here, these emotions move to the cerebral cortex on the right hemisphere, which organizes processing of the subcortical elements, often into visual, auditory, and kinesthetic images. Next the energy contained in the images moves on to more complex areas such as the prefrontal and orbitofrontal cortex, where it becomes available for reflection, an activity that links and integrates previously disconnected elements of lived experience.

A person who perceives suffering but immediately becomes disembodied and dissociated from feelings of terror and horror never connects the reality of the suffering to his or her higher cortical wisdom, empathy, and compassion. If fear and terror are disembodied, suppressed, repressed, or dissociated, the neural energy may become "stuck," leading to a numb depression and immobilization. The neural arousal from terror may also move into the emotional circuit of rage, a state of hyperarousal. Both of these reactions can be confusing to people who have experienced trauma and to their loved ones.

The Cerebral Cortex Sorts Out the Messages from Subcortical Structures

As the most recently evolved and most complex structure of the human brain, the cerebral cortex receives complex messages from the brain stem and limbic system and sends messages back down to the body. If the messages have made it up the vertical structures of the brain, through the neural networks that form the path, the higher cortical processes can integrate and create meaning from the messages and then incorporate that meaning back into the body. See Figure 2.3.

To make adaptive and wise decisions regarding the meaning of neural arousal and emotion, the cerebral cortex is dependent on current perceptions that bring accurate messages from the body, brain stem, and limbic system. The cerebral cortex spans both the right and left hemispheres. On the right hemisphere, the cerebral cortex is able to synthesize messages from the bodily-based subcortical regions of the brain into images and archetypes. It then sends this new meaning over to the left hemisphere to formulate a spontaneous logical, sequential plan of action.

If perceptions of terror and horror have been numbed by dissociation, the innate processing pathways are interrupted and the meaning of the emotion is distorted. When people disregard neural-based sensations and emotions, the cerebral cortex is vulnerable to distorted imagination, faulty logic, and maladaptive reactions. Without an embodied way of knowing oneself and others, empathy and compassion are built upon an idea without substance and endurance. Without the engagement of the body, people become driven by a disconnected imagination or an overly idealized belief. They might have an intention to empathize or show compassion, but

RIGHT HEMISPHERE PROCESSING FROM THE BOTTOM UP

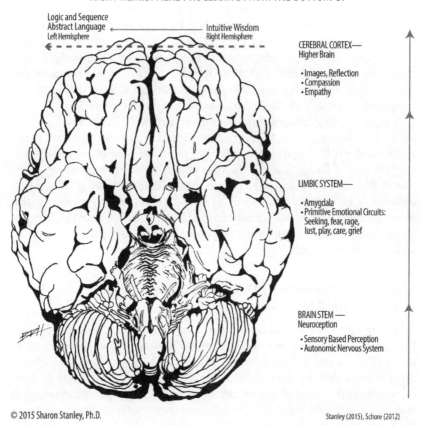

Logic and Sequence
Abstract Language
Left Hemisphere

Intuitive Wisdom
Right Hemisphere

CEREBRAL CORTEX—
Higher Brain

• Images, Reflection
• Compassion
• Empathy

LIMBIC SYSTEM—

• Amygdala
• Primitive Emotional Circuits:
  Seeking, fear, rage,
  lust, play, care, grief

BRAIN STEM —
Neuroception

• Sensory Based Perception
• Autonomic Nervous System

© 2015 Sharon Stanley, Ph.D.   Stanley (2015), Schore (2012)

Figure 2.3 Right Hemispheric Processing

The right hemisphere organizes incoming stimulation; first with perception, then into sensations that generate movement and primitive emotions that then are transformed into sensory-based images and archetypes. Reflection on the contents of this process reveals meaning that is available to the left hemisphere for abstract, logical knowledge.

without embodied empathy they are not viscerally moved to be fully present for another. What they say and do is not supported by what they know and feel—people who have experienced trauma know this instinctively.

To operate effectively, the vertical system of the brain requires billions of neural networks that have optimal connections between subcortical parts and higher cortical areas of the brain. See Figure 2.4. These networks can be formed in a fraction of a second with myelinated neural connectivity between the right-hemispheric brain of one person and the right-hemispheric brain of another. In other words, somatic-based empathy creates neural networks or pathways within the brain and between brains.

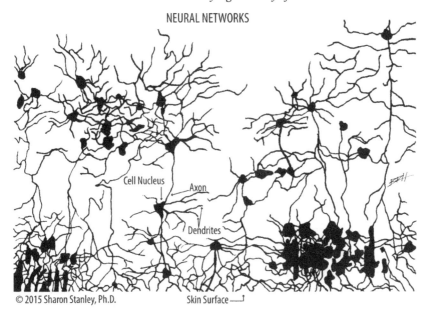

NEURAL NETWORKS

Cell Nucleus

Axon

Dendrites

© 2015 Sharon Stanley, Ph.D.   Skin Surface

Figure 2.4 Neural Networks

Changes in the connections of neuron-to-neuron produces new neural networks that form into pathways for a different flow of information and energy.

These networks form a vertical evolutionary hierarchy connecting the brain stem, limbic system, and cerebral cortex. Arousal messages are sent from bodily-based perceptions up the vertical network of the brain to the highest cortical structures for highly refined human meaning. What happens when there are interruptions to the vertical organization of the brain?

Trauma and the Vertical Structure of the Brain

Early, emotionally noncontingent interactions between a caregiver and an infant impede optimal development of that infant's brain (Beebe et al. 2012) by thwarting the creation of neural connections between the brain stem, the limbic brain, and the cerebral cortex. When people are traumatized, the primitive, subcortical, survival-oriented parts of the brain (elements of the brain stem and the limbic system) continue to be active, yet are disconnected from each other and the higher cerebral cortex. When the brain is out of alignment with itself, the primitive arousal system can take over, creating havoc and confusion for a person suffering from trauma and making mature, authentic, and empathic behavior all but impossible.

Despite this inner suffering on subcortical levels, a person who has experienced relational-developmental trauma can present as highly competent, relationally connected, and calm. Yet under this "apparently normal part" (van der Hart, Nijenhuis, and Steele 2006) can be hidden bodily-based states of anguish and terror that emerge from dissociative processes in night terrors and dreams (Kalsched 2013), physical illnesses (Scaer 2005; Frewen and Lanius 2015) and emotionally absent, noncontingent relationships (Shore 2012). These relationships appear "normal" on the outside but lack the presence of embodied, coherent emotional attunement and fail to offer the nurturing necessary for attachment and connection, an essential element for a life of vitality, joy, creativity, and meaning.

While early relational-developmental trauma results in the absence of connection between the higher cortical and subcortical structures, shocking aversive events may simply interrupt this connection. The purpose of the disconnection is to survive, to avoid unbearable sensory-based suffering, and to protect the self from knowing what it doesn't want to know. Baron-Cohen calls this a kind of "mindblindness" (quoted in Fonagy et al. 2005). According to Kalsched, when trauma occurs, "The essence of the child—the creative, relational, authentic innocent spark of life which is at the very core—goes into hiding, deep in the unconscious" (quoted in Sieff 2006, 69–70). This separation results in dissociation, a primitive, bodily-based defense against overwhelming affects and emotions (Schore 2008). Either way, as an attempt to obliterate meaning or avoid the overwhelming affects, the result of this split is an intrinsic, neurological kind of immaturity that limits intimate relationships, creativity, and growth and development.

The interweave of early relational-developmental trauma and shocking aversive events disrupts neural networks in the brain, so relational practices for healing trauma, such as the development of an intersubjective relationship and compassionate embodiment of dissociated elements of the aversive experience, can be important for resolving shocking aversive events. With aversive events trauma, there is an impact in a fraction of a second, an intense arousal and vivid impression that is retained and connected with the initial impact of an experience. This impact contains what was perceived in the moment and the explicit subjective memory of the experience as well as the body's sense of emotions and images in the moment.

In relational-developmental trauma, the impact of what happened does not carry the high intensity of neural arousal nor the vivid perceptions, emotions, and images that we see in shock events. Relational-developmental trauma creates more of a sense of loss, deprivation, and pervasive emptiness rather than a strong impact in the moment. It involves an absence of relational connectivity that fosters unbearable anguish and an urge to obliterate meaning, while the impact from aversive events lives as a hyperaroused moment in time, hidden in fixed-action patterns.

Much of the injury from trauma, whether relational-developmental or aversive events, lies deeply embedded in the brain stem. At the center of the brain stem is the activity of the autonomic nervous system, a body-wide system that is designed to detect cues of danger, life threat, and safety. Stephen Porges' (2011) polyvagal theory of the autonomic nervous system is an evolutionary-based perspective that describes the primary brain circuits and specific neural states that stimulate processing in the right hemisphere. It provides helping professionals with an orientation to the dynamics of neural arousal, which can guide therapeutic interventions.

The Polyvagal Theory of the Autonomic Nervous System

Porges uses the term *polyvagal* to distinguish between the main branches of the vagus nerve—the ventral vagal and the dorsal vagal—distinctions that are critical to understanding and treating neural states of complex trauma. See Figure 2.5.

The vagus nerve is a complex blend of neural pathways originating in the brain stem. It consists of parasympathetic fibers that run from the body up to the brain, and then back down from the brain stem to the face, larynx, pharynx, heart, lungs, digestive, and reproductive organs. The vagus nerve provides motor and sensory activation from the neck to the face, and down to the heart and other organs. At least 80 percent of vagal fibers are afferent; that is, they conduct impulses from the periphery of the body up to the brain stem, a fact that amplifies the need to somatically track sensory-based impulses that arise from the body.

The ventral vagal and dorsal vagal have a wide range of independent functioning and may collaborate or conflict with each other. When they are collaborating, we feel a sense of personal unity and wholeness. When trauma occurs, they conflict—the vagus can become fused with the sympathetic circuit—binding fear with social engagement or fear with immobility. The fusion between fear and vagal states may be adaptive in times one needs to survive, such as during war, disasters, or sustained violence in the family. Yet these fusions are maladaptive in times of relative safety.

In therapeutic encounters, it is extremely useful to discern the current state of arousal of the different vagal circuits as well as the activity of sympathetic arousal in both people. There are five states of neural arousal: low arousal, hypoarousal, optimal arousal, high arousal, and hyperarousal. See Figures 2.6–2.10. Most people are unconscious of subtle rises and drops in arousal. Through a conscious awareness of cues regarding arousal, we can somatically sense the activation of the ventral and dorsal vagal. The ventral vagal indicates a readiness for social engagement, for example, we can feel ourselves want to connect with another, while the activation of the dorsal vagal signifies a need for deep sleep and other restorative functions that require immobility. When trauma occurs and sympathetic circuits of fear become fused with vagal states of social engagement and immobility, life and relationships become complex and confusing. This fusion, sometimes called coupling or binding, of vagal and sympathetic circuits creates unconscious internal conflicts, disturbing sensory experience,

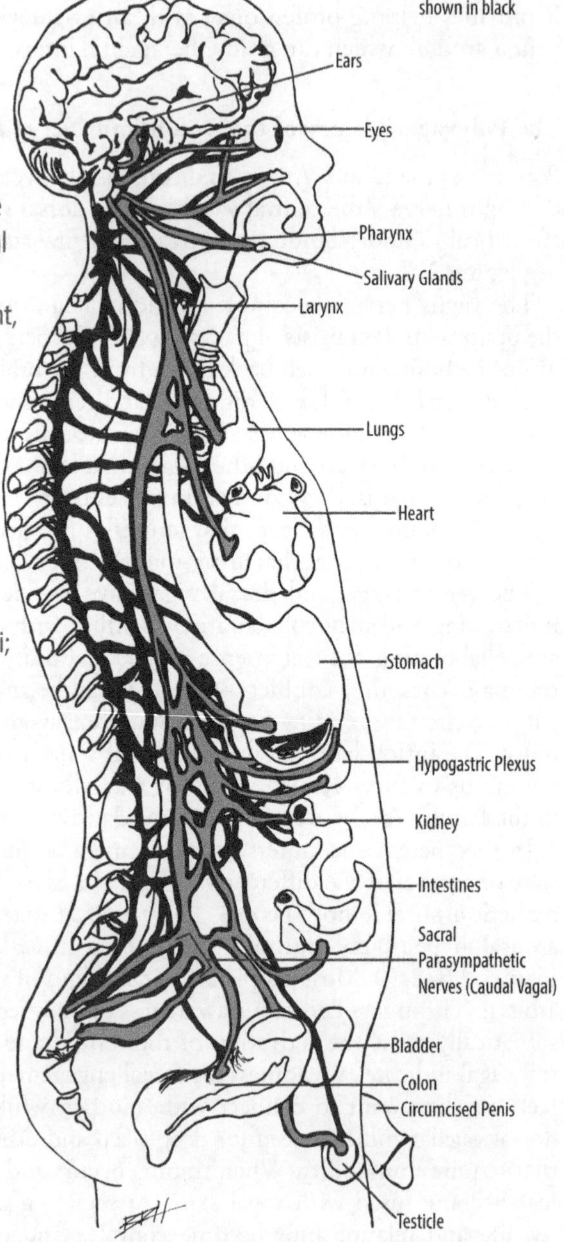

AUTONOMIC NERVOUS SYSTEM INNERVATION - POLYVAGAL

Polyvagal (PV)
shown in gray

Sympathetic (S)
shown in black

The polyvagal theory specifies two distinct functional branches of the tenth cranial nerve, the ventral vagal and the dorsal vagal. The ventral vagal supports social engagement, while the dorsal vagal supports immobilization. Stimulation of vagal parasympathetic fibers slows heart rate; lowers blood pressure; dilates the pupils; increases the perceived strength of auditory stimuli; constricts the smooth muscles of the bronchial tree; stimulates the glands of the bronchial mucosa; promotes peristalsis in the gastrointestinal tract; relaxes gastrointestinal sphincters; and stimulates the secretion of gastric and pancreatic juices.

Ears
Eyes
Pharynx
Salivary Glands
Larynx
Lungs
Heart
Stomach
Hypogastric Plexus
Kidney
Intestines
Sacral Parasympathetic Nerves (Caudal Vagal)
Bladder
Colon
Circumcised Penis
Testicle

© 2015 Sharon Stanley, Ph.D.

Figure 2.5 Autonomic Nervous System

POLYVAGAL THEORY: NEURAL-EMOTIONAL STATES LOW AROUSAL

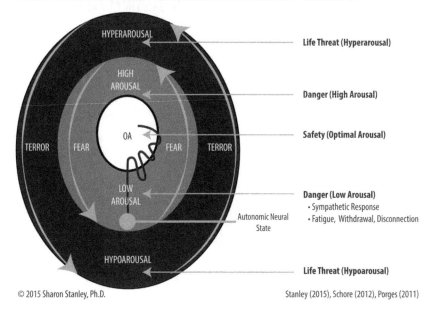

Figure 2.6 Low Arousal

During states of low arousal the dorsal vagal immobility circuit is compromised with fear and sympathetic arousal.

POLYVAGAL THEORY: NEURAL-EMOTIONAL STATES HYPOAROUSAL

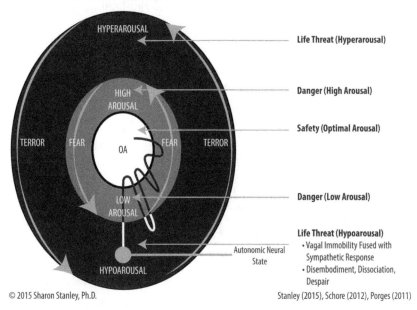

Figure 2.7 Hypoarousal

During states of hypoarousal, the dorsal vagal immobility circuit is bound with terror from intense sympathetic arousal and initiates bodily-based preparations for death.

POLYVAGAL THEORY: NEURAL-EMOTIONAL STATES OPTIMAL AROUSAL

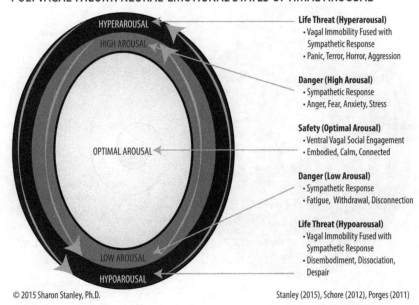

HYPERAROUSAL

HIGH AROUSAL

OPTIMAL AROUSAL

LOW AROUSAL

HYPOAROUSAL

Life Threat (Hyperarousal)
- Vagal Immobility Fused with Sympathetic Response
- Panic, Terror, Horror, Aggression

Danger (High Arousal)
- Sympathetic Response
- Anger, Fear, Anxiety, Stress

Safety (Optimal Arousal)
- Ventral Vagal Social Engagement
- Embodied, Calm, Connected

Danger (Low Arousal)
- Sympathetic Response
- Fatigue, Withdrawal, Disconnection

Life Threat (Hypoarousal)
- Vagal Immobility Fused with Sympathetic Response
- Disembodiment, Dissociation, Despair

© 2015 Sharon Stanley, Ph.D.   Stanley (2015), Schore (2012), Porges (2011)

Figure 2.8 Optimal Arousal

The ventral vagal circuit of social engagement is dominant and facilitates the negotiation of perceptions and reactions from fear, terror, and horror.

POLYVAGAL THEORY: NEURAL-EMOTIONAL STATES HIGH AROUSAL

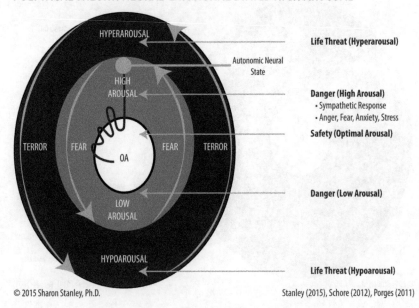

HYPERAROUSAL

HIGH AROUSAL

TERROR FEAR   FEAR TERROR

OA

LOW AROUSAL

HYPOAROUSAL

Autonomic Neural State

Life Threat (Hyperarousal)

Danger (High Arousal)
- Sympathetic Response
- Anger, Fear, Anxiety, Stress

Safety (Optimal Arousal)

Danger (Low Arousal)

Life Threat (Hypoarousal)

© 2015 Sharon Stanley, Ph.D.   Stanley (2015), Schore (2012), Porges (2011)

Figure 2.9 High Arousal

A neural state of high arousal occurs with sustained sympathetic activation due to a perception of danger.

POLYVAGAL THEORY: NEURAL-EMOTIONAL STATES HYPERAROUSAL

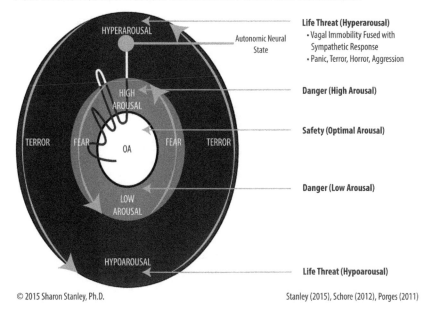

© 2015 Sharon Stanley, Ph.D.   Stanley (2015), Schore (2012), Porges (2011)

Figure 2.10 Hyperarousal

A neural state of hyperarousal occurs with a perception of extreme danger and little protection.

contradictory emotions, and a loss of inner guidance. Let's take a closer look at these circuits.

The Ventral Vagal Circuit

Stimulated by perceptions of safety, the ventral vagal system is myelinated to provide spontaneous, immediate communication and transformational change between the face, ears, eyes, throat, larynx, pharynx, heart, and lungs. See Figure 2.11. When the ventral branch—the front neural connections of the vagal nerve—is activated, we are able to socially engage, regulate, negotiate, nurture, care, and empathize with others through compassionate connection—and put the brake on sympathetic arousal of fear. These interpersonal connections prompt the body to release oxytocin, which supports the social engagement process.

The ventral vagal stimulates the somatic muscles that control facial expressions, mouth movements, speech, eating, and hearing. The ventral vagal is also part of a neuronal network regulating the heart and bronchi to promote calm and self-soothing states. The brain-face-heart connection is an integrated neural circuit that cues others to our changing neuroceptions through subtle muscular changes in the face—a critical aspect of human communication.

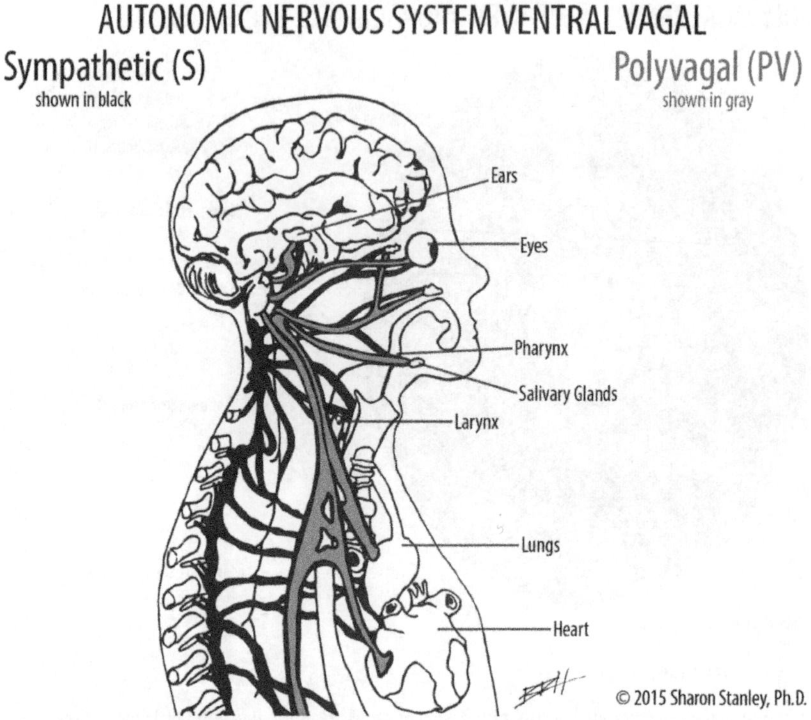

AUTONOMIC NERVOUS SYSTEM VENTRAL VAGAL

Sympathetic (S)
shown in black

Polyvagal (PV)
shown in gray

— Ears

— Eyes

— Pharynx

— Salivary Glands

— Larynx

— Lungs

— Heart

© 2015 Sharon Stanley, Ph.D.

Figure 2.11 Ventral Vagal

The myelinated ventral vagal circuit facilitates rapid communication from organs of perception to the brain to put the "vagal brake" on sympathetic arousal.

Porges (2011) encourages practitioners to help people suffering from trauma activate the vagal brake—a sustained relational connection that puts the "brake" on adrenal-cortical sympathetic arousal. This can be accomplished through embodied empathic interactions as well as interventions that focus attention on relationships that stimulate vitality, connection, and a sense of well-being. The considerable effectiveness of the ventral vagal in quelling traumatic reactions lies in the myelination of the axons of this circuit.

The Sympathetic Nervous Circuit

The sympathetic circuit runs on either side of the spine like a chain of pearls and branches out to connect with muscles and organs throughout the body. See Figures 2.12 and 2.13. To mobilize the body to defend, protect, or withdraw, the hypothalamus activates two systems: the sympathetic nervous system and the adrenal-cortical system. The sympathetic

AUTONOMIC NERVOUS SYSTEM INNERVATION - SYMPATHETIC

Sympathetic (S)
shown in black

The sympathetic nervous system, its fibers originating in the spinal cord, extends along either side of the spinal column from the base of the skull to the coccyx. This forms complex sympathetic plexi in the neck, thorax, and abdomen, which, when stimulated, work in conjunction with the adrenal medulla to mediate a full bodied response called the sympatho-adrenal response. This response causes increased sweating; dilates the pupils; accelerates heart rate and increases blood pressure; increases blood sugar; dilates the lungs' bronchial passages; constricts blood flow to the gut, thereby decreasing gut peristaltic action; decreases blood flow to the kidneys and reproductive organs; and increases blood flow to all major muscle groups. This coordinated response forms the basis for the "fight or flight" reaction.

Polyvagal (PV)
shown in gray

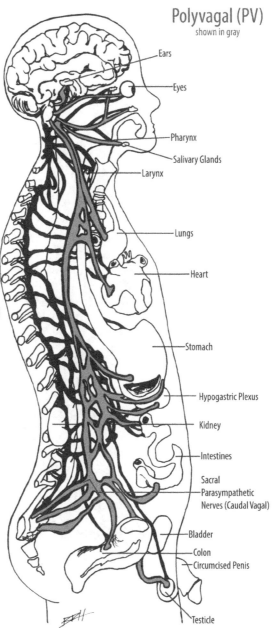

Ears
Eyes
Pharynx
Salivary Glands
Larynx
Lungs
Heart
Stomach
Hypogastric Plexus
Kidney
Intestines
Sacral Parasympathetic Nerves (Caudal Vagal)
Bladder
Colon
Circumcised Penis
Testicle

Figure 2.12 ANS

Sympathetic neural pathways transport signals from the body to the brain muscle to accelerate the heart rate, constrict blood vessels, and raise blood pressure to protect the body from perceived danger.

AUTONOMIC NERVOUS SYSTEM INNERVATION

Sympathetic (S)
shown in black

Polyvagal (PV)
shown in gray

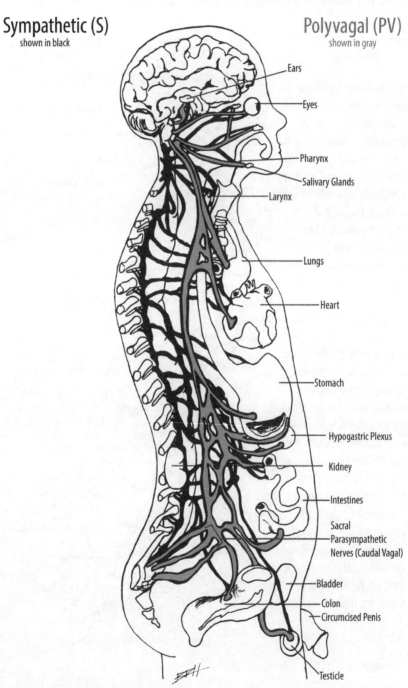

Ears

Eyes

Pharynx

Salivary Glands

Larynx

Lungs

Heart

Stomach

Hypogastric Plexus

Kidney

Intestines

Sacral
Parasympathetic
Nerves (Caudal Vagal)

Bladder

Colon

Circumcised Penis

Testicle

© Sharon Stanley, 2015

Figure 2.13 ANS

Both sympathetic and vagal circuits innervate muscles and organs throughout the body.

nervous system uses nerve pathways to initiate reactions in the body, and the adrenal-cortical system uses the bloodstream. This is a very important distinction to note for the treatment of trauma. While we may be able to tolerate the sensations of sympathetic arousal—even enjoy a little fear of the unknown—the activation of adrenal-cortical toxins in the bloodstream has a harmful effect on the body. Somatic awareness of the initial sensations of sympathetic arousal helps people learn to apply their vagal brake before adrenaline and cortisol flood the body—a component of self-regulation.

Arousal of the sympathetic nervous system and the adrenal-cortical system triggers a number of bodily-based changes including shallow breath, contraction of muscles, dilation of the eyes, increased heart rate, release of adrenaline and cortisol, slowing of the gastrointestinal system, and immobility of the genitals (Nuland 1997). If a perception of danger continues, the combination of a chronic adrenaline and cortisol flow creates a stress reaction that strains the immune system and the cells of the bones, organs, and muscles.

The combined effect of these two systems, the sympathetic arousal and the adrenal-cortical activation, organizes mobilization to aggress or withdraw from danger. When the hypothalamus tells the sympathetic nervous system to kick into gear, the overall effect is that the body speeds up, contracts in preparation for a burst of expansion and action and becomes generally very alert. For example, if a young child drops her ball and steps into traffic to retrieve it, her caregiver must take action quickly. The caregiver's sympathetic nervous system sends out impulses to glands and smooth muscles of the organs and tells the adrenal medulla to release epinephrine (adrenaline) and norepinephrine (noradrenaline) into the bloodstream. These stress hormones prepare the muscles to run and protect the child. At the same time, the hypothalamus releases corticotropin-releasing factor (CRF) into the pituitary gland, activating the adrenal-cortical system and preparing the body to deal with a sustained threat. If attempts at defense are not successful, the instinct to protect may become immobilized, and it may be difficult to spontaneously protect someone again. In this case, the dorsal vagal state of immobility has fused with the sympathetic arousal of adrenaline and cortisol.

The sudden flood of epinephrine, norepinephrine, and other hormones secreted in sympathetic arousal causes changes in the body that can be sensed somatically, such as increased blood pressure and heart rate, which feel like tightness in the temples and chest. Increased visibility of the white part surrounding the eye indicates dilation of the pupils—an aroused state. Pale skin indicates constriction of the veins, a result of stress, as well as increases in blood glucose levels. With this activation, striated muscles tense up and the smooth muscles of the viscera relax to allow more oxygen into the lungs. This relaxation in the viscera can give a false sense of calm in the middle of a crisis. However, all is not well; the digestive and immune systems slow or shut down, and a person can have trouble focusing on small tasks.

When people perceive danger for extended periods, such as during times of war or sustained abuse, the activation of the sympathetic nervous system and the adrenal-cortical system becomes chronic, and fixed-action patterns develop to sharpen the ability to perceive danger and life threat through the eyes, ears, and body sensations. For example, a person may continually scan with their eyes, ears, and nose for cues of danger or threat. This state of hypervigalence allows people to successfully adapt to survival conditions, but it can also become a chronic state with fixed-action patterns, leading to mental and physical illness. Sustained intense levels of sympathetic arousal with adrenal-cortical activation result in a neural state of hyperarousal, fostering "aggressive terror" (Schore, personal communication) that is difficult to reverse, despite times of peace, without bodily-based relational help from another.

With the knowledge of another gained through somatic awareness and empathy, practitioners can deactivate sympathetic arousal with the vagal brake (Porges 2011). Stimulation of the vagal brake allows a traumatized person to tolerate recall of traumatic memories and incorporate sympathetic arousal and vitality into the body without the infusion of toxic adrenaline and cortisol into the bloodstream. In times of real danger, the instincts for adrenal-cortical reactions are available, but the unconscious activation of the toxic hormones from past fears has been differentiated from present moment lived experience, saving the body's reserves from unnecessary depletion.

The Dorsal Vagal System

The dorsal vagal is the lower part of the vagus nerve linking the viscera and internal organs, in the region of the gut beneath the diaphragm, with the brain. See Figure 2.14. The dorsal vagal system produces immobility in the system, such as deep sleep, yet when activated by perceptions of life threat it fuses with sympathetic circuits reducing metabolic output with shut-down behaviors, a state that is potentially lethal to humans (Porges 2011). The dorsal vagal is not myelinated, so messages move more slowly from the gut to the brain than those from the myelinated ventral vagal. The dorsal vagal circuit regulates muscles associated with visceral functions in the lungs, diaphragm, heart and stomach, including peristalsis of the GI tract, and respiration. Responsible for heart rate, dilation of blood vessels, and blood pressure, the dorsal vagal system creates a bodily-based state of partial or full immobilization when we feel safe and ready to rest and restore. This circuit communicates immobility and the body goes into a still state to conserve energy. Because the dorsal vagal is unmyelinated, this state of immobility comes on gradually in a dreamy kind of way, often feeling like a surrender into the sensations of the body as we fall into a deep sleep. The dorsal vagal without fear also provides the quiet peace of mind to nurse and nurture a baby and initiates a motionless bliss following sexual intercourse or, at times, during meditation.

AUTONOMIC NERVOUS SYSTEM DORSAL VAGAL
Sympathetic (S)
shown in black

Polyvagal (PV)
shown in gray

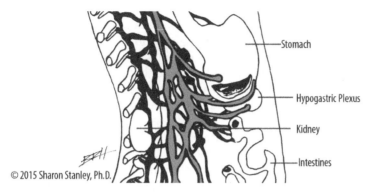

© 2015 Sharon Stanley, Ph.D.

Stomach

Hypogastric Plexus

Kidney

Intestines

Figure 2.14 Dorsal Vagal

The dorsal vagal circuit of immobilization is not myelinated and changes more slowly than the ventral vagal.

However, the dorsal vagal state of immobility can also be at the core of a traumatic experience. When the sympathetic system becomes fused with the dorsal-vagal immobility system in a moment of trauma, a person enters in a state of "immobility with fear"—an arousal state of helpless terror. For example, if a resting baby in a dorsal vagal surrender to immobility is startled awake and frightened, there is a good chance that the dorsal vagal immobility will become momentarily coupled with the brain circuit of sympathetic arousal, creating immobilization with fear. The young baby is totally dependent on a caregiver to soothe, regulate, and differentiate the immobilization from the fear. This differentiation requires that the caregiver acknowledges and joins with the affective distress of the baby to bring her back into a ventral vagal connection of love and calmness through contingent interactions (Beebe et al. 2012). The sympathetic arousal can be relatively short-lived if there is no adrenal-cortical activation. The caregiver can restore regulation through eye gaze, facial nonverbal communication, rhythm, contingent vocal communication, and just the right amount of touch. If there is adrenal-cortical activation, it can take longer to soothe and restore regulation as the activating chemicals need time to dissipate.

The most significant danger from an adrenal activation and sympathetic arousal is an increasing high intensity that suddenly shuts off and drops into a collapse, a dissociated state of chronic "immobilization with fear" that may look like a "good baby," but can begin a lifetime cycle of disembodiment, dissociation, and depression. For example, if a baby is screaming with terror in his crib, in a hyperaroused state, and the parent consistently ignores the scream, the baby can drop down into dissociation, a neural state of immobilization with fear. This fall from hyperarousal first happens when the adrenal-cortical activation reaches a level that is unendurable and the dorsal vagal circuit is activated, dropping the traumatized person into collapsed immobility.

Neural states that are influenced by "immobilization with fear" are challenging to treat physically and psychologically for a number of reasons. First, as implicit memories, they are often hidden in fixed-action patterns in the body and are out of awareness for the person suffering from trauma. When the feeling of this neural state is brought into awareness, the sensations of this collapsed neural state are associated with intense feelings of failure and defeat.

Chronic, shame-based neural states appear in dissociative and depressive disorders. When aversive events occur, shame is at the core of the trauma, with a sense of failure to create safety. In relational-developmental trauma, shame motivates dissociation, an escape from the unbearable and the creation of a "self-contained dream" (Bromberg 2011). In both forms of trauma, shame is a dropping down from states of interest and excitement or a hyperaroused sympathetic state, to a hypoaroused dorsal vagal state of "immobilization with fear." When the therapeutic dyad is able to regulate arousal states and surrender together to the dorsal vagal state of immobilization without fear the physical sense of shame transforms into a healthy sense of humility.

Conflict and Fusion between the Ventral Vagal and Dorsal Vagal

Porges (2011) attributes various emotional, mental, and medical disorders to competitive conflicts between the ventral vagal and dorsal vagal, particularly when the dorsal vagal has coupled with sympathetic arousal and is locked in conflict between immobility and fear. The different vagal states may have oppositional or complementary outputs to the same target organ. For example, during play, the ventral vagal circuit of social connection helps people stay in contact with each other yet explore the edges of fear through small doses of sympathetic arousal. If the arousal of the ventral vagal circuit of social engagement trumps the arousal of the sympathetic circuit, play is successful and participants can enjoy a bond of social engagement. If the ventral vagal arousal is lost for either participant, play can feel like bullying, harassment, or even the terror of life threat. When a child perceives his or her life is threatened in this kind of play, the neural state of "immobilization with fear" can take over and the child can collapse into patterns of blame, shame, helplessness, and powerlessness.

When the ventral vagal circuit of social connection has fused with arousal of sympathetic fear as in children's rough play, the result can be anxiety, anger, and aggression. These emotions can be differentiated from their bodily-based sensations through skillful somatic practices and interventions. Therapeutic interventions may involve an oscillation of phenomenological neural states and emotions to clearly differentiate the fused elements and then integrate them in a creative new neural network.

Fusion of Ventral Vagal, Dorsal Vagal, and Sympathetic-Adrenal-Cortical Arousal

Some forms of extreme trauma, such as the loss of breath while held down or being sexually abused by someone who has been trusted, involves the activation and fusion of several circuits—the ventral vagal, the dorsal vagal, and the sympathetic-adrenal-cortical system—creating a state of global high intense arousal or hyperarousal. The fusion of these circuits makes the differentiation of emotions and sensations during therapy challenging. The loss of relational trust causes the ventral vagal to become tightly fused with sympathetic arousal. The activation of the dorsal vagal and intense sympathetic arousal results in "fear with immobilization" with collapse, dissociation and disorganized behaviors. The impact of such an overwhelming event lies in the binding of the nervous system and forging a cohesive neural state of hypoarousal. A sense of relational betrayal combined with aversive trauma at the hands of a formerly trusted person, can be challenging to differentiate and embody. People with these neural fusions are often categorized in diagnostic language, such as depressive, dissociative, bipolar, borderline personality, or even schizophrenic. The intensity of this neural fusion in complex trauma can range from mild to severe, resulting in more severe diagnosis. The profound loss of trust becomes global in a person's life, complicating most relationships.

Clinically, I have found that in cases of complex trauma I must first focus on activating the ventral vagal circuit of relational connection with tenderness and sensitivity. Some somatic models of trauma advocate for the arousal of the sympathetic circuit to conquer the felt sense of immobility with restoration of the thwarted instinct of power, anger, and rage. Yet with complex trauma, the containment of the intersubjective relationship is used to develop the strength and resilience to tolerate the activation of sympathetic defenses and immobility states. With the safety, strength, and confidence of the resilient ventral vagal system in place, the dorsal vagal circuit can release the terror, bringing rest and restoration deeply into one's inner core, the viscera. When the ventral vagal and dorsal vagal collaborate rather than compete, the viscera releases the hidden sense of shame and failure.

Changing the Neural-Emotional Patterns from Trauma

Guided by Porges' research, we can trust that the root of complex trauma lies in neural-emotional states of "immobility with fear," the fusing of the immobility response with intense sympathetic arousal. How do helping professionals assist people suffering from complex trauma in uncoupling this neural bind? Interventions in the peripheral nervous system and their *sensors and effectors* allows the nervous system to change their interaction with the environment (Romesin and Verden-Zoller 2008). Sensors are the sensations we feel when we perceive changes in the environment—either from within the body or from the outside world. Sensors stimulate the amygdala, the autonomic nervous system, and other parts of the brain. Effectors carry the messages from the brain back to the body and stimulate glands and muscles to act in accordance with the brain's current version of reality. See Figure 2.15.

To make specific changes in this system, we first fine-tune our sensory perceptions. Aided by embodied awareness, we can look more closely, hear

PERIPHERAL NERVOUS SYSTEM

Somatic practices and interventions stimulate new sensory awareness and movement in the context of the intersubjective field.

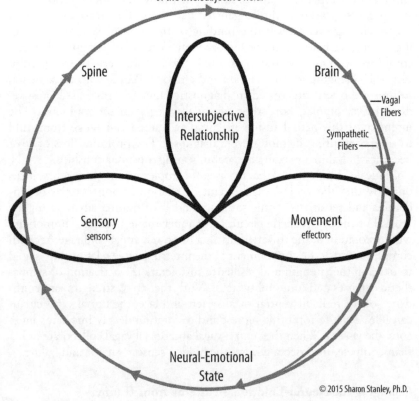

© 2015 Sharon Stanley, Ph.D.

Figure 2.15 Peripheral Nervous System

The peripheral nervous system is outside the brain and spinal cord and connects them with sensory organs, and other organs of the body, muscles, blood vessels, and glands.

more accurately, and feel more actively in the moment, a mindfulness that can shift habitual autonomic fixed-action patterns from trauma. When we bring awareness and specific language to our immediate sensory perceptions, we alter input to the brain and the messages the brain sends to the body, the effectors. The messages the brain sends to the body can then descend as warnings of danger or life threat or assurances of safety.

For example, let's say you detect a change in the weather. Perceptual-based sensors detect subtle changes in your environment and carry the message to various areas of the brain. The right hemisphere of the brain swiftly processes the incoming information and sends new messages via effectors directly to the glands and muscles. If the glands and muscles have gotten the message that this shift in the weather is life threatening, they prepare for death with dissociation. If the muscles and glands get messages of danger, they activate aggressive defenses including the energy to flee. With messages of safety, they restore optimal arousal with relaxation, connection, and ease.

We create change in this cycle by first interrupting the fear-based sensory messages that are on their way to the brain, and cause tension, contraction, and tightness. Faint internal movements are felt as the messages coming from the brain, such as gripping in the gut, swirling in the heart, or dropping down. We can enter into this fear-based conversation of the nervous system with safety and create small shifts in sensations and activate micromovements that indicate a new flow of information and energy. That which has been autonomic can become accessible to consciousness and in coherence with the current reality. This subtle interruption and transformation of sensory perception and voluntary micromovement requires containment within a trusted safe relationship and new affective experiences to create more adaptive perceptions. In Chapter 3, we'll explore how safe relationships affect the brain and nervous system through attachment and how helping professionals can assist clients in developing resilience following attachment disruptions through regulation of the nervous system.

References

Atleo, E. R. 2004. *Tsawalk: A Nuu-chah-nulth Worldview*. Vancouver: University of British Columbia Press.

Beebe, B., F. M. Lachmann, S. Markese, K. A. Buck, L. E. Bahrick, H. Chen, P. Cohen, H. Andrews, S. Feldstein, and J. Jaffe. 2012. "On the Origins of Disorganized Attachment and Internal Working Models: Paper II. An Empirical Microanalysis of 4-Month Mother-Infant Interaction." *Psychoanalytic Dialogues: The International Journal of Relational Perspectives* 22(3): 352–374.

Bromberg, P. M. 2011. *The Shadow of the Tsunami: and the Growth of the Relational Mind*. New York: Routledge.

Fonagy, P., G. Gergely, E. L. Jurist, and M. Target. 2005. *Affect Regulation, Mentalization and the Development of Self*. London: Karnac.

Frewen, P., and R. Lanius. 2015. *Healing the Traumatized Self: Consciousness, Neuroscience Treatment*. New York: Norton.

Hecht, D. 2014. "Cerebral Lateralization of Pro- and Anti-Social Tendencies." *Experimental Neurobiology* 23(1): 1–27.

Kalsched, D. 2013. *Trauma and the Soul: A Psycho-Spiritual Approach to Human Development and its Interruption*. London: Routledge.

MacLean, P. 1990. *The Triune Brain in Evolution: Role in Paleocerebral Function*. New York: Plenum Press.

McGilchrist, I. 2009. *The Master and His Emissary: The Divided Brain and the Making of the Western World*. London: Yale University Press.

McGilchrist, I. 2010. "Reciprocal Organization of the Cerebral Hemispheres." *Dialogues in Clinical Neuroscience,* 12(4): 317–334.

Nuland, S. B. 1997. *The Wisdom of the Body*. New York: Norton.

Panksepp, J., and L. Biven. 2011. *The Archaeology of Mind: Neuroevolutionary Origins of Human Emotion*. New York: Norton.

Porges, S.W. 2011. *The Polyvagal Theory: Neurophysiological Foundations of Emotions Attachment, Communication, Self-Regulation*. New York: Norton.

Romesin, H.M., and G. Verden-Zoller. 2008. *The Origin of Humanness in the Biology of Love*. Edited by P. Bunnell. Charlottesville: Imprint Academic.

Scaer, R.C. 2005. *The Trauma Spectrum: Hidden wounds and Human Resiliency*. New York: Norton.

Schore, A.N. 2008. "Regulation Theory and the Paradigm Shift: From Conscious Cognition to Unconscious Affect." Unpublished presentation at the UCLA Extension and Lifespan Learning Institute Conference, Los Angeles, CA, March 7.

Schore, A.N. 2012. *The Science of the Art of Psychotherapy*. New York: Norton.

Schore, A.N., and R.P. Newton. 2013. "Using Modern Attachment Theory to Guide Clinical Assessments of Early Attachment Relationships." In *Attachment-Based Clinical Work with Children and Adolescents*, edited by J.E. Bettmann and D.D. Friedman, 61–98. New York: Springer.

Sieff, D. 2006. "Unlocking the Secrets of the Wounded Psyche: The Miraculous Survival System That Is Also a Prison." *Caduceus* 69–70: 2.

Thompson, P. 2007. "Down Will Come Baby: Prenatal Stress, Primitive Defenses and Gestational Dysregulation." *Journal of Trauma & Dissociation: The Official Journal of the International Society for the Study of Dissociation (ISSD)* 8(3): 85–113.

Tick, E. 2014–2015. "Healing the Wounds of War: Native perspectives on restoring the soul." *Parabola*, 39(4): 64–71.

Van der Hart, O., E.R.S. Nijenhuis, and K. Steele. 2006. *The Haunted Self: Structural Dissociation and Treatment of Chronic Traumatization*. New York: Norton.

3 Good News! The Brain Can Change!

> The idea that the brain can change its own structure and function through thought and activity is, I believe, the most important alteration in our view of the brain since we first sketched out its basic anatomy and the workings of its basic component, the neuron.
>
> (Doidge 2007, xvi)

Attachment and Optimal Development of Human Beings

People suffering from traumatic experience can actually change the connectivity of their brains through bodily-based relational connection (Schore 2012). To understand why and how this works, we must first explore the conditions that lead to optimal development in children. Optimal development occurs when the highest quality of relational and community care is given to children, enabling them to flourish (Gleason and Narvaez 2014). New standards for optimal development are emerging from attachment research between parents and children (Main, Hesse, and Goldwyn 2008), developmental neuroscience (Schore 2012; Porges 2011), the child-rearing practices throughout the globe called "responsive parenting," and children's socialization within a culture (Narvaez et al. 2013, 2).

At a basic level, a consistent perception of physical and emotional safety is essential for the optimal development of a child's brain and body. This sense of safety fosters the ability to engage in nurturing social relationships and begins before birth. A developing prenate is deeply embedded in the body of the mother and intimately shares her experiences of stress, safety, danger, and life threat (Thompson 2007). For the prenate and growing child, perceptions of danger and life threat interrupt growth in connectivity of the brain, resulting in chronic bodily-based states marked by fear, anxiety, terror, and horror that fuel dissociation and aggression. The sensitivity of early caregivers, particularly "maternal responsivity," is critical to a secure attachment, empathy, regulation, and conscience (Narvaez et al. 2013, 2).

If early interpersonal connections are consistently safe, emotionally nurturing, and socially stimulating, children develop *a secure attachment* with states of mind that predict the quality of intimate relationships throughout life (Main 2010; Siegel 1999; Schore 2003, 2004, 2012). Secure attachment occurs when consistently attuned, resonant, and regulated parents and others can "feel with" a child, make sense out of a child's inner world, and respond with contingent, empathic interactions (Beebe and Lachmann 2014). Reciprocal emotional communication allows a child's brain to create a scaffolding that can support a lifetime of resilience to aversive experience (Narvaez 2014).

Children who are securely attached are able to increase their capacity for coregulation and self-regulation as they grow. *Coregulation* is a pattern that is developed in the infant-parent relationship through affective interactions of reciprocity and changes of rhythm with attention to eye gaze, facial expression, gestures, and vocalizations (Mazokopaki and Kugiumutzakis 2009) and is tied to optimal development through holding, breastfeeding, and play within a community (Gleason and Narvaez 2014). Coregulation supports a child's ability to go out into the environment and explore, developing self-regulation, and then return to relationships for coregulation.

Children with insecure and disorganized attachment are not parented with adequate emotional and social responsivity or sufficient coregulation to regulate perceptions of danger and life threat. Children with an *insecure attachment* are unable to consistently trust the presence of their caregivers as a source of regulation and comfort, while the trust of children with *disorganized attachment* is even more compromised. Feeling simultaneously drawn to the protection of the parent yet frightened and resistant to coming closer, children disassociate from their confusing feelings, resulting in disorganized behavior. This conflict and these feelings lie contained in the body and mind as implicit memories.

Children with insecure and disorganized attachment tend to feel lonely much of the time, perceiving themselves as separate and isolated. Unlike children who are securely attached, they learn to *autoregulate* on a primitive level, finding solitary ways to manage arousal with movements like repetitive rocking, spinning, and aggressing; disembodiment; dissociation; and other fixed-action patterns.

When infants and young children find themselves with little or no emotional resonance and an absence of a reciprocal, interactive response to their nonverbal emotional communication, they may ultimately withdraw with a "still-face," a dissociated facial expression (Tronick 2007). Withdrawal from social engagement in the present moment is a silent survival strategy that can begin very early in life and continue throughout the life span, interrupting development and growth.

Attachment and States of Mind

As children grow, their internal patterns of early relationships emerge as states of mind (Main, Hesse, and Goldwyn 2008) that include sensory, emotional, imaginal, and reflective dynamics in any given moment. It's helpful to think of states of mind as the way consciousness wanders from moment to moment, sometimes creatively and at other times repeating perceptual errors from prior affective experience (Smallwood and Schooler 2015). When a state of mind is organized, the body and brain can process incoming stimulation into a cohesive experience. However, perceptions of fear and terror, arising when children are emotionally neglected and abused, can lead to disorganized states of mind, wounds that limit the ability to process new information.

States of mind can shift quickly (Stern 2004). These fast autonomic shifts can be observed in the behavior of babies and are often confusing for parents if they are not attuned to the inner worlds of their children. Adult states of mind can shift quickly also; we are simply more skilled in hiding our changing reactions, creating confusion in ourselves and our most cherished relationships. An embodied, intersubjective relationship is essential for discerning one's own current state of mind and that of another and regulating emerging dysregulated states.

Attachment patterns formed in childhood persist with surprising consistency. Through in-depth interviews of participants as they recalled their early experiences with caregivers, Mary Main (2000) researched adult attachment states of mind through the Adult Attachment Inventory (AAI). During the interview, adults with a secure attachment were easy with the topic, their memories accurately reflected the phenomena, and they were able to develop a flow of coherent ideas regarding attachment. Flexible, attentive, and coherent in their thinking, they displayed a sense of ease with imperfections in themselves and others—showing compassion, forgiveness, and acceptance.

The AAI results determined that adult insecure attachment has two patterns: Those with a dismissive pattern tended to idealize their parents or childhood—or insisted on a lack of memory of childhood—and actively dismissed the need for attachment relationships. They were remote from feelings and interested in activities or objects rather than relationships. Adults with a preoccupied pattern tended to speak in confusing and noncollaborative ways when describing past relational experience. They expressed anger toward primary attachment figures and blamed themselves or their parents.

Another major pattern that the interview detected was disorganized/unresolved attachment, a state of mind where people unsuccessfully denied the intensity or nature of trauma, felt like they deserved it, tried to "push it out of my mind," and displayed both disoriented speech and a fear of being taken over by the abusive person (Kilpatrick, personal communication). People with a disorganized or disoriented attachment pattern live with a very high arousal of fear combined with immobility—although they may have adopted defensive strategies to mask it—due to a history of unresolved abuse or trauma.

Researchers such as Schore, Beebe, Lanius, Newton, and others are combining findings from attachment research and developmental psychology to form developmental neuroscience or "modern attachment theory" (Schore 2012), which links the failures of insecure and disorganized attachment with losses of neural connectivity in the brain and dysregulated neurological reactions that result in adult relationship failures, physical disease, and mental health issues (Schore and Newton 2013). From a clinical point of view, implicit memories of past perceptions of danger and life threat in less than nurturing relationships offer an entry into efforts to change the brain. By changing the habitual perception of fear and terror to safety in embodied, attuned relationships and reorganizing the habitual neural states of mind from trauma, innate processes of growth and development can resume.

The good news is that repairs can be made and optimal development can be restimulated through affective regulation therapies (Schore and Schore 2014) and embodied relational somatic practices particularly in the context of communal support for optimal development (Gleason and Narvaez 2014). First, let's take a closer look at the origins of attachment disruptions and how the trauma of one generation can be passed on to the next through caregiver relationships and the environment, perpetuating individual and cultural cycles of relational injury, violence, illness, and neglect.

The Multigenerational Transmission of Trauma Predicts Attachment Disruptions

Researchers Schore and Schore (2014), Beebe et al. (2012), and others have established that a mother's inability to communicate emotionally with her infant results in relational-developmental trauma and point to evidence that the origins of trauma run much deeper: they are embedded in historical trauma, generational injuries, and the ecological dysfunction of families, communities, and nations. The loss of emotional support, education, and nurturing for young parents usually begins well before the parents were born (Yehuda et al. 2000; Ehlers et al. 2013; Danieli 1998).

Traumatic experiences are created in part by the environment when family, community, and cultural-based systems do not acknowledge nor support the struggles of people raising young children. Oppression; racism; poverty; slavery; genocide; sexism; the environmental contamination of water, air, earth, and food; and the generational transmission of suffering from war and violence are present in communities throughout the globe. These violent dynamics divert a communities' focus from the responsibility of raising children, healing wounds, and restoring a collaborative and interactive attention to human growth and development. The price of doing nothing is high because the trauma of one or a few can affect the neurobiology of generations to come in our interconnected world.

Researchers like Danieli (1998) have documented the multigenerational trauma legacies of Indigenous people on several continents, survivors of the Holocaust and the atomic bombings of Japan during World War II, as well as the genocide in Cambodia. Cindy Ehlers et al. (2013), Rachel Yehuda et al. (2000), and others have shown how Native Americans have an unusually high risk for post-traumatic stress disorder (PTSD) from traumatic incidences, particularly in early adulthood. The experience of slavery in the United States has also been shown to be particularly devastating to future generations (DeGruy 2005).

Danieli (1998) describes how healing from trauma "must take place in all of life's relevant dimensions or systems and cannot be accomplished by the individual alone" (7). The ruptures of communal trauma create survival patterns of fixity or chaos in individuals, a loss of free flow, and a sense of being stuck in destructive states of mind. The fixity or chaos results in the vulnerability of the individual and his or her progeny to further trauma and illness. For example, Sir Richard Bowlby (2014) describes a pilot study by Jane Sherwood that traces the losses and trauma of sixty families with dementia and sixty families without dementia through the maternal line. Sherwood found a direct correlation between the losses and trauma experiences of grandmothers and the incidence of dementia in their grandchildren as they aged.

The hidden social and neurological dynamics of trauma do not die with the person who directly encountered the event. Rather, the remnants of trauma live on through ordinary, yet highly significant survival patterns, including silence about the trauma (Danieli 1998), splitting the emotional aspects of suffering from ordinary daily functions (Van der Hart, Nijenhuis, and Steele 2006), and in the attachment process between parents and infants (Schore 2012).

The comprehensive research of the AAI (Main, Hesse, and Goldwyn 2008) reveals how parents with unresolved implicit traumatic memories pass on the inability to regulate and securely attach with their offspring. The sensitive and embodied perception, attunement, resonance, and reciprocity parents need to interact with their children can be dulled by survival self-states following a traumatic experience. When in a disembodied, dissociative, or disorganized state of mind, parents do not see the disappointment, hear the sorrow, or sense the pain of their children. The gates of perception that connect them to others become fixed in the moment of trauma and result in patterns focused on their own survival.

If parents impaired by trauma are unable to regulate their own autonomic and emotional states, and resolve their unprocessed traumatic experiences, they unconsciously pass on the living wounds of their trauma to their children by failing to sense, feel, and know them. A young infant has no explicit recall of emotional neglect because the injury occurs during the early development of the right hemisphere of the brain, a time when the explicit memory system of the left hemisphere has not developed. Early exclusivity of the right brain means that implicit memories are formed into habitual states of mind that begin in the prenatal experiences and extend up to three years of age (Schore and Newton 2013). Without resolution or relational support, an infant who has experienced emotional neglect grows into an adult who implicitly passes on attachment-based relational trauma in their states of mind as they interact with their own children. People who have experienced relational-developmental trauma are often unable to sense their own embodied presence, so their knowledge of their own children will be abstract and vague rather than physically connected to them as unique persons. Children born to parents suffering from unresolved trauma live in an unconscious sea of loss and grief, distressing states of mind with implicit memories of unbearable sensations, emotions, and images that contribute to generational cycles of insecure and disorganized attachment.

Case 2.1 Kerry: Changing Neural Patterns in Relationship

The unconscious urge to protect oneself from anguishing sensations of emotional neglect and abuse results in chronic states of hyperarousal and hypoarousal. The mental states of insecure and disorganized attachment are passed down to the next generation with 85 percent reliability (Main, Hesse, and Goldwyn 2008). This was the case with Kerry, a 62-year-old woman who struggled to cope with intense depressive symptoms— stemming from attachment failures—that left her feeling helpless, isolated, and terrified. Working together, we traced Kerry's symptoms in part to sensory-based implicit memories before and after her birth to her fifteen-year-old mother, who did not acknowledge that she was pregnant and was terrified to give birth.

Kerry was born in the bathroom of a high school, her mother assisted by a startled nun. Over time, Kerry was adopted by her maternal grandmother, a woman who was not able to provide emotional nourishment. These early experiences contributed to Kerry's chronic depressive symptoms and formed "dissociative gaps" in her explicit memory, implicit events that were not available to her conscious memory system (Main, Hesse, and Goldwyn 2008). Research on memory indicates that lived experience, even before birth, is held in the implicit memory system of the right hemisphere of the brain. Implicit traumatic memories emerge as fragmented sensory data with "skills and habits, emotional responses, reflexive actions, classically conditioned responses" (Van der Kolk, McFarlane, and Weisaeth 1996, 281) and chronic symptoms of physical and mental illness.

Kerry experienced horrific prenatal experiences with her birth mother, who attempted a painful self-induced abortion several times. As an infant and child, Kerry then endured emotionally neglectful experiences with her adoptive mother, who had emigrated from Northern Ireland with her parents at a young age. The adoptive mother followed what Danieli (1998) calls the "conspiracy of silence" in withholding any information of the extensive and brutal family trauma that led to their refugee status in Canada. Both of Kerry's mothers had histories of depression, anxiety, and dissociation, states of mind that preclude reciprocity, attunement, and resonance with a vulnerable child. Lacking the ability to regulate intense emotions themselves, both mothers were ill equipped to coregulate a traumatized infant and disturbed child.

By the time Kerry came to see me, she wore a "still-face" (Tronick 2007). The deep lines etched in her brow, cheeks, and chin silently told her story of a lifetime of intense suffering. Our first challenge was to create an intersubjective relationship, a process that required me to stay embodied, attuned, and resonant with the cues of her inner world that she provided in her face, posture, tone of voice, and dialogue. I watched carefully for subtle shifts in her eyes, face, voice, and body posture, and attempted to feel the dissociated inner sensations she was too terrified to feel. I needed to attune, resonate, and sense Kerry in a tender way, without drama or angst, to keep the arousal of her fear to a minimum. Too much compassion would have terrified her and too little would have reinforced the emotional neglect she had endured from her earliest days.

In the beginning, I often made mistakes in attuning to her, but she continued to have patience with me as I came to sense how she felt and learned how to be with her in the long silences when it seemed nothing was happening. At first, I found the silences uncomfortable. When I stopped trying to fill the silences, I was able to somatically sense and acknowledge the unformulated pain of her early years, and momentarily embody her numbed anguish.

I found that our silences could be rich and connective through nonverbal forms of communication. As I learned to embody her dissociated anguish in small doses, she recognized it on my face, in my eyes, and in my tone of voice. I alternated between feeling her disembodied anguish and inviting an empathic connection, which provided a spark of aliveness for both of us, a sense of connection that was a relief from fixity and numbness. My embodied, nonverbal oscillation between our shared sensory experience of anguish and an invitation to empathy formed a rhythm that Kerry was able to slowly embody. This play with rhythm lifted her depressed states of mind into moments of aliveness through vitality affects. Vitality affects go beyond mirroring to restore deep neurological, rhythmical patterns that Malloch and Trevarthen (2009) have called *communicative musicality*— a shared rhythm that forms authentic human connectivity. Communicative musicality energizes relationships and is essential in the development of the self (Malloch and Trevarthen 2009). While mirror neurons trigger the spontaneous imitation of movement, engagement in the rhythm and play of vitality affects creates an embodied empathy.

Neither Kerry's mother nor her grandmother was capable of engaging in the subtle, emotional interactions of vitality affects during her infancy and childhood due to their own disorganized attachment patterns. Specifically, what essential ingredients were missing in Kerry's relationships with her caregivers?

Biological Reciprocity

Emotionally neglectful interactions in the early years of a child's life, including those coming from good intentions or misguided love, can result in the absence of an innate spontaneous vitality. The loss of innate vitality can instill a child with a felt sense of emptiness, isolation, and alienation.

In contrast, emotionally congruent interactions, such as gazing, singing, holding, soothing, and providing vitality affects, can "promote the inter-generational transmission of resilience" (Schore 2012, 165). Emotionally congruent interactions where a child is sensed, felt, and known (Beebe et al. 2012) generate biological reciprocity—a key ingredient missing from Kerry's relationships with her mother and grandmother. Mutual eye gaze, vocal interaction, authentic gesture, and tender touch offer rich and mean-ingful episodes of rhythmical biological reciprocity and stimulate vitality. These modes of communication can regulate intense arousal from uncon-scious perceptions of danger and life threat and contribute to the secure attachment of a child. In the first year, a child is able to process social infor-mation that is spontaneously communicated through touch, vocalizations, and expressions on the face and eye muscles—dramatically accelerating the development of the brain.

The biological and emotional congruency between infants and caregiv-ers not only predicts a child's brain development but also the ability to reg-ulate intense emotional states. If this congruency is not accomplished in infancy, it is remedial and can be repaired with coregulation in attuned and responsive relationships (Beebe and Lachmann 2014). Helping profession-als can use the basic modes of nonverbal communication between infants and caregivers—sensing, feeling, and knowing the other with attuned eye gaze, vocal tone, facial movements, gestures, and touch in an interactive, rhythmical fashion—to repair the loss of biological reciprocity in older children and adults.

Having missed many relational developmental milestones in her child-hood, Kerry was open and interested, yet guarded, in our nonverbal connection through eye gaze, facial movements, and vocalizations as we established an intersubjective relationship. During our nonverbal yet highly communicative moments together, Kerry's face began to reveal childlike expressions of fear, terror, sadness, joy, and sometimes contentment.

In my long silences with Kerry, the nonverbal communication was intense, reciprocal, and transformative for both of us. Our eye gaze was particularly interactive; as we began working together, Kerry often averted her eyes to look down and to the left at the floor. I would join her and look to the same place on the floor and then briefly gaze at the space around her face, being careful to avoid invading her with a direct eye gaze. After some time, she began to experiment with quick glances at my face to assess my reactions to her. As we experimented with different modes of commu-nication, the rhythm began to generate vitality affects. In addition to eye gaze, our body posture, breath, and subtle gestures, all distinct, expressive communicative modes, created comfort between us at times, distress at others. My nonverbal, yet active vocalization was met with interest and attention. Sounds of prosody or mother-ese, such as *ohhh*, *umm*, and *hummm* let Kerry know I was tracking her very subtle exploration with right-hemispheric ways of communication. Through sensing and knowing, I would match the tone of my prosody to the developmental age I sensed in her. Early in our work together, she stated that she felt "at home" just being quiet with me.

When Kerry and I did exchange verbal communications, it was not the content that was important but the underlying pattern of nonverbal attunement and resonance that helped us connect. The melody, rhythm, tone, and prosody of the human voice communicates authentic emotions, interactions that can be confusing if they are not expressing sincere emotions. The voices of others affect the brain development of a child, unconsciously producing sounds that communicate safety, danger, and life threat. When we perceive safety in the tone of voice of another, we feel free to enter into more complex emotional communications. If we detect insincerity, danger, or even subtle threat in the tone of another's voice, our emotional connection is interrupted and our defenses take over.

In addition to eye gaze, voice, and gesture, physical touch communicates emotion. Babies and adults can unconsciously sense whether they are loved through the quality of touch. Touch can also communicate unacknowledged anger, dislike, impatience, and disgust, powerful messages to an undefended body. According to Feldman, Singer, and Zagoory (2010), the synchrony of touch between a mother and baby "alters vagal tone and cortisol reactivity," shifting intense emotions (quoted in Schore and Newton 2013, 17). Vagal tone, a neural state that is free from constrictions of fear, predicts whether we find social interactions enjoyable as opposed to scary or threatening. With safe and loving connection, people shift out of sympathetic arousal and terror and into a vagal tone that supports social connectivity or drop into vagal states of immobility for restorative rest. In the following section, we'll take a look at the neural change processes that lead to the development of a strong vagal tone.

Changing the Brain: Epigenesis and Neuroplasticity

Relational-developmental trauma is primarily a right-hemispheric wound, an interruption of the innate processing of the right hemisphere, which transforms incoming perceptions to sensations, sensations to movement, movement to feelings and emotion, and emotions to images. Fortunately, disruptions to this innate processing system can be identified and altered. The first type of change we will discuss is *epigenesis*—the shaping of genetic expression through lived experience. According to Leckman and March (2011), epigenesis reveals how early maternal care impacts the genome in brain development, predicting health and disease (quoted in Schore and Newton 2013). Mental states, whether of safety, grief, terror, or horror, are passed on through epigenesis, leading to modifications in development across generations.

Panksepp and Biven (2012) acknowledge that while we inherit many strengths and weaknesses from our parents, much also emerges from how we are reared. "Epigenesis is an experience-dependent change that occurs to genes, typically after we are born. One of the ways genes can change is through the variation in the degree of gene expression. All the cells of the body have the same genes, but in each cell only some of the genes are active or "expressed." When the strength of gene expression is environmentally either decreased or increased, we call it epigenesis" (240). With repair through affective embodied relational experiences, children can lead very different lives than those of their parents and ancestors. Relational nurturing creates new neural pathways for perception, awareness, states of mind, and new knowledge, positively influencing the brain from conception through old age. Epigenesis is not the only process by which the brain can change.

Neuroplasticity refers to the brain's capacity to reorganize its 100 billion neurons into new neural networks that have different synaptic connections. This change process allows the brain to learn, and alter areas of functioning, particularly following traumatic experiences. Doidge (2007) describes how the brain can adjust its structure, optimizing circuits to suit a specific activity and asserts that "children are not always stuck with the mental abilities they are born with; the damaged brain can often reorganize itself so that when one part fails another can often be substituted; if brain cells die, they can at times be replaced; many circuits and even basic reflexes that we think are hardwired are not" (xix). This research indicates it is possible to enter into the implicit memory system and change injured and distorted functions of the brain. For example, Kerry and I were able to alter the effect of her neglectful experiences into a stronger sense of vitality and connection. How exactly does a brain that is suffering from the effects of neglect or injury learn to adapt to a nurturing experience?

The brain changes through two processes: synaptogenesis and myelinogenesis (Siegel 2010). To reorganize itself through *synaptogenesis*—for example, to learn new information—the brain forms new synaptic connections between intact neurons and those that have been damaged. *Myelination* refers to the fatty myelin sheath that coats the axons on the nerves of the ventral vagal social engagement system that moves information and energy very quickly through neural networks. With the growth of myelination through responsive relationships, neurological change can occur swiftly; fear is transformed with connection to others. Changing the brain through lived experience is not random. It requires precision and accuracy to avoid understimulation, overstimulation, and more injury. For example, an intact neuron might be part of a neural network that is contained in the care circuit, which is involved in caring for life, animals, family, and friends. As a child learns to help his peers in a community service activity, we would want to stimulate the care circuit, but not overload it with responsibility beyond the child's current capacity. Growth experiences need to link what is already known with new learning and must be tailored to a tolerable level of arousal.

The change process of *myelinogenesis* occurs in affective embodied relationships, creating rapid shifts in vagal states. Reorganization through myelinogenesis occurs when the myelin sheath of the ventral vagal circuit, the social engagement system, which includes the face, voice, neck, heart, and lungs, is stimulated. Siegel (2010) claims myelinogenesis is one hundred times more effective than synaptogenesis. Changes that occur through social engagement are spontaneous, immediate, and transformative (Porges 2011).

So how can professionals go about helping their clients suffering from trauma replace dysfunctional neural networks with new neural networks? Regulation is grounded in perceptions of safety in the present moment, so by bringing attention to the dynamics of the body, neural states in moments of relational safety, and appropriate somatic interventions, intense emotions from trauma can be felt and coregulated into new meaning.

Earned Secure Attachment through Embodied Attunement, Resonance, and Responsivity

Regulation of intense emotions is the hallmark of resilience—our ability to discern cues that indicate danger and turn to collaborative relationships to manage threats, rather than activate defensive reactions. Professionals can help another coregulate and eventually self-regulate the effect of intense emotions because "the right hemisphere continues its growth over the life span, thereby allowing for therapy-induced plasticity in the system" (Schore 2012, 107).

In the absence of a secure attachment, the right-hemisphere is not able to fully process lived experiences. The restoration of an *earned secure attachment* requires an intersubjective relationship where both people are sensed and known to each other so they can effectively coregulate intense emotions and make sense out of lived experience.

To create secure attachment, both caregivers and professional helpers must foster a sense of embodiment within themselves, a way of living where the mind and body have a congruent connection. A simple way of saying it is—we feel what we know and we know what we feel. On the outer part of our brain, the cerebral cortex maps body parts and movements in the somatosensory cortex. Damasio (2010) explains how the somatosensory cortex, which houses the current version of one's self, maps the body in the brain, synthesizing the felt sense of the mouth, the ears, the eyes, the toes, and all the parts of the body for a sense of embodiment and self-in-relation. See Figure 3.1.

SENSORY MOTOR MAPS IN THE BRAIN

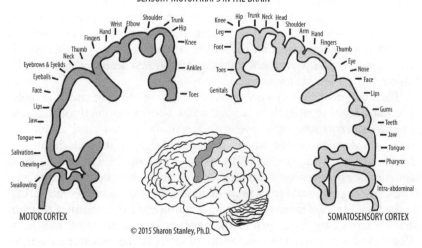

MOTOR CORTEX   SOMATOSENSORY CORTEX

© 2015 Sharon Stanley, Ph.D.

Figure 3.1 Somatosensory & Motor Cortex Chart

Sensations and movements are mapped in the brain for future guidance.

While embodiment is natural for a securely attached child, it is a profound achievement for a traumatized person, particularly one suffering the effects of complex trauma, like Kerry.

People with depression and other symptoms of hypoarousal are unconsciously disconnected from the anguishing sensations in their bodies. For example, Kerry came into therapy with little awareness of her body. In a rare moment of laughter one day, I asked her where she felt this moment of happiness in her body. She looked startled, then offended and told me clearly that she didn't feel anything in her body. Slowly during our coregulation, Kerry was able to identify sensations in her environment, then little by little, in her hands, feet, and face, particularly when she would touch those places. More consistent and deeper embodiment within her viscera developed as we used somatic practice to process difficult emotions in the context of our relationship. Somatic practices are first silently utilized by practitioners, and then as people learn to self-regulate and increase their ability to tolerate uncomfortable sensation, they gradually develop their own ability to use somatic practices. An embodied caregiver or helping professional silently fosters bodily-based connectivity in the brain of the traumatized person, which allows for more complex and spontaneous forms of communication.

Just as embodiment allows a parent to spontaneously attune, resonate, and respond to the dissociated emotions of a child, helping professionals use somatic practices to attune, resonate, and respond to distressing states of mind to assist those suffering from trauma. To attune is to intentionally focus on the specific rhythms of another's presence. Resonance is feeling the sensations, vibrations, peristalsis, and pulsations in the other's body as well as one's own body, enabling someone to actually feel with another. Attunement and resonance are the bodily-based foundations of empathy. When one feels felt by another, they know that they are alive and connected. Trauma brings feelings of isolation, alienation, and separation, while "feeling felt" in a "moment of meeting" transforms trauma from chronic sympathetic arousal to states of vagal social engagement. The Boston Change Process Study Group (2010) proposes that "a moment of meeting" between two people is an event that rearranges implicit relational knowing (6). It creates a new context where past experiences can be reorganized, a moment where subjective realities and implicit memories can change.

To create dynamics for changing the brain in people of all ages, helping professionals can replicate the attuned, resonant, and reciprocal communications between a secure infant and parent. They respond with an eye gaze that feels just enough, vocalize similar sounds, attune and resonate with cues communicated through the movement and gestures of the mouth, face, arms, legs, spine, and voice. Replicating early patterns of mutual communication and vitality affects helps children, adolescents, and adults to establish an inner, rhythmically based self-regulation.

Strengthening Vagal Tone

Connections through attunement, resonance, and reciprocity help develop a strong vagal tone and shift symptoms of complex trauma. With a strong vagal tone, the habitual states of sympathetic arousal transform into strength and humility in relationships. Coregulation and social engagement then emerge to assure survival of both self and other in times of authentic danger and life threat through embodied practices.

To develop a strong vagal tone, states of hyperarousal must be somatically felt with another, and down-regulated within an embodied intersubjective relational field. Chronic states of hyperarousal may contain memories where a defense was mounted but was not fully successful; the defense was thwarted in its efforts to restore feelings of safety in the moment. Embodied presence, mindfulness awareness, somatic empathy, and other somatic interventions can shift the states of aggression, anger, and terror into a sense of peace, containment, and calmness. However, in my experience, states of hypoarousal are more challenging to regulate.

A neural state of hypoarousal is created by an unconscious recall of memories where the person was without resources to mount or sustain a mobilized defense and felt helpless and powerless. Hypoaroused states of disembodiment, dissociation, and depression require a highly flexible, embodied empathic connection with another to stimulate vitality affects. When helping professionals perceive glimpses of the neural state of "immobility with fear," they need to stay embodied and physically and emotionally close to the person suffering from trauma, yet not so close as to create alarm. The goal is to uncouple fear from immobility, a process that occurs over time in a safe relationship, when the fixity of sympathetic arousal of terror is uncoupled from the dorsal vagal system of immobility.

During this process, the energy from released terror may suddenly shoot up into hyperarousal, fueling an impulse toward aggression. With close empathic proximity, emotionally and physically, helping professionals can coregulate and help channel the survival energy into a felt sense of power, mastery, and then prosocial emotions. Stimulating the ventral vagal state of social engagement prompts feelings of nurturing and acceptance of strong states of power. If fear released from immobility goes into the limbic rage circuit, the terror and rage must be contained within the relational field; otherwise a sudden catharsis of trauma can become violent if too much moves too fast. While encountering these rapid shifts, helping professionals can pay close attention to the neural state behind the emotional circuit of rage—the sensations in the body that indicate hyperarousal—and encourage the energy and affect to move through the relational therapeutic field in an affective embodied experience. This may be the first time that the person suffering from trauma experiences intense neural and emotional arousal while being held in a caring relationship and is fundamental for integration of the self and the creation of new bonds that lead to secure attachment.

Embodied connection with people experiencing chronic states of hypoarousal is not for the cautious or faint of heart. Helpers run the risk of awakening their own unresolved trauma and need to be prepared for their own unexpected reactions. However, the gift of awakening the hidden energies of a person's life force through vitality affects becomes an opportunity to deepen the intersubjective field and find healing for one's own implicit pain and suffering.

References

Beebe, B., F. M. Lachmann, S. Markese, K. A. Buck, L. E. Bahrick, H. Chen, P. Cohen, H. Andrews, S. Feldstein, and J. Jaffe. 2012. "On the Origins of Disorganized Attachment and Internal Working Models: Paper II. An Empirical Microanalysis of 4-Month Mother-Infant Interaction." *Psychoanalytic Dialogues: The International Journal of Relational Perspectives* 22(3): 352–374.

Beebe, B., and R. M. Lachmann. 2014. *The Origins of Attachment: Infant Research and Adult Treatment.* New York: Routledge.

Bowlby, R. "Bowlby on Schore: How Allan Schore Changed our Views of Childhood and Old Age: Is Infant Attachment the Missing Link in Dementia?" Lecture notes from the Annual Interpersonal Neurobiology Conference, Los Angeles, CA, March 14, 2014.

The Boston Change Process Study Group. 2010. *Change in Psychotherapy: A Unifying Paradigm.* New York: Norton.

Damasio, A. 2010. *Self Comes to Mind: Constructing the Conscious Brain.* New York: Pantheon Books.

Danieli, Y., ed. 1998. *International Handbook of Multigenerational Legacies of Trauma.* New York: Plenum Press.

DeGruy, J. 2005. *Post Traumatic Slave Syndrome: America's Legacy of Enduring Injury and Healing.* Portland: Joy DeGruy Publications.

Doidge, N. 2007. *The Brain That Changes Itself: Stories of Personal Triumph from the Frontiers of Brain Science.* New York: Penguin Viking.

Ehlers, C. L., I. R. Gizer, D. A. Gilder, and R. Yehuda. 2013. "Lifetime History of Traumatic Events in an American Indian Community Sample: Heritability and Relation to Substance Dependence, Affective Disorder, Conduct Disorder and PTSD." *Journal of Psychiatric Research*, 47(2): 155–161.

Feldman, R., M. Singer, and O. Zagoory. 2010. "Touch Attenuates Infants' Physiological Reactivity to Stress." *Developmental Science* 13: 271–278.

Gleason, T., and D. Narvaez. 2014. "Child Environments and Flourishing." In *Ancestral Landscapes in Human Evolution: Culture, Childrearing and Social Wellbeing*, edited by D. Narvaez, K. Valention, A. Fuentes, J. McKenna, and P. Gray, 335–348. New York: Oxford University Press.

Leckman, J. F., and J. S. March. 2011. "Developmental Neuroscience Comes of Age." *Journal of Child Psychology and Psychiatry* 52(4): 333–338.

Main, M. 2000. "The Organized Categories of Infant, Child, and Adult Attachment: Flexible vs. Inflexible Attention Under Attachment Related Stress." *Journal of the American Psychoanalytic Association* 48: 1055–1096.

Main, M. 2010. "Cross-cultural Studies of Attachment Organization: Recent Studies, Changing Methodologies, and the Concept of Conditional Strategies." *Human Development* 33(1), 48–61.

Main, M., E. Hesse, and R. Goldwyn. 2008. "Studying Differences in Language Usage in Recounting Attachment History: An introduction to the AAI." In *Clinical Applications of the Adult Attachment Interview*, edited by M. Steele and H. Steele, 31–68. New York: Guilford Press.

Malloch, S., and C. Trevarthen. 2009. "Musicality: Communicating the Vitality and Interests of Life." In *Communicative Musicality: Exploring the Basis of Human Companionship*, edited by S. Malloch and C. Trevarthen, 1–11. Oxford: Oxford University Press.

Mazokopaki, M., and G. Kugiumutzakis. 2009. "Infant Rhythms: Expressions of Musical Companionship." In *Communicative Musicality: Exploring the Basis of Human Companionship*, edited by S. Malloch and C. Trevarthen, 185–208. Oxford: Oxford University Press.

Narvaez, D., 2014. *Neurobiology and the Development of Human Morality: Evolution, Culture and Wisdom.* New York: Norton.

Narvaez, D., L. Want, T. Gleason, Y. Cheng, J. Lefever, and L. Deng. 2013. "The Evolved Developmental Niche and Child Sociomoral Outcomes in Chinese 3-year olds." *European Journal of Developmental Psychology* 10(2): 106–127.

Panksepp, J., and L. Biven. 2012. *The Archaeology of Mind: Neuroevolutionary Origins of Human Emotions.* New York: Norton.

Porges S. W. 2011. *The Polyvagal Theory: Neurophysiological Foundations of Emotions, Attachment, Communication, and Self-Regulation.* New York: Norton.

Schore, A. N. 2003. *Affect Regulation and the Repair of the Self.* New York: Norton.

Schore, A. N. 2004. *Affect Dysregulation and Disorders of the Self.* New York: Norton.

Schore, A. N. 2012. *The Science of the Art of Psychotherapy.* New York: Norton.

Schore, A. N., and R. P. Newton. 2013. "Using Modern Attachment Theory to Guide Clinical Assessments of Early Attachment Relationships." In *Attachment-Based Clinical*

Work with Children and Adolescents, edited by J. E. Bettmann and D. D. Friedman, 61–98. New York: Springer.

Schore, J. R., and A. N. Schore. 2014. "Regulation Theory and Affect Regulation Psychotherapy: A Clinical Primer." *Smith College Studies in Social Work* 84: 2–3, 178–195.

Siegel, D. J. 1999. *The Developing Mind: Toward a Neurobiology of Interpersonal Experience.* New York: Guilford.

Siegel, D. J. 2010. *Adult Attachment: Interpersonal Neurobiology and Psychotherapy.* Audio CDs. Lifespan Learning Institute Conference.

Smallwood, J., and J. W. Schooler. 2015. "The Science of Mind Wandering: Empirically Navigating the Stream of Consciousness." *Annual Review of Psychology* 66: 487–518.

Stern, D. N. 2004. *Forms of Vitality: Exploring Dynamic Experience in Psychology, the Arts, Psychotherapy, and Development.* Oxford: Oxford University Press.

Thompson, P. 2007. "Down Will Come Baby: Prenatal Stress, Primitive Defenses and Gestational Dysregulation." *Journal of Trauma & Dissociation: The Official Journal of the International Society for the Study of Dissociation (ISSD)* 8(3): 85–113.

Tronick, E. Z. 2007. *The Neurobehavioral and Social-Emotional Development of Infants and Children.* New York: Norton.

Van der Hart, O., E. Nijenhuis, and K. Steele. 2006. *The Haunted Self: Structural Dissociation and the Treatment of Chronic Traumatization.* New York: Norton.

Van der Kolk, B. A., A. C. McFarlane, and L. Weisaeth, eds. 1996. *Traumatic Stress: The Effects of Overwhelming Experience on Mind, Body, and Society.* New York: Guilford.

Yehuda, R., L. M. Bierer, J. Schmeidler, D. H. Aferiat, I. Breslau, and S. Dolan. 2000. "Low Cortisol and Risk for PTSD in Adult Offspring of Holocaust Survivors." *American Journal of Psychiatry* 157(8): 1252–1259.

4 Embodiment

Coming Home to Our Bodies

When I allow myself to experience my body as a sacred instrument capable of receiving and generating sensations, I start to notice that my attitude about my body becomes more impersonal. I am teaching myself to listen to the sensations resonating in my flesh and to differentiate between sensations originating without and sensations originating from within. As I allow others to affect me, I have to hold more firmly onto my own center of awareness.

(Woodman 1992, 15)

The Roots of Embodiment

Embodiment has been a somatic practice of mindful attention toward internal sensory-based data for people throughout history. Those who lived in hunter-gatherer societies had to stay connected to their bodies and the bodies of others in order discern the dangers in the environment and to survive as a group. All aspects of traditional life from hunting, root digging, camping, moving camps, berry picking, child rearing, and ceremonial dancing were held together by the shared body of human beings working in relationship with each other and with the elements of the universe (Matheson 2001).

A number of scholars have examined the ancestral practices of small nature-based societies (Diamond 2012; Narvaez 2014; Cozolino 2013) because they provide a natural baseline for optimal development of self-regulation and concern for others, fostering behaviors that are essential for healthy human functioning and moral development (Narvaez et al. 2013). The ancient practice of embodiment is associated with enhanced emotional and physical health, the development of prosocial relationships, low interpersonal violence (Narvaez 2014), and effective conflict management (Diamond 2012).

Despite the many personal and communal benefits fostering a sense of embodiment can provide, states of disembodiment are pervasive and contribute to the growing tide of trauma occurring throughout the world. People who have experienced trauma often live disconnected from their own bodily-based nature. They are usually unconscious of their disembodiment and how it negatively affects their behavior, emotions, and relationships, particularly their child-rearing practices—creating a whole new generation that lacks embodiment and is therefore more susceptible to experiencing complex trauma. To enter into the neurologically based paradigm shift of healing, the first step is to develop a personal practice of embodiment. Embodying our sensations, emotions, and life as it is, complete with joy, sorrow, struggle, conflict, and injustice, reveals the truth of our current existence. Knowing that truth allows us to take responsibility for our actions and support others to know the truth of their lived experience.

Embodiment: The Key to Feeling Ordinary Lived Experience

Embodiment is grounded in habitual awareness of one's inner world and the environment through clear bodily-based perceptions. To embody the lived experience of a particular moment means to viscerally feel sensory, motor, emotional, and imaginal experience rather than funnel arousal into mental concepts, ideas, and categories (van Manen 1990). Offering direct phenomenological contact with the world, embodiment is a primary expertise for helping professionals (Schore 2009). The word *embody* means "to provide with a body, incarnate, make corporeal; to embody a spirit; to collect or include into a body: organize, incorporate" (Webster's Unabridged Dictionary 2001). This definition offers guidance for the process of embodiment, yet the abstraction of this language fails to describe the feeling sense of embodiment.

What *does* it feel like to be embodied? Embodiment is characterized by a felt sense of grounded aliveness, vitality, calm yet active presence in the moment, a keen awareness of subtle internal and environmental shifts, and a sense of belonging to a larger realm. People who are embodied have "one eye looking in and one eye looking out" (Kalsched 2013) and can discern the subtle differences between self and other—especially in moments of emotional identification (Scheler 1970). (Emotional identification refers to the unconscious projection of one's own buried emotional experience onto another.) The "one eye looking in" somatic awareness stimulates vitality and activity in the muscles and viscera while the "one eye looking out" is alert to change and novelty. The "one eye looking in" detects the results of perception of the "one eye looking out." With this dual perception, we can reflectively adapt our inner world to function in the outer world *as it is* and adapt our behavior to be consistent with the external world *as it is*. This process is the development of acceptance, wisdom, and grace that comes from our intersubjective relationship with the world.

The ideas and thoughts of embodied people are congruent with the sensory experience of their bodies, and their bodies are the fundamental source of knowledge. People who are embodied express authentic emotion through facial expressions, gestures, postures, and voice, and are open to receiving such nonverbal communication from another. Their perceptions are marked by curiosity and engagement in the fluid, ever-changing spirit of life as it is, rather than rumination and obsession about what they or others should be. In other words, they are physically and mentally present and attentive to the energy in the moment. Spirit and energy in this sense means vitality, fullness, and transcendence within the body and mind, which spontaneously expand into the environment.

With embodiment, one's own inner subjective world is fluid, dynamic, alive, and outgoing, naturally leading to interest and curiosity about the inner world of another. Embodiment is a way of knowing that instills a sense of continuity of the self and forges energetic connections with others. These embodied connections are the only way we can truly feel loved. Studies reveal that comforting touch influences the self-regulation of children and a mother's attitudes about touch predicts the child's level of empathy for others (Narvaez et al. 2013). Without the embodied touch of a loving other, we lose a sense of aliveness. Somatic practices that deepen embodiment, such as awareness, empathy, inquiry, intervention, and reflection are ways of being that allow people to be affectively touched by another and slowly incorporate traumatic experiences to restore the natural process of human development.

Though a sense of embodiment offers an abundance of knowledge about oneself and the environment, North American culture has moved away from the ancient embodied ways human beings once knew themselves and the world. A shift away from embodied ways of living and child rearing results in reduced sociomoral functioning in adulthood and the observation that "Western brains are not developing optimally" (Narvaez et al. 2013, xviii). Diamond (2012) argues that modern industrial societies are inferior to traditional societies in areas of emotional and social development, areas that require embodiment including child raising, caring for the elderly, settling conflicts, and avoiding stress related to noncommunicable diseases. However, now evidence-based theories are returning to age-old ancestral practices that rely on bodily-based wisdom to restore the values of affect regulation and social-emotional development in parenting, education, and mental and physical health (Cozolino 2013; Narvaez 2014). As Max van Manen (1990), writes, "It [embodiment] is both new and old."

Lessons on Relational Embodiment from the Chamorro

Many Indigenous people around the world have relied on embodied ways of knowing for community survival, and remnants of this way of life exist in many regions. One such place is Guam, where I had the privilege of living among the descendants of the Chamorro people in my twenties. Accompanying my husband, I arrived on this small island in the Marianas eight months pregnant with my first child. The people there lived close together with few material possessions and depended on somatic ways of knowing and relational interdependence. They intuitively guided us through birthing two babies and supported us in rearing our children as we adjusted to life on a foreign island.

When my oldest son was born a month after our arrival, the community held a celebration for him, welcoming him as one of their own. They treated his colic with herbs and bananas from their yards. Perhaps most importantly, their loving humor was always present, a "lifting up" that kept my homesickness at bay. Their relationships with each other and with us were filled with their somatic ways of being, including heartfelt affection, touching, embodied child raising, respect, compassion, humor, caring, and generosity. The Chamorro word for their relational way of being, *inafa'maolek,* means to "do good for each other," and to show respect for family, community, and the elderly. These core values, passed down from ancient times, surprised and awakened me to my embodied self.

Historian Morris Berman (1989) differentiates cultures that value somatic ways of knowing, like the ancient heritage of the Chamorro, from those that impose authoritarian standards of thought while suppressing bodily-based ways of knowing. Somatic experiences, whether ancient or contemporary, assist people in fluidly shifting perceptions of themselves and others through embodied ways of seeing, listening, knowing, exploring, intervening, and reflecting on meaning. These experiences form an embodied sense of self-awareness that is distinct from the usual left-hemisphere ways we think about ourselves in Western culture, ways of knowing that form a conceptual self-awareness. In the following section, we'll explore the difference between embodied self-awareness, a direct feeling of the self—located in the right hemisphere of the brain—that changes from moment to moment, and conceptual self-awareness, an abstract way of knowing about the self that can endure for a lifetime.

Embodied Self-Awareness vs. Conceptual Self-Awareness

Allan Fogel (2013) distinguishes between conceptual self-awareness and embodied self-awareness. Conceptual self-awareness is distinct from present moment felt sense. It has a logical, explanatory quality that is expressed in abstract language. Embodied self-awareness emerges from the lived experience of the moment. It is spontaneous, ever changing, and felt through sensations, emotions, images, and reflection on that experience.

Embodied self-awareness is a direct encounter with inner knowledge while conceptual self-awareness is a secondhand description of a past perception. Conceptual self-awareness often develops in retreat from painful life events and attempts to explain or avoid troublesome feelings and emotions. Severed from bodily awareness, conceptual self-awareness is distant from direct knowing or feeling. For many, a discussion based on conceptual self-awareness is the focus in helping relationships, an abstract conversation lacking the flow of energy and information and intense neural activity necessary to change the brain.

Embodied self-awareness reveals knowledge that can be expressed through movements, gestures, images, and spontaneous nonverbal or artful verbal means, and stimulates the firing and rewiring of neural states in the moment. This way of inner knowing can be communicated through a flash of light in the eyes, an uplifting or down-turning of facial muscles, or an instinctive shift in body posture. Consider someone who is close to death and is unable to form words or move her body. An embodied sense of self-awareness still allows her to communicate intense emotions—sorrow, joy, and compassion through the eyes, and a soft, open face. When one is in a state of receptive embodiment, he or she can perceive the moment-to-moment expression of another's embodiment and the brains of both are changed in the process.

The intersubjective joining of two embodied people creates a new synthesis of inner subjective realities, a somatic interpersonal knowing that can be perceived by each and sometimes sensed by onlookers. People may try to describe these encounters by the emotions that flow through them, such as feelings of love, tenderness, nurturing, and connection. Or they may sense a numinous quality and call them spiritual relationships. However, what is most significant to the participants of embodied communication is the sharing of specific knowing in a moment in time that activates the change process of neural networks, causing us to become different. Embodied somatic connection in a safe relationship is needed to release perceptions of fear from conceptual self-awareness and enter into the ancient inner realms of bodily-based wisdom and guidance.

How can we know whether we are in a space of conceptual awareness or embodied somatic awareness? Conceptual self-awareness has a distant quality about it. It may bring about feelings or describe feelings but it is not in direct contact with the sensory elements of feelings. Conceptual self-awareness is a habitual way we think about ourselves that may not have any relationship to who we are at the core; it may be called our self-image. There is a familiar, repetitive, somewhat stale quality to the words or images used to label and evaluate experiences. Conceptual self-awareness can be distorted by trauma and form the ruminations that fuel depression.

Ideas of conceptual self-awareness can be generated by the failure to protect the self. When shocking aversive events occur or when people have been involved in relationships characterized by consistent emotional neglect, they have a tendency to value the subjective perceptions of others over their own embodied self-perceptions and to consider the subjective opinions of others and culturally based perceptions as truth. Concern about the perceptions of others may influence people to try to live by conceptual systems, religious rules, teachers, and gurus; however, ultimately this way of knowing results in neglect of the perception of inner, direct spiritual wisdom of the body. I do not advocate living only by inner subjective perceptions, but rather finding a balance between the inner wisdom and the wisdom known universally throughout the world and over eons of human history, particularly that of cultures that live close to nature. Embodied self-awareness invites us on a communal path that may be new in the dominant Western human social structures, a way of being that brings our unique self into full expression in relationships and in the world.

Speaking the Embodied Truth

In contrast to the repetitive phrasing that arises from conceptual self-awareness, expression of the embodied self is characterized by freshness and vitality, generating life and interest in the listener. The use of freshly formed words, the "spontaneous language" (Merleau-Ponty 1973) of embodied self-awareness, provides guidance and meaning to lived experience. *Spontaneous language* refers to the words that flow naturally from perceptions based on embodied somatic awareness. It reveals a truth that "shows through and envelops us rather than being held and circumscribed by our minds" (Merleau-Ponty 1973, xii). Spontaneous language is direct, evocative, and emerges from the subjective felt sense. Glimpses of embodied self-awareness can be described in words, developed in art, or portrayed in archetypes that communicate the universal human experience of bodily-based wisdom.

This intense interaction of spontaneous language between two people has a synergistic effect that can transform both into higher states of consciousness and knowing. When participating in embodied social engagement, neurologically based sensations, primitive emotions, and intrinsic images move from the body up to the face, forming very subtle, spontaneous muscular movements in and around the eyes, mouth, jaw, and neck, ultimately forming into spontaneous language. The movement of these muscles is a powerful form of communication of subjective inner experience, one that an infant is highly attuned to for connection.

Eye gaze, movements of the face, and the sound of one's voice form one experience; to dissect it with an unconscious message of the face in conflict with the tone of voice creates confusion and causes breaches in relationship. The flow and rhythm of nonverbal somatic communication and the wisdom of spontaneous verbal language can be breached when one or both people abdicate embodied self-awareness and seek safety from intimacy in conceptual self-awareness. Energetically, a breach in embodied presence is the equivalent to turning away or erecting an invisible, yet felt barrier from the other. Let's examine more closely how disembodiment splits the self to create a conceptual sense of self-awareness.

Disembodiment Creates a Fragmented Self

The dualistic values of Western culture often conspire to split people between their emotional body and their mental ideas—creating a state of disembodiment. What does this dualism look like? McGilchrist

(2009) states that this way of thinking results from an imbalance in the way we use our brains. He claims that we live in disembodied ways that distort our perceptions and split thinking into opposites of the same reality. Emotional ways of knowing are demeaned when we live in disembodied ways. "Emotion is inseparable from the body in which it is felt, and emotion is also the basis for our engagement with the world. . . . In keeping with its capacity for emotion, and its predisposition to understand mental experience within the context of the body, rather than abstracting it, the right hemisphere is deeply connected to the self as embodied"(66). This split begins to knit together when we embody sensory-based data, emotions, and imaginal lived experience in the right hemisphere of the brain.

The left hemisphere is not interested in the body as the "intersection between ourselves and the world at large" and can fragment bodily-based experiences from mental activity (McGilchrist 2009, 67). When living in chronic disembodied states, people ignore the critical messages of their bodily-based sensations and emotions, creating alternative, ideal states of being that are out of touch with the reality of their lived experience. Children who have their emotions ignored find ways to split their sense of self to find protection and love.

Lisa Mortimore (2013) describes the result of disembodiment to one's sense of self: "The fragmented self is at home in a disembodied state and content to rely on knowledge garnered through logic and reason. . . . When we divide ourselves into parts we lose the connection to the whole of who we are and our inner connection. Our disembodied selves, disconnected from nature, are severed from the very source that affords us life" (23–25). This disconnection results in distorted perceptions, emotional blindness, shallow relationships, loss of meaning, and mental and physical illness. A healthy infant is born embodied, so how is embodiment lost?

When traumatic events and neglectful emotional experiences occur, critical aspects of the self become disconnected from awareness, reducing a sense of aliveness in the body. People can lose embodiment, which carries an inherent sense of value and the vital spark of life—the inner sense of divinity (Kalsched 2013)—when they are forced to adapt to less than nurturing environments. Survival self-care systems (Kalsched 2013), which diminish one's sense of embodied wholeness, allow people to adapt to frightening ways of living. Survival self-care systems lack the innate vitality of the life source and the effective processing of right-hemispheric sensory-motor, vestibular, visual, auditory, proprioceptive, and visceral ways of knowing that come with embodiment. The perceptual distortions of survival self-care systems may form into aggressive behavior or withdrawal, but beneath both the high arousal and the low arousal is horror and terror (Schore, personal communication), emotions that are highly contagious, even to helping professionals.

How do we heal the split of the disembodied mind? How do helping professionals restore their own embodied selves and reclaim their inner unity to support people who are suffering in fragmented states?

Restoring Embodiment

Embodiment provides the path through which helping professionals can guide clients in integrating forces of aggression, manipulation, and dissociation that emerge from terror and horror. The process of healing trauma involves the courage to feel and tolerate painful and unacceptable emotions that have been hidden beneath aggressive thoughts and behavior with mental and physical withdrawal into safety. As even young children know, having a companion in frightening times makes it easier to feel and move through the intolerable. The work of healing trauma is to slowly uncover the intense emotions and unbearable sensations that lie in bodily states and find a way to embody them. In other words, the terror and horror that was overwhelming in the moment of trauma is still alive under arousal states of aggression and withdrawal. When these states are felt with another, one's survival self-care system is no longer needed; a person can return to the natural process of development as an embodied, incarnated human being. People incarnate when their innate vitality comes to life, when they are embodied and present in the flesh, when the parts of themselves that were separated in trauma are made whole.

With conscious awareness of the mind in the body, there is a return of an inner aliveness. This sense of aliveness becomes a way of knowing that awakens and reunites the aspects of the self that have been severed from each other, the disconnected parts of the inner world. As trauma survivors come home to live in their bodies, rather than in the realm of abstract thoughts, conceptual self-awareness, and ever-cycling inner ruminations, they are able to sense and feel themselves in relationship with the environment, the earth, and other living beings. To do this, they slowly learn how to fully experience whatever sensations and emotions that might emerge in the moment in the context of an intersubjective relationship. They return to reality, where awareness of bodily-based perception is used as a fulcrum to sense the world.

Over time, experiences of embodiment create a consciousness that goes beyond simply noticing the body. Through the practice of somatic reflection, this consciousness represents a complex synthesis of the knowledge, wisdom, and truth of the body, mind, and spirit (Merleau-Ponty 1973). With an embodied consciousness, helping professionals are able to remain mindfully present to the most disturbing sensations, emotions, and images that arise in relationship while offering compassion and engaging in practices of coregulation and self-regulation, rather than subtly withdrawing into disembodiment and dissociation. So often, I have witnessed helping professionals, including myself, touch into another's inner world of terror and horror and immediately withdraw to analysis, treating the extreme states as problems to be solved. An alternative option is to notice the terror, feel it in one's own body, feel the connection with the other, and open to wonder and curiosity about the sensations of this emotion.

The shift from being unconsciously gripped and held by terror in the brain stem to inquiring about the sensory dimensions of the terror engages higher cortical structures that allow for the regulation of neural states and emotions (Tucker 2007). Traumatized people can sense when helping professionals are willing to be with them in this state and when they are curious about the terror. They can also learn ways to move through the terror, namely coregulation, which makes it possible to engage with the other in feeling the distress and then move together toward deeper social engagement. It is unlikely people can stay embodied over time without developing thorough practices of coregulation and self-regulation—skills that build resilience to aversive experiences. Coregulation can bring highly aroused states down into social engagement while upregulating despairing, depressed states.

With intention and support for coregulation, embodiment can grow in and through adversity, creating an open, accepting consciousness laced with vitality and engagement with life. Embodiment begins with an intention to be present to phenomenological moment-to-moment encounters with one's own bodily-based sense of self in interactions with others and in the environment. People with an embodied consciousness are able to attend to phenomena that exist in the present moment—especially the moments that bring terror and horror. They avoid resisting reality and practice incorporating the knowledge of reality into an ever-expanding consciousness.

The practice of developing an embodied consciousness begins with the practitioner. Then with patience and coregulation, a practitioner can help clients slowly experience their own sense of embodiment with coregulation as they heal from complex trauma.

The Embodied Practitioner

The incorporation of traumatic memories into a tolerable felt sense in the body is best accomplished in relationship with a skilled, embodied other; it's not always a self-help process. When alone, a bodily-based recall of traumatic memories can unconsciously trigger defenses that arose in the moment of trauma. On the other hand, an embodied practitioner is uniquely able to help people suffering from symptoms of trauma—chronic states of anxiety, anger, and rage that often loop with states of disembodiment, dissociation, and depression.

A sense of embodiment allows practitioners to enter into somatic awareness and somatic empathy, an attuned and resonant bodily-based empathic relationship with another. Somatic empathy in the intersubjective, therapeutic relationship lays the foundation for somatic inquiry, a phe-nomenological process of discovery into hidden aspects of lived experience. A practice grounded in caring curiosity, authentic interest, and compas-sion, somatic inquiry is based on an intention to help another through gaining a deeper knowledge of the other. Within the containment of lov-ing empathy and inquiry, a person suffering from trauma slowly begins to feel safe. When safe and contained in an intersubjective relationship, they slowly embody their dissociated sensations and emotions and bring implicit memories from traumatic experiences into the intersubjective field. This somatic-based processing reveals surprising information. Inner secrets become available for change, transformation, and reconsolidation. The secrets can be deeply personal, such as the discovery of one's intrin-sic value or a dissociated memory of guilt or powerlessness that helps to make sense out of the confusion of the trauma. As the dissociated memo-ries are revealed, creative somatic interventions offer opportunities for the transformation and incorporation of the traumatic memory. With somatic reflection, the embodied practitioner and person suffering from trauma recall the integration of small changes in relationship dynamics and iden-tify new associations, emotions, and images that create more expansive meaning.

Practitioners can foster their own sense of embodiment by attending to sensory-based experience while alone and with another. Conscious of pos-ture, attentive to the subtleties of what they see, hear, and feel, embodied practitioners grow in the practice of engaging deeply in their inner world and environment. The practice of embodiment encourages observation of the subtle sensations, movements, and emotions arising out of bodily-based awareness. When clients enter into implicit traumatic memories that are laced with terror and horror, there can be a contagion of emo-tions that can affect helping professionals, unconsciously resulting in dis-sociated states of mind. Practitioners working with trauma survivors can learn to remain conscious of their own somatic awareness in the moment, and learn to repair it when they find themselves spacey, disconnected, and dissociated, depending on the severity of the emotional contagion. If the contagion evokes an unresolved trauma for the practitioner, it is essential to consult with another as soon as possible. One of the most important benefits of a practitioner who is embodied is that he or she can create a timely repair of enactments that happen with emotional contagion.

Transferring States of Embodiment

Each of us has multiple aspects of ourselves that emerge in different situ-ations. For example, as a mother, grandmother, teacher, psychotherapist, and friend, I have multiple ways of relating to people. These habits seem to come out of separate parts of me, one part that is quite young and that loves to play, particularly with children; another part, a kind of a nomad, that is reluctant to stay settled in the same home for years at a time, and a part that loves to accompany people in discovering their strengths, vulnerabilities, and true selves. A poet from the Celtic tradition describes the different aspects we each hold: "While there is a fundamental self in each of us that makes us different from everyone else, this self should not be constructed as being merely a singular subjective center. Rather, there is a multiplicity of selves within us. But all our selves do cohere into one presence" (O'Donohue 2010, 6).

I imagine O'Donohue's coherent self, the "one presence," as an embodied way of being, despite multiple aspects of the self. This embodied way of being is a sense of self that emerges when consciousness is located in the body and people feel their bodies exist in space and time. For people who have experienced trauma, specific aspects of the self carry intense emotions and drop out of awareness in order to function in ordinary life. We call these "not me" aspects of the self, dissociated self-states or parts.

Kalsched (2013) speaks of dissociated experiences in moments of trauma that are open to supportive spiritual forces that offer unconscious ways of knowing one is not alone, help is on the way, and life will be restored. The dissociated, disparate, and conflicting aspects of the self, created during moments of trauma, can be differentiated, re-embodied, and incorporated into a sense of self. With somatic practices of awareness and observation, practitioners can intervene by inviting attention to different parts of the body in order to gradually create a sense of embodiment that can integrate the dissociated parts. Practitioners might suggest a relational, focused attention to sensations and movements of the feet, legs, and lower trunk of the body, an awareness that guides the neurological flow of energy down through gravity to lessen intense arousal in the brain. A somatic observation stimulates higher cortical organizing energies to focus on brain stem arousal of uncomfortable sensations or limbic system arousal of intolerable emotions. Exercise 4.1: Grounding and Restoring Rhythm explores how to use movement to diminish dissociation and stay present in the moment. See page 200 of the appendix.

According to Damasio (2010), "we can ask the more complex levels of the self to observe what is going on at the simpler levels" (104). The mind with a self is grounded in biological processes, and from an evolutionary point of view, the thrust of sensory-based neural states and primitive emotions emerge from the brainstem to create specific emotional circuits in the limbic brain. Emotions arise from the body as well as from the cerebral cortex. The body is continually mapped in the brain while the brain needs ongoing updates from the body to coordinate vital life functions with ease. The representations of the body in the brain are "essential for the creation of the self" (104).

Somatic empathic connections allow one person's embodied state to transfer to another and simulate the other's body state (Damasio 2010). Alfred Margulies (1989) speaks of an imaginative process that allows us to experience the subjective, physical inner world of another. This dynamic within relationships has traditionally been described as transference and countertransference in psychotherapy and is an aspect of a two-person enactment. When unconscious of this imaginative process, helping professionals can experience emotional identification and infection, dynamics that negatively affect relationships. A somatic, conscious intention to experience and monitor an intersubjective field in the present moment can minimize the dynamics of transference and simulation. The capacity for a simulated transference from the body state of one person to the body state of another described by Damasio (2010) is a turning point in the neuroscience of helping relationships. "Transferring" states of embodiment from the therapist to the patient, a two-person relational mode of helping, is encouraged (Bromberg 2011; Schore 2012). In a two-person mode of healing relational-developmental trauma, the embodied helper provides a connection, vitality, and patterns for the transformation of disembodied and disavowed relational experience of the patient.

Damasio (2010) asserts: "Maps of the body in the brain can be simulated as if they were occurring even if it is not true. Because we can depict our own body states, we can more easily simulate the equivalent body states of other. The range of phenomena denoted by the word empathy owes a lot to this arrangement" (104). In other words, the body state a helping professional brings to another can transfer a healing dynamic to relieve suffering. The embodied "one presence" O'Donohue references can support another to incorporate multiple, dissociated, discordant selves into one presence.

Changing the Brain through Embodied Awareness

Somatic practices for helping professionals begin with the formation of the intersubjective field and stabilization through that relationship to regulate intense affect. Once the intersubjective field has been established, helping professionals can then invite a person who has experienced trauma into embodied awareness through very small phenomena of perception. Practitioners may begin with attention to sensations and movement when a person is talking about a pleasant experience, or exploring images and emotions when a person is in a pleasurable neural state. As awareness of the body begins to awaken in these tolerable neural states, the process of embodiment begins, a state that a person who has suffered from complex trauma may be experiencing for the first time.

Early embodiment exercises may focus on sensory experience in the environment such as the effect of the light or colors in the office on the person, the texture of fabric, or the feel of bare feet on a carpet. I often ask people to slowly orient to the environment of my office, to move their eyes, head, neck, and shoulders, to slowly explore the light, color, shapes, and space in the room. Then I ask them to notice how they feel in their bodies in this moment. Exercise 4.2: Fostering Mutual Embodiment, Exercise 4.3: Weaving a Cocoon for Protection, Exercise 4.4: Feeling Embodied Compassion, and Exercise 4.5: Listening to the Voice of the Body are ideal for practicing embodiment for both helping professionals and clients. See pages 201–202 of the appendix.

Bodily-based awareness communicates essential information to the brain, an awareness of aliveness and a sense of self (Damasio 2010). Damasio (2010) argues that the first manifestations of the mind arise in the brain stem, and processing begins in felt body states. "Body and brain are engaged in a continuous interactive dance. Thoughts implemented in the brain can induce emotional states that are implemented in the body, while the body can change the brain's landscape and thus the substrate for thoughts" (96). Damasio (2010) points out that the communication between the body and the brain is a two-way interaction, the body-to-brain signals permit the brain to witness the activities of the body and allow the body to inform the brain of changes.

The body informs the brain about changes in the state of both striated and smooth muscles, the walls of the arteries, the gut and bronchi, the amount of oxygen and carbon dioxide in any region of the body, the temperature, the presence of toxic chemicals, and a vast range of information about the environment. This is essential information if the brain is to provide corrective changes to mitigate danger or any threats to life. In times of disembodiment and dissociation the somatosensory and motor cortex is mapped with the distortions inherent in the disconnection. This distortion of the brain is a misrepresentation of reality fostering a breach with bodily-based experience and perception.

We can change our brains by restoring the presence of accurate information regarding the environment and the internal world. The brain can then use that information to map the body in a new way within the somatosensory and motor cortex. When we bring somatic awareness to feelings of vitality and movements of sensation in the present moment, the somatosensory and motor cortex adapt to the reality of the present moment, influencing how motion, emotion, and motivation is subtly created in the body.

This body-to-brain and brain-to-body communication becomes a loop that reinforces the intense emotions of trauma. However, we can sense this loop through our own embodiment and influence the endless cycle of trauma with somatic awareness of vitality and meaning rather than states of rumination and depression. Catherine Kerr (2011) from Brown University found that somatic awareness and attention was the key to unlocking the body-brain patterns of rumination. When we enter the sensory realm and pay attention to bodily sensations, with a high level of detail, Kerr (2011) reports there is a lower risk of depression, the perception of chronic pain diminishes, and the immune system is strengthened. Subtle awareness of bodily sensations takes us out of "rumination" networks of the brain.

In body-to-brain communication with a person who has experienced complex trauma, the body may inform the brain of areas of chronic muscular contractions or flaccidity, distress in the digestive, respiratory, or circulatory system, and a general felt sense of pleasure or disease. In ordinary daily life, incoming data and stimulation is processed and organized by nonconscious communication between the different parts of the body and the brain. Data that has been processed and organized becomes information if it reduces uncertainty and meaningfully fulfills a need (Tucker 2007).

Tucker hypothesizes that "the mind evolved from the brain's mechanism of bodily control" (12). The function of the brain is to organize experience into meaningful information by first integrating sensory and motor patterns. The mind operates with bodily mechanisms from the inside out and then the outside in. The inner core holds the networks of the viscera that form emotional experience while the outer shell forms somatic ways of knowing; control is managed by the higher cortical structures. The communication between the outer core, the somatic ways of knowing reality, and the inner core—the needs and emotions of the viscera—is the foundation of intelligence (Tucker 2007). With intention, we can bring awareness to our bodily states in the moment. Each intentional shift from worry and dissociative rumination to present moment bodily-based somatic awareness becomes a step toward changing the brain.

As we recognize how the outer shell, the somatic ways of knowing, can transform the inner core, the needs and emotions, the practice of somatics becomes a critical catalyst for change. The following chapters explore practical ways to implement this change; however first, we will explore some of the practices Indigenous cultures around the world use to restore embodiment and heal from trauma.

References

Berman, M. 1989. *Coming to Our Senses*. New York: Simon and Schuster.

Bromberg, P. M. 2011. *The Shadow of the Tsunami: and the Growth of the Relational Mind*. New York: Routledge.

Cozolino, L. 2013. *The Neuroscience of Education, Optimizing Attachment & Learning in the Classroom*. New York: Norton.

Damasio, A. 2010. *Self Comes to Mind: Constructing the Conscious Brain*. New York: Pantheon.

Diamond, J. 2012. *The World Until Yesterday: What Can We Learn from Traditional Societies?* New York: Viking.

Fogel, A. 2013. *Body Sense: The Science and Practice of Embodied Self-Awareness*. New York: Norton.

Kalsched, D. 2013. *Trauma and the Soul: A Psycho-spiritual Approach to Human Development and its Interruption*. London: Routledge.

Kerr, C. 2011. "The Neuroscience of Somatic Attention: A Key to Unlocking Contemplative Practice." [Webinar]. March 21. Center for Contemplative Mind. Retrieved from: http://vimeo.com/39205220

Margulies, A. 1989. *The Empathic Imagination*. New York: Norton.

Matheson, D. 2001. *Red Thunder*. Portland: Media Weavers LLC.

McGilchrist, I. 2009. *The Master and His Emissary: The Divided Brain and the Making of the Western World*. London: Yale University Press.

Merleau-Ponty, M. 1973. *The Prose of the World*. Edited by C. Lefort. Translated by J. O'Neil. Evanston: Northwestern University Press.

Mortimore, L. 2013. "Embodied Ways of Knowing: Women's Eco-Activism." PhD diss., University of Victoria, ProQuest (NS28393).

Narvaez, D., J. Panksepp, A. Schore, & T. Gleason, eds. 2013. "The Value of Using an Evolutionary Framework for Gauging Children's Well-being." In *Evolution, Early Experience and Human Development: From Research to Practice and Policy*, 3–30. New York: Oxford University Press.

Narvaez, D. 2014. *Neurobiology and the Development of Human Morality: Evolution, Culture, and Wisdom*. New York: Norton.

O'Donohue, J. 2010. *Four Elements: Reflection on Nature*. New York: Harmony Books.

Scheler, M. 1970. *The Nature of Sympathy*. Brooklyn: Shoe String Press.

Schore, A. N. 2009. "Attachment Trauma and the Developing Right Brain: Origins of Pathological Dissociation." In *Dissociation and Dissociative Behavior Disorders: DSM-V and Beyond*, edited by P. F. Dell and J. A. O'Neil, 107–141. New York: Routledge.

Schore, A. N. 2012. *The Science of the Art of Psychotherapy*. New York: Norton.

Tucker, D. 2007. *Mind from Body: Experience from Neural Structure*. Oxford: Oxford University Press.

Van Manen, M. 1990. *Researching Lived Experience: Human Science for an Action Sensitive Pedagogy*. New York: SUNY Press.

Webster's Encyclopedic Unabridged Dictionary of the English Language. 2001. New York: Gramercy.

Woodman, M. 1992. *Leaving My Father's House: A Journey to Conscious Femininity*. Boston: Shambhala Publications.

5 With Trauma "the Spirit Leaves the Body"

"'Fearful' experiences can take an infinite variety of forms, but all involve a communication between the spiritual and the physical."

(Atleo 2004, 73)

As Berman (1989) tells us, trauma is not new to the human experience; healing principles and practices have been refined in somatic-based cultures for thousands of years. To learn from Indigenous and traditional cultures, we must respect each practice within its own context and be sensitive to the misappropriation of cultural practices. While it would be presumptuous for me to replicate the rich stories, songs, dances, ceremonies, and social structures of other cultures, it is important to explore specific common human experiences for healing complex trauma that has been lost to Western culture. The challenge is to discern the essential elements of traditional cultures to learn how to expand and enhance our own cultural ways of interacting and healing while respecting the integrity of contributing cultures.

In some cases, there is more overlap between Western approaches to healing trauma and Indigenous practices than one might think. Disciplines such as neuroscience, the social sciences, anthropology, and philosophy—particularly phenomenology—have all contributed to the new paradigm for the healing of complex trauma and are highly congruent with practices of many Indigenous cultures. Human growth and development has happened for 99 percent of history in Indigenous culture (Narvaez 2014). Current Indigenous cultures provide a link to optimal human development and healing its injuries and interruptions. Some common denominators include a right-hemispheric approach with reliance upon an individual's subjective bodily-based way of knowing; respect for intersubjective influences; interest in developing affective transformative practices; and time and resources dedicated to arts, music, contemplative practices, and dance, experiences that can convert the chaos of trauma into relational resources and integrate imaginal symbolic experiences with bodily-based ways of knowing. Each of these common elements is present in the three Indigenous healing practices explored in this chapter—ceremony, spiritual energy, and community.

Ceremony

Perhaps one of the most important lessons Indigenous cultures can teach us about recovering from complex trauma is that healing practices can be amplified through ceremony, a set of actions that create a crucible for the dynamics of change. Ceremonies can hold the intense, chaotic, undifferentiated energies of trauma and allow transformation to occur in a natural, communal way, restoring interconnectedness and inviting the fragmented elements of the right hemisphere to come back into cohesion. In addition to healing trauma, people throughout history have engaged in ceremonies to unify communities and engage together in the unknown mysteries of lived experience, preventing and preparing for inevitable moments of adversity and chaos.

Some Afro-Brazilian communities use ritual and ceremonies from the Umbanda tradition to heal from the multigenerational legacy of trauma caused by four hundred years of slavery. Participating with them in healing practices for over seven years, I noticed their ceremonies were characterized by the following: a right-hemispheric orientation; the voice and vision of their spiritual leader's alignment with the natural forces of energy—the earth, air, sun, wind, leaves, water, fire, and stones; Afro-Portuguese Catholic prayers; the reenactment of ancient stories; and the benevolent incorporation of Afro-Brazilian and Catholic archetypes. Participants dressed in clothing from the era of slavery, yet the garments were white, a symbol of purity. From my perspective, the ceremonies reenacted the universal human journey from slavery to freedom with the help of beloved spiritual entities. Guided in a call-and-response, the dancers would embody the rhythm of the song and move in a circle. Subtle changes in the rhythm embodied the small transformations from slavery to freedom, leading to the incorporation of the spiritual entities. The dance began with movements that looked like reenactments of dissociated compliance, then transitioned to an awakening with gestures of resistance and anger, intensifying into determined empowerment. The empowerment transformed into strength and confidence and was completed in the embodied spiritual joy of young children. When initiates had incorporated a spiritual entity into their bodies, they were able to bless, heal, and teach with divine powers.

Returning from Brazil each year with new vitality for living my life, conducting my practice, and teaching my students, I identified two principles of the Afro-Brazilian ceremonies that I adapted into my work: *conversion* and *metabolization*. These change processes first transform the implicit subcortical neurological effects of trauma and then restore the fragmented right hemisphere to cohesion and collaboration. In the language of neuroscience, healing trauma requires the conversion of the survival-oriented amygdala to the more highly evolved brain circuit that trusts embodied communal relationship (Narvaez 2014). The loving relationships of the Umbanda community, brought together by a gifted spiritual leader, created a nurturing environment with the containment and safety necessary for the conversion from distrust to trust, vigilance to caring, and isolation to interdependence. Following this change, participants became fully embodied in a rhythmical movement and relationally supported to process, or metabolize, their emotions through movement of their bodies, incorporating their healing entities and archetypes.

Like the Afro-Brazilian community, Indigenous people around the globe are revitalizing ancient ceremonies to recover from the trauma of colonialism, genocide, loss of ancestral land and water and the mandatory attendance of their children in residential schools, a cruel practice that tore apart many Indigenous communities. First Nations ceremonies are embodied, relational, and connected with ancestors, animals, the land, and members of the community (Atleo 2004). Grounded in creation myths, the sound and rhythm of drums, ritual movement of ancient dances, and singing the inherited songs awakens the active imagination for incorporation of the stories that guide the lives of participants.

While conducting a trauma training with a First Nations tribe, a participant introduced me to *oosumich*—a practice of ritual cleansing that prepares one to face adversity that Atleo writes about (2004). Tom was a big man who loved to laugh. He had a history of traumatic injury from his longshoreman work, a childhood spent in residential schools, and a life permeated by multiple forms of oppression from colonialism. Tom told me it was difficult for him to trust someone who was as "white" as I was, a reference to my cultural ways of thinking, feeling, and communicating.

During the first week of trauma training in this community, Tom volunteered to join me in a somatic demonstration. It was clear that I had said or done something upsetting and he wanted to set things right. He did not use words to describe his truth so we entered into a bodily-centered exploration. We stood together in the middle of the room, each with our feet firmly grounded on the earth. I invited him to feel the sensations within. He let me know a strong sensation was deep in his gut and moving up through his chest. As he felt it, I invited him to make contact with my hands and allow the energy to come from his guts through his heart and then his arms and hands while we maintained eye contact. I held a soft gaze with him as he slowly allowed this inner sensation to mobilize and move through his arms. He found that I was responding with contingency to his emotions, in a slow motion form, and that I was able to physically and emotionally meet the intensity of his sensation, so together we could allow our aroused energy to move through into completion and connection while we maintained relationship with each other. As the energy and mobilization completed, our eyes met and we each saw the other as we were, human beings from different cultures, but somehow related.

Then suddenly, Tom left the group. I had seen a light in Tom's face that indicated to me that something had shifted within him. His eyes had met mine with a new warmth and connection, so I knew that the encounter was helpful for both of us. Still, I had no idea of what might happen next.

Several hours later, Tom reappeared. During our demonstration together, he had brought awareness to his inner sensations so that emotion was no longer hidden in his gut. He had left the training to complete *metabolization* of his emotions with a traditional cleansing ritual, the *oosumich*. In accordance with this ritual, Tom disrobed, scrubbed with fresh cut cedar boughs, bathed in the cold river, and then donned an unworn white shirt. He explained the spiritual meaning of the *oosumich* ceremony to the group and how wearing a white, previously unworn garment signified the beginning of a new phase of life. Atleo (2004) describes *oosumich* as a ritual cleansing that stimulates the body's own healing energies as well as building courage, determination, and endurance since "existence is inherently dangerous" (92). Ki-ke-in, a Nuu-chah-nulth man, says that the *oomsuch* (there are different spellings of the same experience) helps us to "organize ourselves spiritually so that we can be strong when something needs to be done (Hoover 2000, 215) Following that experience with Tom, there was a new level of trust and a sense of lightness in the group.

All cultures celebrate essential elements of life in different forms of ceremony. A ceremony involves encounters that contain and hold the disturbed energy of trauma along with the natural healing forces of life. In many ways, the encounters of the new paradigm in Western healing practices, right-brain-to-right-brain affective embodied experiences that Schore (2012) advocates, are ceremonies that bring essential elements together for healing trauma. The ceremony can be a contained intersubjective dialogue between two people or a group; it might be a meditation, or the experience of sharing and embodying imagination and dreams, dancing, music, or other expressive forms. The elements that make it a ceremony include embodied intersubjective relationships, the rituals of sacred, uninterrupted time, the development of bodily-based rhythm and movement, and somatic relational exploration of internal and environmental influences on human experiences.

Throughout many years of participating in ancient healing ceremonies, I have noticed that the ceremonies for transformational change begin with clear intention and deep respect for bodily-based ways of knowing and relational connection. Ceremonies welcome and integrate supportive relationships with animals, the earth, plants, guides, and ancestors. Social engagement, stimulated by the ventral vagal circuit, is continually strengthened to be the first line of defense in traumatic moments rather than isolation with sympathetic arousal used for individual survival. Participants in these ceremonies value connection between the people, land,

and other beings; the wisdom of lived experience through elders; and attunement, resonance, and interconnectedness of all elements of nature. Creative ceremonies for building and restoring relationship, cleansing as a discipline, and moving with rhythm and incorporation of spiritual energies facilitate change for communities, while restoring a personal sense of innate individual wholeness and connection with that which is larger than the human experience. Ceremonies bring the fragmented elements of dissociative experiences together in an alive and pulsing container for acknowledgment, conversion, metabolism, and transformation of lived experience. How do we translate these elements into practices of psychotherapy, medicine, and education?

In developing a ceremonial encounter for healing trauma in a one-on-one relationship, we need a clear and caring intention for ourselves and the other, honoring the unique intersubjective relationship in that moment, and giving careful bodily-based attention to space, time, energy flow, and connection between participants and the environment. The intention for a healing ceremonial encounter is based on core human values, such as the Chamorro concept of doing good for others, the loving kindness of Buddhism, and the unity of love and pain—a Nuu-chah-nulth principle (Atleo 2004).

To clarify my intention, before a person comes into my office for psychotherapy, I meditate on my experience of them, bringing the person to mind and attending to what arises in me. I recall vivid moments of earlier encounters. I might notice anticipation, concern, trepidation, intrigue, curiosity, or caring. I then notice my internal somatic reactions to my meditation, regulating any arousal that emerges. In the meditation, I wonder what might be needed. Rather than planning a protocol or technique, reflecting and wondering about the other prepares me for authentic engagement where we can come into an embodied present moment experience of safety and intersubjectivity to continue our exploration and incorporation of dissociated traumatic memories.

Following intention is the greeting, a "moment of meeting," a reunion experience, that sets the initial conditions of the encounter and the conversion from sympathetic arousal to social engagement. The greeting is mindful, involving a respectful presence and welcome, a moment of eye gaze, naming of the other, and physical guidance with gesture and movement into the space where the therapeutic encounter will occur. Like a ceremonial dance, this embodied greeting sets the theme of relational caring, respect for the person, and is often communicated through nonverbal gestures. I offer tea or water and personally prepare refreshment for my guest, a symbolic preparation for the refreshment our encounter will provide for each of us. With this attentive, ritual beginning, the energy of a ceremonial session builds, engaging us in the embodied intersubjective field and the containment to convert and regulate difficult arousal states of fear and immobility into relational connection. Following regulation, we enter into a somatic-based inquiry and the emergence of "just enough" new material to metabolize in our relationship. New inner material may have come from emerging implicit or explicit memories, intuition, dreams, reflections, or from the intersubjective field. As the new material is phenomenologically explored, amplified, differentiated into opposites, oscillated, integrated, and then embodied into the current felt sense, the sense of interconnectivity grows. Often a time of silence is needed for synthesis with a rich and full nonverbal presence of each to the other. The closing of a session involves a coreflection on our shared experience, naming subjective and intersubjective dynamics. This shared inquiry in the reflection period allows the right-hemispheric processing to translate into the more abstract language of the left hemisphere.

For many, these ceremonial encounters, or affective embodied experiences, are described as spiritual, expansive, and "lightening," yet distinct from religious overtones and able to translate into meaningful knowledge that shifts the distorted perceptions of trauma.

Wisdom of Spiritual Energy

The right hemisphere of the brain holds the wisdom known as spiritual experience. Spiritual experience, for me, is that which has been embodied and processed from unknown hidden parts into new interconnected images and valued wisdom. The right hemisphere requires a kind of vitality, a spirit, to reorganize its fragmented elements. Following the conversion of chronic neural states of sympathetic arousal into relational interdependence, the incorporation of bodily-based lived experience with symbolic, imaginative realms, the metabolism, restores wholeness and a sense of spiritedness to individuals and communities. With the container of ceremony and the animation from the intersubjective field, the splinters from trauma are innately linked in the right hemisphere. We can easily see the radiance of individuals when their spirits are alive in their bodies. With the conversion of fear to love, the accumulated defenses and memories from trauma can slowly be metabolized by shared affective embodied experiences into a sense of self-in-relation and growth in maturity and development.

Nuu-chah-nulth scholar Atleo (2004) describes a natural relationship between the physical and the spiritual. Spiritual experience is divided into two categories: experiences that arise from the spiritual realm and experiences that stem from human activity, such as "fasting, dreams, ritual cleansing, praying, petitioning, waiting, and chanting" (72). Spiritual realm experiences consist of practices like the Afro-Brazilian Umbanda, which values bodily incorporation of divine energy and forces of nature, and Christian mysticism, which fosters a direct, loving relationship with the divine.

For Atleo, all spiritual experiences, those initiated by the spiritual realm and those initiated by human intention, are forms of communication between the spiritual and the physical. While human spiritual abilities are respected and valued, they are "very limited in comparison to the great powers available from the spiritual realm" (74). Atleo (2004) encourages people to pay attention and listen to the spiritual realms rather than totally rely on human-initiated disciplines and practices.

The worldview of the Nuu-chah-nulth (Atleo 2004) moves between humans, animals, and the divine, with a sense of the spiritual embedded within the physical. Communication with animals in ordinary daily life, particularly in moments of prayer and visioning, is significant in the relationship with spiritual realms. While logic, reason, and spiritual practices are respected and valued, intuition is known as a spiritual communication, one that is highly valued (Atleo 2004).

An exploration of my own Indigenous legacy led me to study Celtic spiritual practices in Ireland and Scotland, practices that are still flourishing today. While teaching in Iona, a small, isolated island off the coast of Scotland, I toured a fifth-century abbey that contained the remains of an ancient convent for women dedicated to the healing arts and was also where the famous Book of Kells was written in the Middle Ages (Hull 2012). One evening, I unexpectedly witnessed a ceremonial festival that enacted stories of oppression, war, resistance, and spiritual healing dating back fifteen centuries. To prepare for the festival, the community invited the children of Iona to create their own Book of Kells to describe the events on the island since the original book was written. In the full moon of a magical May night, the festival dancers and performers replicated a fifth-century celebration with fire, movement, music, procession, ancient props, and dramatic enactments pertaining to the Book of Kells. As I watched the festival, I found myself fully engaged in a ceremony, following the procession down to the water where ancient replicas of the Irish boats were moored and the children's Book of Kells were placed in a leather boat for the trip back to Ireland. The boatmen began to row the small craft away from the dock and under the light of the moon. In a transformative moment, I intuitively knew an aspect of my own ancestral history that filled my being. The energy of the past is often invisible, somewhat like the remains hidden in an archeological site. As we bring these energies to light, healing and restoration can occur.

A common dimension of the Celtic "green" way, Indigenous traditions, and Afro-Brazilian Umbanda practices lies in how people are embodied and strive to live in interdependent relationship with each other and their inner worlds—healing the past, each other, the land, nature, community, and the spiritual energies of the universe. In her feminist-arts informed research on embodiment and eco-activism, Lisa Mortimore (2013) found that some eco-activists experience a personal reciprocal communication with the wind, trees, and mountains. Healing trauma is not just a psychological technique, but an ancient practice of embodied healing by a socially engaged community that does not begin just after an aversive event. Rather it is a way of living that prepares for adversity and actively converts, metabolizes, and incorporates all lived experience, including what we consider trauma, into sacred and powerful energies.

Clinicians can engage and promote this spiritual way of living by expanding their perceptions of nature, self, and other in relationship to a larger realm and worldview. Spiritual practices where they continually struggle to be transparent and loving in their ordinary relationships and immerse themselves in the rhythms of the land through walking in the forest, sitting by the shore, watching the sky and its changes, and mindful gardening can reweave the bonds with the natural world. Imagination can also be a portal to these realms of unity and connection. As we watch a sunset, we can imagine what plant and animal life as well as the elements of the universe would want to say to us. Interactions with trees, birds, and plants reminds us we are not alone on this planet. A Japanese practice of walking in the forest is widely acclaimed to be healing to the spirit while a similar Buddhist-based meditation as developed by Jon Kabat-Zinn (2005) is used for healing in many institutions.

The Power of Community

For thousands of years, Indigenous people relied on relational, cultural resources for healing, particularly those that embraced one's individuality and promoted social-emotional inclusion in the community (McMillan 1999). During the trauma trainings I conducted with them, Indigenous participants recognized that the core knowledge of trauma—the bodily base, historical legacy, and the restoration through somatic practices—was familiar to their culture, embedded in traditional teachings, songs, and ceremonies. This knowledge had become invisible through repression of traditional practices by colonial governments and was recognized by a community leader, as the "new/old way of trauma healing."

During these trainings, I became a learner, and the wisdom of the ancient heritage that was invisible within me and within the participants became our teacher, and so it was here that I consciously became aware of the power of the community to heal trauma that goes far beyond one-on-one encounters. During the trainings, many of the participants were able to uncover dissociated patterns of trauma and implicit memories from oppression. When these moments occurred, individuals with emerging cues of dissociated trauma did not want to leave the group to work one-on-one with a facilitator, a common practice in training groups. Rather, when a person felt the emergence of trauma they opted to participate in demonstrations of somatic healing practices within the whole group, who—sitting in a circle together—would hold hands, relying on the invisible yet powerful cultural and spiritual resources that connected them to help guide them in the recovery of vital elements of the self. The Indigenous people were not afraid of appearing weak, "unprofessional," or vulnerable to others as I often noted in other groups and were able to support and assist each other in healing.

For example, one day in the training, a participant named Henry spontaneously recalled a memory of his past. A small child in the bush with his father and grandmother, he recalled suddenly being picked up by a priest and carried away on a horse. This practice—gathering Native children and taking them to mandatory residential schools where they were forced to assimilate to white culture—began in the late 1870s and continued into the late 1990s. Run by an agreement between the government and organized religious groups, the schools were harsh places where many of the students were subjected to severe physical, emotional, cultural, sexual, and spiritual abuse.

Surprised by the intense sensations of the arousal that accompanied the recall of his repressed memory, Henry reached for the hands of the people next to him as he somatically entered into the implicit memory of the traumatic events. The terror, horror, and immobility with fear from long ago was fully alive in the present moment, yet was shared and contained by the surrounding people who loved him. Henry described his terror as a young boy and then how he had learned to survive imprisonment in the residential school. He held tightly to the hands that joined his; the hands around the circle formed a community-based, ancient container for their anguish. After approximately twenty minutes of vivid recall, he looked at the hands touching his and the circle of familiar faces and slowly began to return to present moment reality. The chaos of the traumatic memory began to convert into relational connection, differentiating the past from the present moment.

As Henry became calm and present in the moment, I invited him to notice what he was sensing in his body. He became silent and then his body spontaneously startled with a sharp movement. "Something came into me," Henry said, "I don't know what it is." As I invited him to continue noticing what was happening and to stay connected to the people near him, his startle diminished and he became curious. He then recognized what had come into him: "It's me, it's my Self." His face softened and radiated with light. Henry released the hands that held his and said with confidence, "That was not a breakdown, it was a breakthrough."

Later as the group reflected on the day, one of the elders recalled that she had known Henry as a little boy before his capture and then again as an adult, and yes, the spirit of the boy that he was, had come back into his body and she was grateful. The elder had a vision where she could now see his ancestors around him dancing in celebration. She said that she knew that with his leadership their community would be able to heal and become a stronger healing presence for each other and in the world.

With the support of his community and culture, Henry incorporated his authentic self, the "one presence," his spirit, into his body. With this incorporation, his body was able to restore the vitality of the self in the context of relational support. The elder described the effects of residential school trauma as the "spirit leaving the body," a concept similar to disembodiment, disconnection, and dissociation. Henry experienced healing when his implicit memory system revealed details of a *dissociative gap*, an amnesic memory characterized by intense neural states hidden under the survival patterns he needed to endure the residential school. The elder who revealed the vision of dancing ancestors recognized the moment of reembodiment, or incorporation of his spirit as significant, not just for Henry, but for the well-being of the community, restoring health to people from the past as well as those to come.

A strong community where people are welcomed *as they are* and are connected through their heritage, through day-to-day living and shared arts and culture offers a sense of home for people suffering from early trauma and a solid container for the restoration of wholeness for an individual. To heal trauma in Western culture, we need to find embodied ways to work together in small groups, processing the affective, emotional experiences of our lives on a continual basis, and provide resources for those who are currently experiencing traumatic events including abuse, poverty, disempowerment, genocide, disaster, and oppression. In Chapter 12, we will explore ways clinicians can form into small groups to study the research on trauma, build sustaining relationships, and process their own trauma in safe and nurturing ways.

Incorporating Indigenous Ways of Knowing into Western Culture—Case 5.1: Phil

Ceremony, spirituality, and engagement in relational communities are affective embodied experiences that can be incorporated into a Western approach for healing trauma. In this section we'll explore how I drew from the intersubjective relationship, Indigenous ways of knowing, and social engagement practices to work with Phil, a retired man in his sixties who experienced early attachment trauma.

When Phil first came to see me he was struggling with escalating addictions and the depletion of financial resources due to excessive gambling. His career was marked by his ability to financially organize through the left hemisphere while right-hemispheric processes of bodily-based awareness, emotion, and imagination were fragmented, dissociated, and invisible. As we began to talk about his life, Phil revealed he was "bothered" by memories of his early relationship with his mother and other family members. A young Jewish woman, his mother had grown up in Europe during World War II and had spent several years hiding in a monastery. Following the war, his mother married a soldier and came to the United States. When Phil was six months old, his mother was hospitalized with a "nervous breakdown." For eighteen months, until he was two years old, Phil was passed from one relative to the next, and when he was returned to his mother, he completely ignored her and would not allow her to care for him. I wondered if Phil was dealing with states of disorganized attachment, avoiding intimate connection through dissociation in order to inhibit his inner pain.

After a beloved aunt, who he knew had cared for him during his infancy, passed away, Phil started having panic attacks, moments when horror would break through into night terrors and bouts of extreme anxiety during the day. Since his aunt's death, these "past times" had begun to take over his life. I was reminded of the Latin root of the word addiction, *addictus*, meaning to give oneself over to another (Leonard 2001).

During his adolescence and adulthood, Phil's mother's hospitalization and his early life experience of being shuttled between relatives was never mentioned, yet it existed "like a dark cloud of dread" in his implicit memory system. Phil described this "dark cloud" that lived within his viscera as a heaviness in his chest and a constricted, numb belly combined with a restless irritation, cues that the neural states of immobilization with fear were bound in his autonomic nervous system and viscera. During our early sessions, we spent a fair amount of time building a relationship together, participating in moments of silent presence, mindfully engaging in practices of grounding and embodiment, and engaging in dialogue in an effort to convert his sympathetic arousal into relational trust. The mutual intersubjective relationship that grew between us gave us both a sense of warmth and connection—an *affective embodied experience*—and gradually brought Phil into the connectivity of human relationship as his primary response to ordinary experiences. However, buried as dissociative states, were implicit traumatic memories that could erupt in intense reactions under emotional stress.

One day, while talking about an upcoming visit with his adult son whom he had not seen in many years, Phil had a panic attack in my office. This was the intrusion of immobilized terror from his dysregulated autonomic nervous system that had previously been inhibited by his dominant left hemisphere and his addictions. His son had called Phil, telling him he would arrive in a week, bringing his twenty-year-old daughter, and wondering if they could talk about family history. As Phil told me about the impending visit, his hands became rigid, turned cold, and he struggled to breathe, all signs of dissociated hypoarousal and immobility with fear. When I asked Phil if he would like to hold my hands, he reached out. Moving closer, I could sense a rigidity deep within his body. As I touched his hands, a shiver went through my body, and I felt and tasted an ice-cold terror and horror. Through the cold sensations in my body, I recognized the neural state of life threat or shock that moved between us. Phil observed my spontaneous reaction as I felt the sensations of intense fear, horror, and terror. His eyes were wide open, deep brown irises surrounded by a sea of white. As I looked into the terror in his eyes, I felt and acknowledged the terror; my heart was beating fast and my viscera held a rush of chaotic sensations. While embodied, I observed and witnessed my own reaction with interest and curiosity. I grounded myself, sensed my feelings of love for Phil, oriented to the regulating elements in my office, the art, the light, and color, and the water, trees, and sky outside my window. I then met his unmoving stare with a soft gaze and easy, rhythmical voice. I acknowledged that what had happened to him as a child was truly awful, and in this moment he was now safe, his body could breathe, and we were both able to attend to his feelings. I assured him that I would stay with him while these feelings revealed what we needed to know.

In a soft voice, I asked Phil if we could begin caring for him by noticing his feet. He slightly nodded his assent. In response to my inquiry, Phil became aware that my feet were close to his and he could feel the contact. I invited him to simply notice how it felt in this moment to feel me with him. His hands within mine, I asked him if he could feel our hands connecting. With this inquiry, I could feel a slight vibration in his hands and a subtle warming. I nonverbally responded to his shift with a little pressure from my hands. As we watched and felt our hands together, they continued to warm, tingle and vibrate, and I intuitively recalled the simple hand-to-hand touch that had allowed the First Nations people to endure the anguishing return of dissociated affect with others. I invited Phil to notice that we were here in the present moment, the past was leaving, and old memories were slowly moving out of his body. Similar to the experience of Henry holding the hands of people close to him, I was transmitting the concern and caring that is shared in my community to Phil. Without my experience of belonging to a strong and interconnected community, I am not sure it would have been possible for me to offer this connection to another. The felt presence of another living, breathing person in the moments when a dissociated memory emerges allows the terror to be contained and the immobility to be shared and then converted into relational engagement. It was essential that I hold an inner awareness of my connections to nature right outside my window: the trees, water, sky, and light and all the loving relationships of my life. I needed to stay embodied as I reacted with contingency to his shifting emotions, meeting them, and responding with my intuition, not necessarily therapeutic techniques. It was also important that we had converted the signals of an activated amygdala, the fear, to energy for relational connection over and over in our work together prior to the panic attack.

Traumatic memories of shock continued to emerge as we held hands. Phil's face was pale, he began shaking, and spontaneously moving his body. He said he was very cold so I covered Phil with a warm blanket and continued to hold his hands, containing his intense energy in our intersubjective field. This containment was a vigil, part of a sacred ceremony that holds the dissociated terror and horror as we moved toward acknowledging, converting, and incorporating energy into our intersubjective field.

This experience in therapy was a "moment of meeting" (The Boston Change Process Study Group, 2010), a change mechanism of developmental neuroscience described in Chapter 3, but more poetically known as *transformation* in cultures that enjoy right-hemispheric dominance. The processes of conversion from one arousal system to another and metabolism, the integration of fragmented energy into a whole, is necessary in the transformation of trauma. Phil's experience was similar to both Henry and Tom's encounters with deeper aspects of the self. Containing these moments of transformation in a subtle ceremony allowed Tom to experience a sense of renewal; for Henry it was the restoration of his own spirit.

After about five minutes of shaking and settling, a deep restorative breath moved through Phil as he slowly opened his eyes, a breath that marked the conversion of the brain circuits from a terrorized immobility system to an engaged relational system. He had come through the implicit traumatic memory experience, "a breakthrough, not a breakdown." His eyes had softened and a warm mutual gaze was now possible. We communicated wordlessly for a period of time before I asked Phil what he was noticing in the moment. His hands were warm and had released mine following our nonverbal but potent communication. With that nonverbal message, I moved my chair back into my usual place. This shift was an indicator that the intense moment of change, the conversion from one brain circuit to another, was now integrating and freeing his vitality and imagination to metabolize his implicit memories.

As Phil considered my inquiry, he softly said he was thinking about his mother. He had a spontaneous image of her as a deeply frightened teenager, near the age of his granddaughter. (Previously, he had been struck by the physical resemblance between his mother and a photo of his granddaughter.) In a fleeting image that emerged in our silence together, he recognized a place of safety and comfort for his mother.

We slowly began to incorporate the image of this safe and comfortable place for his mother into our bodily-based intersubjective field—and the image moved along in time. I inquired into the specific phenomena and energy of the image slowly and carefully. In Phil's imagination, the place of safety was a small monastery where his young/old, Jewish mother was covered in the robes of a monk. He was an older monk who held his mother's hands as she slowly warmed to the safety, compassion, and presence he and his community could offer.

With the image of his mother finding safety and connection through the archetype of a monk, Phil was able to incorporate the message of safety, compassion, and bodily-centered protection that his mother was not able to communicate when he was an infant. Just as the Indigenous people trusted the spiritual energies of ancestors, through his spontaneous imagination, Phil was able to restore his trust in his deceased mother.

Recognizing the intense spiritual energies of protection from ancestors and archetypes, I recognized Phil's addictions as ways that he had learned to protect himself from the implicit traumatic memories of the terror and horror of his early life that threatened his consciousness. Kalsched (2010) notes that violent memories often emerge in emotionally positive times as caring, trusting relationships begin to offer hope and opportunity for growth. With his addictions, he was able to dissociate from the intense anguish and enter into the dissociative "flow" at the casino, yet these addictions were also persecuting him, holding him hostage to humiliation and shame.

In a bodily-based reflection in the next session, I found out that both Phil and I sensed the protective love his mother had for him in his transformative image, a love he was not able to incorporate until the implicit memory opened him to receive human touch, connection, and embodied imaginal presence. There was more work to come, but Phil's ability to open to the love that he had intuited through his imagination was a turning point in our work together.

Facilitating Change through Differentiation and Linkage

Successful practices for learning, healing, and continuing growth and development—whether Indigenous, traditional, or Western in origin—all begin with the dynamic of differentiation and linkage. For example, in a ceremony, people leave their ordinary life and enter into fluid, altered states where wounded internal phenomena, such as fused brain circuits, can be differentiated and converted into more adaptive and mature patterns.

The process of differentiation first begins with an amplification of the diverse phenomena associated with an experience, such as identifying particular sensations, tracking the movement of emotions, attending to images that appear in conversation, and carefully listening for the embedded moments of vitality and aliveness. With differentiation and amplification, phenomena of the same experience can be separated into polarities. Once the phenomena is contained in polarities, the tension can be held in the intersubjective field. As we feel the tension together, elements of our creative right hemispheres find new ways to come into "right" relationship with each other. For example, in the sessions with Tom, Henry, and Phil, we focused on differentiating the sensory emotional states of trauma from current, relational states of connection.

What makes Indigenous practices, such as the Umbanda rituals and the *oomsich*, so effective in healing trauma, is that they facilitate the differentiation of neural traumatic knots—love fused with fear, terror coupled with immobility, memories lost in dissociative gaps—through affective embodied experiences and intersubjective relationships. As the differentiated elements are held open and separate, unseen forces within the intersubjective field guide the differentiated elements into new and surprising forms of reconnection, linkage, and integration. I consider these unseen forces of present moment lived experience the ultimate healers of trauma.

How does this translate to Western culture? The skill of differentiation in a helping relationship centers on a bodily-based inquiry into lived experience—a phenomenological method of dialogue and exploration that gently discerns the fused parts of a system. *Phenomenology* is a method of discovery that is interested in what it means to be a human being. Similar to the traditional wisdom of Indigenous cultures, it is rooted in the present moment, but seeks to unify the past, present, and future. It is most interested in describing the essence of things independently of presuppositions. Slow and careful differentiation through phenomenological inquiry allows the intense energies of trauma to become available in small and tolerable doses that can be incorporated and linked back into the body, transforming a traumatic memory into new forms of vitality. Differentiation requires conscious, sensitive skills in embodied inquiry while linkage is more mysterious and occurs spontaneously as an innate synthesis of reconnection at a higher level of development.

When differentiated parts of a system are open to new linkages, they can be supported and guided into new connections that foster higher levels of human abilities, such as self-regulation, creativity, kindness, compassion, and empathy. Throughout this book we explore how the innate, yet very often subtle change process of differentiation and linkage can be utilized in the somatic treatment of complex trauma.

References

Atleo, E. R. 2004. *Tsawalk: A Nuu-chah-nulth Worldview*. Vancouver: University of British Columbia Press.

Berman, M. 1989. *Coming to Our Senses*. New York: Simon and Schuster.

The Boston Change Process Study Group. 2010. *Change in Psychotherapy: A Unifying Paradigm*. New York: Norton.

Hoover, A., ed. 2000. *Nuu-chah-nulth Voices, Histories, Objects & Journeys*. Victoria: Royal British Columbia Museum.

Hull, V. 2012. Iona: *A Guide to the Sacred Isle*. Clinton: Storybook House.

Kabat-Zinn, J. 2005. *Coming to Our Senses: Healing Ourselves and the World through Mindfulness*. New York: Hyperion.

Kalsched, D. 2010. "Defense in Dreams: Clinical Reflections on the Multiplicity Necessary for Survival in Pieces." Paper presented at annual meeting of the International Association for Analytical Psychology, Montreal, August 2010.

Leonard Schierse, L. 2001. *Witness to the Fire: Creativity and the Veil of Addiction*. Boston: Shambhala.

McMillan, A. 1999. *Since the Time of the Transformers: The Ancient Heritage of the Nuu-chah-nulth, Dedidat, and Makah*. Vancouver: University of British Columbia Press.

Mortimore, L. 2013. "Embodied Ways of Knowing: Women's Eco-Activism." PhD diss., University of Victoria, ProQuest (NS28393).

Narvaez, D. 2014. *Neurobiology and the Development of Human Morality: Evolution, Culture, and Wisdom*. New York: Norton.

Schore, A. N. 2012. *The Science of the Art of Psychotherapy*. New York: Norton.

6 Somatic Awareness

The Truth of the Mind Begins in the Body

"If you want to understand the beauty of a bird, a fly, or a leaf, or a person with all his complexities, you have to give your whole attention, which is awareness. And you can give your whole attention only when you care, which means that you really love to understand—then you give your whole heart and mind to find out."
(Krishnamurti 1969, 31–32)

Facilitating Collaboration between the Mind and the Body

The practice of somatic awareness begins in embodiment, fostering a compassionate, gentle, and communicative relationship between the mind and the body. Somatic awareness witnesses from within the ongoing communication between the body and mind, between the inner world and outer world, and between the subjective self and the subjective world of another; it is a fundamental way of knowing the truth of one's lived experience. A sustained somatic awareness arises naturally from embodiment, yet, as a therapeutic practice, it can be focused like a laser beam for intentional healing.

Merleau-Ponty (1962) identified perception through the body as the core of all knowing and the subjective sense of self. He recognized that without knowing through the body, one's sense of self is an empty mental abstraction, an idea without a ground, a structure of dry logic and abstract language without a feeling of a heartbeat or breath. Somatic awareness facilitates a collaborative relationship between the body and mind, where the body has an active voice in transforming the mind and the mind processes and refines knowledge—communicating that information back to the body. The practice of somatic awareness initiates the reconsolidation process of traumatic memories, bringing attention to the breaches in the right-hemispheric processing of lived experience.

The practice of somatic awareness is voluntary and requires a higher cortical consciousness of sensory motor reactions, particularly those arising from neuroceptions of safety, danger, or life threat. The right-hemispheric orbital frontal cortex is able to empathically witness and track sensory reactions with compassion as they arise, shift, and transform into new sensations, movements, emotions, and images, organizing lived experience into knowledge. Tucker (2007) theorizes how the somatic "shell" can contain and integrate the intense emotions that lie in the visceral "core," helping us gain control of our lives by making important decisions in the moment and processing the intense emotional implicit memories from early relational-developmental trauma and aversive events. It links the maturity of higher cortical processes with the helplessness of a highly aroused amygdala.

Somatic awareness is a perceptual skill, an ability that comes naturally to people who live in embodied, nurturing relationships. However, to survive, many people from Western culture engage in mindless thinking (Varela, Thompson, and Rosch 1991) and as a result have learned to dissociate from their bodies. However, they can recover the perception of direct bodily-based experience with mindful, intentional practice. Somatic awareness begins with opening our consciousness through the body to deeper levels of lived experience, dynamics that may be invisible and unconscious to others. Body-centered consciousness stimulates the imagination and archetypes, more universal aspects of human ways of knowing. These collective ways of knowing have been shared in traditional cultures and rooted in their oral history of creation and relationship (Jacob 2013). People from Indigenous and traditional cultures, prior to colonization, were firmly grounded in bodily-based consciousness. Those with shamanic and intuitive abilities have honed somatic awareness into a powerful means for living in interconnected ways. They are able to stay sensitive and attuned to emerging subtle perceptions in the moment and to discern the sensations that come from what they see, hear, and feel while inviting corresponding images to emerge that clarify ambiguous situations. In the Afro-Brazilian practice of Umbanda, the leader and community members bring an embodied presence to ceremony with a heightened sensitivity and attunement to visual, auditory, and kinesthetic communication from the shared intersubjective field and the environment. This heightened sensitivity in the brain stem and limbic system accelerates right-hemispheric processing to reveal vivid images and archetypes for protection, guidance, healing, and strength. Let's take a closer look at how somatic awareness affects the brain.

Somatic Awareness Stimulates the Brain and Restores Vitality

Somatic awareness stimulates right-hemispheric processing and reorganization by "putting the spotlight" on neural networks, an intention called "selective attention" that can increase neural firing by 300 percent (Koch 2004). Sensation is the language of the nervous system, informing us continually through neuroceptions (Porges 2011). Attention can be thought of as the ability to concentrate on a particular stimulus while excluding competing ones. Selective attention involves a conscious choice regarding the direction of focus.

Christof Koch (2004) explores how awareness links the current sensory environment to the information from memory banks germane to present-moment situations. "We learn to relate sensory events to positive and negative states so as to guide its behavior" (321). Koch explains that the role of the brain is to plan for multicontingency situations. To do that, the right hemisphere of the brain gathers and processes sensory-motor stimulation, movements, primitive emotions, and emergent images. Sustained somatic awareness of particular areas in the body quickens neural firing. Networks that are actively firing together are wiring together into new neural networks. Those networks that are fused in moments of trauma can be differentiated to fire separately while others can be linked for connectivity. In other words, whatever we attend to or "shine the spotlight on" grows and flourishes neurologically, the spotlight being the practice of somatic awareness while the process of internal linking in the right hemisphere is far more mysterious.

Somatic awareness of the body awakens the energetic life force necessary for the reorganization of the body, mind, and brain. This vitality, often truncated by trauma, is essential for healing and living in the moment in creative, adaptive, and intimate relationships. Vitality is a "manifestation of life, of being alive. We are alert to its feel in ourselves in its expression in others" (Stern 2010, 3). Daniel Stern approaches vitality as a "mental creation, as a product of the mind's integration of many internal and external events, as a subjective experience, and as a phenomenal reality" (4). Current experiences of vitality bring life to trauma-based fixed-action patterns to reconsolidate one's "past experiences, including memories, dissociated experiences, phenomenological experiences, past experiences known implicitly and never verbalized, and in particular 'implicit relational knowing'" (Stern 2010, 11). The fundamental challenge of helping people suffering from complex trauma, particularly those living in states of disassociation, depression, and despair, with neural states of "immobility with fear" is restoring the innate dynamic of vitality. Before we discuss how to use somatic awareness to restore the natural processing of the implicit memory system, let's examine how memories are stored.

Implicit and Explicit Memory Systems

The implicit and explicit memory systems are two of the ways that memories are stored and recalled. Explicit memories begin to form as the left hemisphere comes "online" toward the end of the second year of life. Until then all memories are implicit and navigated by the right hemisphere (Schore 2012). Explicit memories are more accessible because they involve conscious intent to store and to retrieve. We are accessing our explicit memory when we describe a significant event in detail or offer a narrative of our life experience.

Implicit memories are "skills, habits, emotional responses, reflexive actions, and classically conditioned responses" that are linked with the nervous system (van der Kolk, McFarlane, and Weisaeth 1996, 281). Implicit memories range from the survival-oriented primitive reactions of the amygdala and autonomic nervous system to procedural memories, such as tying shoelaces or riding a bike. An example of a more sophisticated, skilled implicit memory is the intricate series of movements a dancer recalls during a performance. Our faces reveal our current implicit memories through small, often subtle, muscular movements that unconsciously divulge the emotions of fear, disgust, curiosity, or compassion. Our voices also disclose unconscious implicit memories in harsh tones or more prosodic ways of speaking. Body postures retain implicit memories of a traumatic past and can be activated when we feel overwhelmed.

Implicit memories are less accessible to consciousness because they are often formed during the early communications of the infant-parent relationship (Schore 2012). Contingent relational patterns formed in childhood experiences are retained as implicit memories on the right hemisphere and are expressed through expectations for how others will act in response to our behavior (Beebe and Lachmann 2014). Beebe describes contingencies as the predictable relation between behavior and consequences that infants learn in terms of their environment and their own behavior. These contingent implicit memories emerge as patterns in our adult relationships. Changing expectations requires the formation of new, implicit learning that occurs in lived experiences with others.

According to Bromberg, the processing of lived experience into implicit memories of the right hemisphere occurs mainly out of awareness, yet it provides us with basic action knowledge about ourselves, the world, and how things and people work. Implicit memories are a way of "just knowing" or "sort of knowing" (Bromberg 2011). The knowledge held in implicit memories may be called intuition or gut knowing and may be difficult to put into words. It's important to note that when a helper's own implicit memories from relational trauma are dissociated and their current somatic awareness is limited, gut knowing or intuition can be dead wrong, leading to enactments. As helping professionals, we *need* somatic awareness to develop authentic mutuality, empathy, and clear intuition. For growth in accurate intuition, helping professionals need to be aware that their perceptions, evaluations, and motivation can be influenced by their own dissociated implicit relational trauma (Bargh and Morsella 2008). Ineffective and disruptive relational experiences, sometimes known as transference and countertransference may be due to a "lack of awareness of the influences or effects of a triggering stimulus and not the triggering stimulus itself" (74). The practice of somatic awareness calls us to a deeper level of knowing self and other than many psychological theories have assumed over the past century. In the midst of our relational dilemmas, if we consider that the unconscious mind is simply unaware of stimuli, knowledge that may be accessed through somatic awareness, it makes sense to wonder and explore awareness of bodily-based sensations, emotions, and imaginal stimuli rather than jump to theory-based interpretation.

Implicit Traumatic Memories

When trauma occurs and there is little or no support available to make sense of what is happening, a person's implicit memory system becomes overloaded and interrupts right-hemispheric processing. Chronic states of anger, aggression, withdrawal, depression, and dissociation can all result from disruptions of this innate processing system. These reactions accumulate into repetitive patterns. Bromberg (2011) states that implicit memories of trauma are not relieved by telling because "procedural" forms of memory are emotional, not cognitive. "High levels of stimulation from the amygdala interfere with hippocampal functioning (memory formation). When this occurs in treatment, and it occurs inevitably, the sensory imprints of experience that are stored in affective memory continue to remain isolated images and body sensations that feel cut off from the rest of the self" (79).

One of the most challenging perceptions for trauma survivors is the differentiation between implicit traumatic memories from the past and present moment experience. A spontaneous bodily-based arousal of fear could mean unconscious associations with prior traumatic experience or it could indicate very real explicit danger in the moment. How can we tell the difference and uncouple the maladaptive fused neural circuits that have "fired together and wired together" in the moment of trauma?

Within the context of an intersubjective dialogue with trauma survivors, somatic awareness can differentiate the sensations and emotions that have fused in traumatic moments. To differentiate sensations from emotions, we *bracket* the emotions and hold somatic awareness of the sensations in the intersubjective relationship. Bracketing is a phenomenological method that acknowledges phenomena, yet consciously sets it aside for a time to attend to more essential phenomena. Bracketing might sound like this: "And when you feel that emotion, I'm wondering what you notice in your body?" Bracketing does not negate or suppress emotion, but opens up a way to directly change the neural states of the implicit processing system.

As people differentiate sensations from emotions, the sensory experience moves along in time and can be incorporated back into the body as another way of knowing, often generating new emotions. This practice strengthens the recognition of barely perceptual cues, making it possible to read the primitive meaning of a neural state before it emerges as an emotion. For example, we can feel a rising up in the chest indicating joy, a contraction in the chest signifying fear, a tightening of the jaw indicating anger, or a dropping down sensation in the face and viscera associated with grief, sadness, and disappointment. Emotions are vivid messages that have significant meaning in our lives, and through the conscious practice of somatic awareness of sensory-based neural states that lie beneath the emotions, we can learn to recognize and shift the neural states of implicit memories of the past that may feel very familiar, or distinctly unfamiliar and "not me." Neural oscillations of attention between sensations and emotions can differentiate the binding of the sensory-emotional experience and open a path for the sensation to become free from the fusion of emotion that happens in a traumatic experience. In the following section, we'll explore the role of somatic awareness in neural oscillations.

Oscillation Regulates Traumatic Memories and Restores Vitality

To better understand the role of somatic awareness in regulating traumatic memories, let's explore what Koch (2004) refers to as the binding problem—how different neural activities such as sensation, vision, light, color, sound, and emotion during trauma form into one perception. Binding, fusing, or overcoupling occurs when neurons fire together and wire together. A traumatic event has visual, auditory, and kinesthetic phenomena that fire and wire together with emotions of terror, horror, pain, and rage. To solve the binding problem, we must harness the power of neuron coalitions, Koch's description of neural networks that encode one precept, event, or concept. Coalitions are born and die in a fraction of a second; members reinforce each other and suppress competing coalitions. Applying this concept to survival powers following trauma, we can see how neurons firing together in one moment fuse many different aspects of trauma together into one experience.

In therapeutic work with traumatic memories, neural coalitions can be differentiated, releasing the fusion and allowing the neurons to relink into more adaptive coalitions in the present moment. In other words, the changing of neural coalitions is a transformative shift in consciousness that creates new neural pathways within the implicit processing system. With somatic awareness, we can select certain neurons for firing and use oscillation of attention to strengthen a bias toward healthy neural coalitions. In other words, with somatic awareness I can choose to bring my attention to the beauty within a person or ruminate on his or her very human limitations.

An inquiry into a traumatic experience within a person's zone of optimal arousal consists of small oscillations between arousal and regulation that are "safe but not too safe" (Bromberg 2011). These oscillations are created by differentiating survival-based inner phenomena with phenomena of relationship, beauty, and interconnection. The differentiation between just right amounts of "safe" phenomena and just right amounts of "not too safe" phenomena generates a creative tension that allows unsafe material to be incorporated into safety. Somatic interventions, such as oscillation, can interrupt and shift maladaptive patterns of implicit memory.

In order for traumatic memories to be processed through oscillation, people must be able to access a sense of vitality. Lost in moments of trauma, vitality can be restored by recalling a nourishing moment of lived experience while holding the images of terror and horror. For example, one summer evening I was enjoying some time with friends on their patio when I became aware of a birdbath in my line of vision. Watching four birds splashing together, I felt an expansion of life within me, an internal sense of delight, an arousal of joy. As I attended to the sensations of this internal movement with a focused somatic awareness, I noticed a surge of energy moving up my chest, opening my heart, and sending tingling sensations through my throat, neck, and face. I took notice of this awakening of vitality within me and later brought it into my daily meditation. I recalled the images of the evening, the faces of friends, the shared conversation in the setting sun, the excitement and splashing of the birds. I then recalled and incorporated the somatic awareness, the felt sense of the arousal of vitality in my chest, throat, and face to strengthen my vagal brake against old survival-based reactions that could emerge.

Small moments of delight surround us, yet when we are burdened by traumatic memories and our own alienation from others, we are not able to see, hear, or feel them. Practice recalling moments of embodied vitality with somatic awareness in Exercise 6.1: Accessing Vitality. See page 202 of the appendix.

Developing the Practice of Somatic Awareness

Somatic awareness begins with intentional perception, attending to the ongoing flow of sensations that form a felt sense of who we are in the moment. It is this flow of information and energy that constitutes our mind (Siegel 1999) and organizes the phenomena of lived experience. As we bring somatic awareness to the felt sense of our bodies, sensations intensify (Koch 2004) and initiate spontaneous movements of vitality (Stern 2010). These internal movements form into primitive emotions. Emotions then move into images, meaning, and thoughts. When images and thoughts are integrated with bodily-based neural and emotional states, new knowledge has been organized.

There are multiple ways to develop somatic awareness, including orienting to the present environment; journaling; mindfulness meditations on the body that map bodily states in the somatosensory cortex, such as eye and voice work, including toning and chanting practices to stimulate vibration and pulsation; massage; and active bodywork including the Rosen Method, Pilates, Tai Chi, yoga, and Feldenkrais—a particularly informative bodywork practice that replaces maladaptive gestures and body movements with graceful sustainable patterns. Other ways to develop somatic awareness include dance and authentic movement as developed by Marion Woodman, attending to emotions of vitality, joy, and connection, and engaging in projects such as playing music and art making, which stimulate perceptual clarity.

Daily practices for somatic practitioners include embodied meditation on lived experience and journaling the felt sense of dreams. Rather than narrating an explicit account of dreams, drawing dream energy and images with oil crayons helps to identify and shift implicit memories. The critical element of these practices is the development of somatic awareness with an interest and curiosity about moment-to-moment recognition of reactions and subtle changes in the body. With mindful somatic awareness, we are able to recognize and track different sensory states, their movement and emotions, and attend to the images that come in the moment, preparing to create shifts through rhythmical oscillation of attention. Exercise 6.2: Honing Nonverbal Somatic Awareness on page 203 of the appendix is a partnered exercise that can help to develop a mindful practice of somatic awareness. In the following section, we'll explore how to bring somatic awareness to areas of tension in the body.

Using Somatic Awareness to Sense Conflict

When a conflict does not ease with left hemispheric analysis and problem-solving strategies, we can enter into right brain somatic awareness to process the experience. To do this, first quiet the body and mind, take a few minutes to settle, watch, and listen to the activity within. Simply notice what is happening in the moment, without criticizing, changing, or influencing the bodily based experience in the moment. Somatic awareness can detect the invisible dynamics of internal processing and bring them into consciousness. Once into consciousness, we can intentionally bring somatic awareness to each sensation, movement, emotion, and image, grounding and energizing the felt sense. It's best to focus initially on vitality, aliveness, and pleasurable sensations; attention to these dynamics energizes and stabilizes the system. Then slowly allow one specific aspect of the conflict, a sensation, emotion, or image, to emerge, one that is within the optimal arousal zone. While maintaining curiosity, simply notice the phenomena. While exploring a sensation, emotion, or image, you may sense a holding, tension, or emptiness, or even nausea. The tension may be felt in voluntary striated muscles, such as the arms, legs, or hands, or the smooth involuntary muscles of the viscera, the organs.

If there is tension, nausea, or a sense of emptiness felt in the viscera, it is likely to be an emotionally charged dissociated implicit memory. A person may not be able to fully incorporate a sudden release of that emotional energy—leading to a retraumatization. The release of intense emotional energy is best accomplished within the optimal arousal zone in the context of a caring relationship.

For the purposes of this example, let's say there is a holding sensation in my right leg. I bring an inner gaze to the leg and observe the edges of the "qualia," the sensory data as it comes into awareness. When observed from an embodied perspective, sensory-based data awakens and begins to move (Koch 2004). This movement of sensation may be swift or slow, pleasurable or unpleasant, or even extremely uncomfortable. The sensory data may move down through the feet, with an urge to walk, run, or flee. In this case, somatic awareness activated a tension in the leg that released a sensory flow of energy instructing the body to physically move. Somatic awareness has revealed discomfort in the current environment and the bodily-based urge to run or withdraw. With this somatic cue, I can choose to stay and make micromovements with my leg that approximate running, or I can actually leave and follow my thwarted instinctive sense. In this simplistic example, somatic awareness has revealed an unconscious neuroception, a message from my body that is telling me to physically withdraw. However, the problem is the tension in my leg may not be indicative of present moment experience; it could be the residue of a contraction at an earlier time of a traumatic experience. How can we tell the difference between somatic awareness of the present moment experience and that of an unprocessed past?

When we reflect-in-action, we can consciously and intuitively assess a sensation while holding curiosity and wonder and respond in ways that help us adapt to present moment experience. Reflection-in-action "reshapes what we are working on while we are working on it" (Schön 1983). This curiosity about our spontaneous reactions can lead us into a somatic inquiry, a phenomenological method of discerning truth and meaning of lived experience. If the somatic inquiry reveals our reactions to be the unconscious recall of an implicit memory, we can then process the implicit memory with another or through other active bodywork. Through somatic awareness in the context of an intersubjective relationship, the binding of sympathetic arousal of past fear with the dorsal vagal state of immobility can be differentiated in the growing safety and trust in a relationship.

Even in a state of social engagement, it's important to be cautious when engaging in somatic awareness with trauma survivors. People suffering from complex trauma often experience a variety of bodily-based distress, dysregulation, and discomfort. For example, they may hold intense contractions and pain in the striated muscles as well as the smooth muscles of the viscera (Tucker 2007) with a sense of deadness and emptiness sometimes described as an "inner black hole," or they may feel uncomfortably chaotic sensations throughout the body. As trauma survivors develop bodily awareness, hyperarousal from implicit memories of past traumatic experience can flood into the present moment—retraumatizing them. People who have experienced complex trauma should *not* be asked to sense into the core feelings in their body until intense emotions can be regulated and tolerated. They need attuned relational support to slowly incorporate somatic awareness and to regulate and calm intense arousal of implicit memories. As extreme neural states become regulated, the perception of

bodily-based sensations can be incorporated into an embodied consciousness that permits somatic awareness within the optimal level of arousal. In
the following example, we'll examine how to introduce somatic awareness
into the therapeutic relationship.

Bringing Somatic Awareness into the Therapeutic Relationship—Case 6.1: Patricia

I first met my client Patricia shortly after her divorce. She described her life
as "without color" and "empty," indicators of chronic hypoarousal and a
deficit of vitality. She also reported a chronic tightness in her chest, a binding when she tried to breathe, and continual respiratory illnesses. As we
began to develop an intersubjective relationship, I recognized high emotional charge in her viscera from feelings that had not yet been processed.

One day as Patricia recounted her story in a numb, emotionless way,
I felt tension build in my chest. Talking about the divorce also triggered
Patricia's unconscious breathlessness and cough, indicating to me it was a
good time to bring somatic awareness into our relationship. I said, "Patricia,
I notice that your mind and your body each have a version of what happened to you. I am wondering if we could take some time to listen to your
body." Unaware that there was a nonverbal, bodily-based narrative of her
losses, she was curious to explore it with me. I invited her to bring somatic
awareness to the striated muscles of her shoulders, hands, and arms in the
moment, and then allow them to drop down into gravity and rest.

As Patricia felt the bracing and subtle release in her shoulders, hands,
and arms, her face opened to me with interest and intrigue. She reported
that she felt some vibration and pulsation in her palms, a return of vitality. In fact, her hands were getting hot. I invited Patricia to join me in
slowly opening and closing her hands while we noticed the edges of the
constriction in her chest. As her hands found a rhythm of contraction and
expansion, I observed a shift in her breathing; she was taking in more air
and the rest of her body began to release the constricted bracing that had
been in her posture, eyes, and voice. I observed a general softening in her
face and body. The neural coordination of her breath and heart rate had
reset spontaneously in our relationship. Following her deepened breath,
Patricia opened her eyes and indicated nonverbally she had shifted into
a more connected state, but was on the edge of her optimal arousal zone
as she sensed the pervasiveness of bracing in her usual body states. This
intervention of somatic awareness was enough for that moment; more
would have aroused too much fear to be embodied in the moment. When
encountering people with chronic hypoarousal, it is helpful to move slowly
and access safety and "feeling felt" through somatic awareness to regulate
states of bracing and collapse.

In the encounter with Patricia, somatic awareness of the playful ability to
open and close her hands were differentiated from feelings of immobility

and constriction in her chest creating a polarity. The differentiation was in the neural states, while the linking occurred through our relationship. As I accompanied Patricia in the opening and closing of her hands, I noticed my chest begin to pulse with the rhythm of heart rate variability and ease with the emerging interconnection of the breath and heart. This introduction of somatic awareness helped Patricia begin to release chronic holding of striated muscles, but even more intriguing was the experience of somatic awareness where she could connect her mind with her body.

Early in our work together, Patricia was able to enjoy somatic awareness as she became aware of her own joyful physical and emotional states in the moment. At the same time, she was feeling the emotional backlog of anguish that had been held in chronic hypoarousal and depression. Patricia required relational support to endure the tension of the polarities and the anguishing sensations of these implicit traumatic memories in her viscera, energy that had been emotionally constricted since early childhood and had appeared in frequent asthma attacks. If we had opened the floodgates to her terror, grief, and anguish in her chest in one cathartic moment, Patricia would have been deeply retraumatized. Instead, we took the spiral path of healing and growth, working slowly on the periphery, continually touching into her zone of optimal arousal, to gain confidence in somatic awareness and our relationship and to reveal and embody the complex, unresolved, dissociated emotions from the past. In the following section, we'll explore the use of somatic awareness to process traumatic memories.

Somatic Awareness and a Case of Complex Trauma—
Case 6.2: Judy and Peter

Judy and Peter, a couple in relationship therapy with me, had both experienced complex trauma in their youth. Over two years of working together, Judy had found that as she became more regulated, her relationship with Peter became more conflicted. When Judy expressed her anguish and suffering, Peter, despite his best intention to be present, would grow silent, drop into hypoarousal, and emotionally withdraw from the interaction.

When Peter spoke about his withdrawal, I listened with somatic awareness to my own internal state as well as Peter's subjective state. Somatic awareness helped me to feel the helplessness of his present state. As I continued to listen, bringing a somatic awareness and presence to Peter, I allowed my face and body to spontaneously respond to him. I realized Peter was beginning to "feel felt" when he connected his gaze with mine and allowed me to hold him in my soft gaze.

After my nonverbal contingent responses, Peter became silent again. Through somatic awareness, I sensed a drop in Peter's neural state and his emotions. I asked Peter what was happening for him and he said he was feeling hurt and rejected. His body posture and tone of voice was much younger than his present chronological age, and I recognized a drop into dissociated affect. Peter described how as a child he would go to his room and sit silently for hours when he felt rejected.

With somatic awareness, I had felt a softness in our mutual gaze, and then a sense of dropping into a feeling of collapse and helplessness with a heaviness in my torso. A somatic inquiry revealed more about Peter's sense of rejection and led to a state of high arousal. Speaking very quickly, Peter recalled vivid traumatic childhood memories that included beatings from older gangs of children and emotional neglect from both parents. As he shared his story, I could feel my cheeks burning and a tightness return to my chest. In Peter's face and posture, and within my own body, I sensed a combination of anger, rage, and helplessness. Peter's jaw was thrust out, his eyes were tight and small, and the pitch of his voice had continued to increase with fear, all cues that Peter was escalating beyond his level of optimal arousal.

I asked Peter if we could to take a few moments to let the intensity settle. I wanted to return to an optimal level of arousal to process his intense emotions. As Peter quieted, his skin tone became pale and blotchy, indicating the shock embedded in his recall of traumatic memories. Peter was cycling between high arousal and low arousal, periodically entering into a state of hypoarousal. It was important to stay close and attune to the present hypoaroused state with a slow, quiet yet intimate embodied presence.

When I asked Peter what he was noticing in this moment, he said he felt a "funny" sensation of nausea, often an indicator of change in the state of hypoarousal. As we acknowledged his nausea, I inquired about other current experiences as a way to orient to the present moment. Peter responded that "he had a bitter taste in his mouth," another cue that his immobilization with fear was starting to differentiate. As I felt, tasted, and acknowledged the discomfort of these sensations, this data formed an image for Peter: he described feeling a "dark ball in his gut," which was now available for transformation.

Responding nonverbally, Judy and I brought embodied awareness and compassion to his visceral suffering. Through somatic awareness, I sensed inner tears well up in me and an energy rising up from my chest that went to my eyes. I held this intensely caring energy in a soft gaze with Peter and said slowly and clearly, "Peter, I am so sorry this happened to you. I am sorry you had to endure years of pain and sadness alone." Peter held the mutual gaze. After a while, he simply said, "Thank you." My heart opened in gratitude. After a few moments of quiet connection, I asked Peter what he was noticing about the ball in his gut. He said it had become softer around the edges and when I asked him if the ball had any movement, he made a small circular gesture in front of his body. This gesture indicated an internal synthesis that was moving within his body, an innate healing energy. I invited Peter to slow the gesture to the rhythm that felt best to him and I joined him in a slow, mindful spiral movement. After a while, Peter's hand dropped and we sat in a companionable silence of optimal arousal for a while. The movement had transformed the image into something new, and I wanted to allow time for it to gestate into its own unique way of being.

I invited Peter to orient again to my office and to his partner sitting nearby. Peter had continued his somatic awareness despite the discomfort until it shifted, holding an awareness of his internal sensory and imaginal experience while reorienting to the present moment. I was aware of two significant aspects of Peter's change in the moment. First, Peter's sensory motor and primitive emotions had been processed internally and formed into an image of a ball. This indicated an initial reconnection of some neural networks that had been severed in his traumatic experience. Second, Peter was able to hold a somatic awareness through deeply uncomfortable moments with a dual awareness of the images and sensations. A third awareness was added when I asked Peter to orient to the present moment environment. The perceptual ability to hold a "multilens perspective" (Stanley 1994) is important in integrating the felt sense of traumatic memories into the body and current relational life. I did not expect Peter's life to radically change with these achievements, but he had begun to embody a portion of his dissociated lived experience.

What happened with Peter? Neurologically, in a moment of trauma, the dorsal vagal brain circuit is rapidly firing in oscillation with the sympathetic system, resulting in frozen terror and horror (Schore, personal communication). We feel frozen in the moment, unable to act, unable to move and the only option is to collapse into dissociation and invisibility. These perceptions of the past are unconsciously and implicitly remembered in the present moment and fuel us into thinking in polarities: either I am helpless in my shame or the other person is the problem.

As we reflected on our shared experience, Peter realized this pattern was familiar. His pattern of hypoarousal was leaving him confused about what was true in the past and what was actually happening in the present, a conflict between two perceptual systems. With two perceptual systems competing for acceptance, it is important to hold the tension of that polarity, ultimately allowing for a multilevel perspective, one of fluid change and wisdom. For this to happen, the shame that is locked into the gut like a "dark ball" needs to come into somatic awareness. Only then can shame be transformed into the humility one needs for authentic love and intimacy.

Embodied Practitioners and Somatic Awareness

The primary value of somatic practices for me lies in the ability to communicate connection, caring, and compassion for people who have been isolated in their suffering from trauma. Somatic awareness is a perception that guides us through the darkness and chaos of traumatic memories. It helps us develop a meta-perspective of our habits of mind that affect the body and brain, allowing us to become embodied witnesses to our own lived experience. The key to the effectiveness of somatic awareness lies in the wholeness and well-being of embodied practitioners. While people who have experienced trauma may be able to adopt a somatic perspective as they regulate arousal, it is primarily the responsibility of the practitioner to foster somatic awareness within the relationship.

It's important to keep in mind that when working with complex trauma survivors who have deep states of immobility with fear, indicators of major therapeutic success may be few and far between, leaving helping professionals frustrated, overwhelmed, and burned out. Attention to small neural shifts allows us to participate in the precise changes needed for healing. As Morris Berman (1989) points out, we unconsciously learn through our dominant Western culture to search for secondary satisfactions of success, rather than the primary satisfaction of somatic sensual awareness of the world around us and the direct experience of loving in troubled moments.

Somatic awareness of the bodily-based experience of loving, a primary satisfaction, is within our control. In our quest for success in helping others heal from trauma, it's easy to bypass the felt sense of truly loving our clients. The critical change element of all healing, loving another is not always a pleasant or easy experience. As Ruddick (1995) points out in her research on maternal love, there can be a wide variety of emotions—fury, rage, boredom, and joy—when loving another. The key to loving is to communicate that you are somatically aware of the pain and anguish of the other. Somatic awareness of another's felt sense results in a person *feeling felt*, a profound communication of love. When a person feels felt, the shared, embodied intersubjective relationship then becomes the crucible for the further development and growth of consciousness.

References

Bargh, J. A., and E. Morsella. 2008. "The Unconscious Mind." *Perspective on Psychological Science,* 3(1), 73–79.

Beebe, B., and F. M. Lachmann. 2014. *The Origins of Attachment: Infant Research and Adult Treatment.* New York: Routledge.

Berman, M. 1989. *Coming to Our Senses.* New York: Simon and Schuster.

Bromberg, P. M. 2011. *The Shadow of the Tsunami: and the Growth of the Relational Mind.* New York: Routledge.

Jacob, M. M. 2013. *Yakama Rising: Indigenous, Cultural Revitalization, Activism, and Healing.* Tucson: University of Arizona Press.

Koch, C. 2004. *The Quest for Consciousness: A Neurobiological Approach.* Englewood: Roberts & Company.

Krishnamurti, J. 1969. *Freedom from the Known.* Edited by M. Lutyens. New York: HarperCollins.

Merleau-Ponty, M. 1962. *Phenomenology of Perception.* Translated by D. Landes. New York: Routledge.

Porges S. W. 2011. *The Polyvagal Theory: Neurophysiological Foundations of Emotions, Attachment, Communication, and Self-Regulation.* New York: Norton.

Ruddick, S. 1995. *Maternal Thinking: Toward a Politics of Peace*. Boston: Beacon Press.

Schön, D. A. 1983. *The Reflective Practitioner: How Professionals Think in Action*. New York: Basic Books.

Schore, A. N. 2012. *The Science of the Art of Psychotherapy*. New York: Norton.

Siegel, D. J. 1999. *The Developing Mind: Toward a Neurobiology of Interpersonal Experience*. New York: Guilford.

Stanley, S. 1994. "The Process and Development of Empathy in Educators: A Phenomenological Inquiry." PhD. diss., University of Victoria.

Stern, D. N. 2010. *Forms of Vitality: Exploring Dynamic Experience in Psychology, the Arts, Psychotherapy, and Development*. New York: Oxford University Press.

Tucker, D. M. 2007. *Mind from Body: Experience from Neural Structure*. New York: Oxford University Press.

Van der Kolk, B. A., A. C. McFarlane, and L. Weisaeth, eds. 1996. *Traumatic Stress: The Effects of Overwhelming Experience on Mind, Body, and Society*. New York: Guilford.

Varela, F. J., E. Thompson, and E. Rosch. 1991. *The Embodied Mind: Cognitive Science and Human Experience*. Cambridge: MIT Press.

7 Somatic Empathy
Encounters of "Feeling Felt"

"I've learned that people will forget what you said, people will forget what you did, but people will never forget how you made them feel."

(Maya Angelou)

What Is Somatic Empathy?

Each of us holds an inner subjective reality, one that is different from any other person and is continually in the process of change as time goes on. A person's inner subjective reality is his or her best attempt to adapt to the environment. When people suffer neglect, abuse, or injury, their subjective perspectives become distorted in order to ensure survival. These distortions live on and become the "demons" or hidden emotions that limit the capacity for growth. As helping professionals, we must become intimately acquainted with another's inner subjective reality in order to access dysregulated neural states and hidden emotions to facilitate the healing process. We come to know the dynamic inner world of another through empathy—a process that provides a person suffering from relational trauma with the essential elements for vitality and social engagement.

Max Scheler coined the term *fellow-feeling* to describe authentic empathy. "In authentic fellow-feeling, there is an 'intentional reference' to the feelings of the other person's experience" (1954, 3). When a person holds the intention to care about another and feels moved to prevent and alleviate pain, a mutual connection begins to grow between the two. Empathy has tremendous power for healing the effects of trauma—isolation, alienation, and shame. Carl Rogers, a psychotherapist who wove phenomenological methods into helping professions, articulates this well: "To my mind, empathy is in itself a healing agent. It is one of the most potent aspects of therapy, because it releases, it confirms, it brings even the most frightened clients into the human race. If a person is understood, he or she belongs" (1986, 129).

However, empathy, has often involved a more cognitive left-hemispheric perspective—an attempt to understand another without feeling with another.

Somatic empathy, on the other hand, requires a right-brain-to-right-brain relationship (Schore 2010)—it is about *feeling felt* rather than simply being seen, heard, or understood. Well supported by clinical research (Beebe and Lachmann 2014; The Boston Change Process Study Group 2010; Schore and Schore 2014), somatic empathy involves a sincere intention to attune, resonate, and imagine the inner felt sense of another in the other's own terms. Somatic empathy is a complex mental, emotional, physical, and spiritual art. Yet with practices of embodiment, somatic awareness, artful inquiry, imagination, and reflection—the core elements of somatic empathy—we can bridge the chasms that separate human beings to construct an alive, resonant connection.

To understand somatic empathy, it is helpful to first explore similar concepts in different cultures. In Confucianism, the concept of *shu* is similar to a somatic definition of empathy (Kalton, personal communication). A professor at the University of Washington, Michael Kalton describes *shu* as the thread that runs through the "Way"—the path leading people to a good and stable society, a communal form of empathy. To live in the Way of *shu*, "one attempts to be centered in the heart and mind of human persons" (Kalton, personal communication). *Shu* describes a form of empathy where one holds the inner world of all others within one's own subjective reality. Holding another's mind and heart within our own means we are never alone; we are part of a vast interconnection and our separateness is simply an illusion.

Many traditional societies and Indigenous people nourish a similar communal form of empathic knowing. The Nuu-chah-nulth writer, Richard Atleo, describes a multigenerational and spiritual aspect of empathy in his culture. "In the Nuu-chah-nulth world view, each family has a direct connection to the Creator through the gifts of the grandchildren" (2004, 29). The family *hahuupa* (teachings) seek to improve all relationships with demonstrations of welcoming, kindness, joy, and love while the primary purpose in life is to strengthen the relationship between all elements of creation. These ancient teachings recognize how both love and pain are natural in relationships, and that feeling pain with another makes loving each other even more precious. The Nuu-chah-nulth culture differs from English language-based cultures, where empathy has been a relatively recent concept, and one that has been often misunderstood as a reflective mental achievement that can occur without full-body participation and awareness of feeling with another.

Somatic empathy is a way of knowing significant aspects of our inner world through direct observation and feeling, without losing continuity of the self—a concept that allows us to have a sense of who we are over time and in changing situations. Critical to somatic empathy is the intention to actively feel the suffering of another while bringing compassion to the felt sense of both (Stanley 1994). Somatic empathy is not static, a knowledge that is ever complete. Rather it continues in a fluid, interpersonal flow of connection and knowing as lived experience changes in the moment. Somatic empathy has the power to strengthen an intersubjective connection with another because it is a receptive and invitational—as contrasted to a projective—form of empathy. What's the difference?

Receptive Versus Projective Empathy

In a secure attachment, receptive empathy occurs when a parent or caregiver is able to perceive the needs, desires, and emotions of children—and feel with them—rather than direct them into ways of thinking and behaving that are incongruent with children's emotions and current understanding of themselves. More forceful forms of empathy, where professionals match and "project" their experience onto another can influence unconscious imbalances in the power dynamics of a relationship and interrupt the intersubjective field. With projective forms of empathy, the practitioner may appear to know more about the client than the client knows about him or herself, recalling disturbing traumatic moments of power imbalances and separation from others. Receptive empathy, on the other hand, allows practitioners to remain curious, interested, and open to the unique subjectivity of the other and be changed and influenced by the other— a humble, vulnerable, and risky way to relate to another, but one that deeply restores the lost empowerment of the person suffering from trauma and opens the intersubjective field to more safety and trust.

When practitioners offer a receptive form of empathy, they are open to surprising revelations about the lived experience of another, instead of theorizing, analyzing, explaining, and interpreting. The practitioner is ready to accept, appreciate, legitimize, inquire, cherish, and explore the unique configuration of another's inner world—and to be surprised as it is slowly revealed in relationship. Receptive empathy breaks through defensive fixed-action patterns of the body and mind to radically change both people in the relationship. The receptive listener functions as an embodied, observant, yet participating witness to welcome the aspects of the other that has been buried in dissociative memories back into relationship. The hospitable nature of receptive empathy allows the authentic self to be awakened, welcomed, acknowledged, and nurtured in relationship, gradually coming into cohesion and continuity.

In clinical practice, I have found that an invitational way of knowing allows people the freedom of constructing their own way of being authentic in relationship. For people who have been traumatized by implicit and explicit demands to submit to the authority of parents, church, school, government, and other oppressive structures, projective forms of empathy may trigger endless enactments that continue in therapy and throughout life. Feeling controlled and interpreted by another in the other's terms can be alienating and shaming. Alternatively, people who have experienced trauma can abdicate their own way of knowing the self and become dependent on and compliant with those in power. Dependency and compliance often occur in fiduciary relationships, those where practitioners, such as religious leaders, therapists, lawyers, and other health-care professionals, hold the power and trust of the other, yet impose their interpretations and projections on the lived experience of the other.

The distinction between projective empathy and receptive empathy is particularly important to people who have experienced neglect, oppression, and traumatic intrusions into the boundaries of the self. Children who have experienced abuse and other aversive experiences may yearn for people to tell them about themselves and fix them, yet resist projective forms of empathy as a survival defense, a dynamic that fuels therapeutic enactments. People who have experienced relational-developmental trauma can sense the empathic receptivity of another and feel the freedom from judgment and interpretation. This freedom allows people to disclose hidden wounded areas without coercion. By offering an invitational, embodied presence in the moment, practitioners *receive* the internal subjective experience of another into their bodies and minds. They sense and discern the intense feelings of the other in the intersubjective field and can self-regulate the shared hyper- and hypoarousal. Observing the influence of their trauma on another, combined with the effects of self-regulation, offers clients new images and possibilities for healing. Receptive somatic empathy can restore hope and resilience to regulate intense affect. This receptive way of knowing can bypass resistance and offer a bodily-based welcome to the other that can touch the inner core of her subjective self, the heart and soul.

Case 7.1: Denise

Perhaps the most powerful aspect of receptive somatic empathy is that it functions as an antidote to immobility with fear—the neural state of shame, dissociation, and depression. Those who are immobilized with fear experience affective glimpses of past terror and horror that they believe are occurring in the present moment. Maintaining somatic empathy with someone who is stuck in immobility can be challenging and can also reveal our own dissociated immobility, a reality I discovered while working with Denise, a psychotherapy client with a history of sexual abuse.

When I first started seeing Denise, she was disassociated and exhausted most of the time. Despite her reported feelings of an "empty numbness," I did not pathologize her or interpret what was happening. Rather, I approached her with a sense of genuine interest and curiosity about her lived experience. But one day Denise claimed I saw her as a whining, immature, and needy client. Her complaint hit home. It was true that I felt overwhelmed by the intensity of her anguish and had withdrawn from being fully engaged with her. In fact, I recalled the day and moment I began to feel frustrated that I was unable to help her enough, and I remember thinking that I truly didn't know what else I could do for her. As I sat with my shame in withdrawing my emotional presence, I realized that *shame* was Denise's strongest emotion. I experienced a direct encounter with shame—its heaviness, ache, and nausea—and realized this was Denise's life. In that moment, I felt and received her lived experience, compassion transformed my shame, and I renewed and deepened my commitment to maintain and deepen somatic empathy with Denise.

Somatic empathy combines an awareness of physical sensations—like the heaviness of Denise's shame—in the musculoskeletal and visceral systems of the body with intuitive processing of emotions and symbolic ways of knowing (Kilpatrick 2000). Symbolic ways of knowing come through embodied attention to dreams with images and archetypes and through reflective processes where wisdom is gleaned from direct contact with the body's way of knowing. For example, you can have a direct perception of a river, yet you can also sense a river as a metaphor or symbol of a fluid, dynamic life. You can taste the water, feel the cool flow on your skin, and at the same time hold the truth of life as a nourishing, cleansing flow of time.

By linking the reorganized sensate with the intuitive, somatic empathy moves beyond many body-centered therapies to incorporate visceral and symbolic ways of knowing through higher cortical structures (Kilpatrick 2000). In other words, the "gut" knowing of the belly and heart can be synchronized with the knowing achieved through poetry, images, and spiritual experience. This somatic link of the lower cortical structures of the brain stem with the higher cortical structures of symbol and archetype offers unexplored options for right-hemispheric processing of traumatic experience.

In addition, somatic empathy creates a potent and powerful intersubjective field between two bodies, minds, hearts, and souls. The intersubjective field is a shared, complex consciousness that develops in relationships between people that offers each person wordless access to the inner world of the other and provides a place where embodied intuition can guide healing. Kilpatrick describes embodied intuition as a "fast-acting mode of communication with an accelerated processing speed that is the primary function of soul connection" (2000, 26–27). A way of knowing that comes from somatic empathy, embodied intuition is not merely an idea, it is held deeply within the viscera as gut knowledge. Terry Marks-Tarlow (2012) maintains that it is through clinical embodied intuition that helping professionals can pick up on and resonate with dissociated emotions in the intersubjective field, which I found to be true in my relationship with Denise.

At first, she and I struggled to establish a mutual intersubjective field. She nonverbally distanced herself from emotional connection a number of times while my subtle "power-over" therapist strategies unconsciously emerged when the depth of her shame, depression, and dissociation frightened me. However, eventually I began to pay closer attention to her unspoken needs, those that appeared in her posture, tone of voice, eye gaze, and gestures. I resisted the temptation to "fix" her problems or mobilize her through stimulating her anger and righteousness regarding her abuse. Instead, we explored and imagined her own perception of her life, together. Over the course of two years, I learned to drop down into a more humble, shared, mutual experience where I was willing to feel Denise's helplessness, rage, and terror without moving quickly to shift her feelings.

It was within this darker, heavier realm of shared sorrow that we explored her intense arousal states and gradually built the relational container, optimal arousal zone, and vitality necessary for processing brutal and numbing memories. Before long we were able to coregulate the fear, anger, and shame in our relationship and process the traumatic memories that generated these emotions. I was fully engaged in her bodily-based emotions, our conversations were dialogical, phenomenological, and reciprocal, and our interactions were contingent on each other's perspective. Our relationship became a two-person embodied psychological experience.

The most significant accomplishment with Denise was the development of somatic empathy in our relationship. The enactment—the unconscious distancing I did to protect myself from feeling the depth of her anguish and her ability to bring that to my attention—may have seemed like a setback at first, but it strengthened our relationship by allowing me to feel what she was feeling. The ability to authentically "feel with another" in a mutual, intersubjective relationship is a foundational goal in becoming an effective helper. The difficulty with somatic empathy lies in feeling the anguish, helplessness, and disconnection with another rather than trying to fix that person's distressing state or withdrawing emotional presence. It is particularly challenging to engage in somatic empathy with people experiencing hypoarousal and symptoms of depression and dissociation, in part because these interactions often unearth dissociative gaps in our own inner world.

The Guises of Somatic Empathy

Scheler (1954) reminds us that empathy has a variety of covert guises that infect our perceptions and distort an authentic knowledge of another. These guises include enactments, emotional contagion, emotional infection, and emotional identification. People suffering from trauma have a fundamental need to feel safe, and when someone feels felt by another, they unconsciously begin to feel safe. However, disruptions in the emotional safety of a helping relationship can lead to enactments (Bromberg 2011). Max Scheler (1954) describes *enactments* as the emotional contagion that occurs in relationship when people unconsciously mistake others for themselves and themselves for others. Enactments support access to dissociated affect in the intersubjective field for both the helping professional and the client

(Bromberg 2011; Schore 2012). Ginot (2009) points out that enactments are often unconsciously formed in empathic encounters. In my early experiences with Denise, I had unconsciously empathized with her dissociated emotions and did not want to truly feel them with her, which led to an enactment. I had not yet acknowledged and processed a similar implicit traumatic memory and I was emotionally contagious and thus responsible for our enactment. Denise's accusation that I saw her as needy opened me to the possibility of finally attending to my own dissociated emotions of shame in consultation with a mentor.

Empathy can also be confused with *emotional infection*, a projection of a feeling that does not involve participation or knowledge of the emotions and feelings of the other. With emotional infection, contagion is involuntary and increases the degree of projection (Scheler 1954). For example, a couple that meets and immediately falls in love and then finds many areas of disagreement may be experiencing emotional infection. They did not take the time and attention to really get to know each other in the other's own terms and may find themselves hurt when the other person fails to live up to their expectations or projections. Emotional infection is likely to become contagious between the two; bickering may increase unless they can find a way to develop authentic empathy for themselves and the other.

Emotional identification occurs when the feelings of another are unconsciously and involuntarily identified as one's own (Scheler 1954). Emotional identification can come about when one is overwhelmed by another and "absorbs" another's emotions. For example, in an inequitable relationship, the emotions of the one who dominates can permeate the fragile layers of the one who is less powerful so that there is little differentiation in the emotional reaction of the two people. As you will see in the example below, helpers often get caught in the dynamics of emotional contagion, infection, identification, and enactment instead of engaging in somatic empathy.

Case 7.2: Bret and Jim

Bret was a therapist who found himself stymied by emotional identification. During our consultations, he described a series of interactions with Jim, his client of five years. Although Jim had been diagnosed with serious personality disorders, Bret saw steady growth and development in him. However, Bret became disturbed when Jim stopped taking his medications and his psychiatrist dismissed him for noncompliance. In his early life, Jim's mother had abandoned her family for a religious cult, one that Jim, his father, and brothers entered into only to comply with the demands of his mother. Bret was concerned because Jim had announced that he was moving to the small community where Bret was quite active and highly connected. Bret felt his own rage to the point of vertigo, yet another part of him felt numb, analytical, and compliant about Jim's announcement.

When Bret perceived that Jim was trying to communicate his own rage and powerlessness about his mother's demand to join a church, he could begin to recognize the emotional contagion and identification that was active in his relationship with Jim. Jim had been effective in communicating the intense immobilization with fear that he had felt in his family, and now that Bret was conscious of his contagion and identification, Jim's decision to move to his small community could be recognized as an unconscious form of communication, one that could be brought into the intersubjective field for processing.

What had been missing from Bret's relationship with Jim was a sense of fellow-feeling, a shared sense of "feeling felt," a deeply personal entering into another's situation that creates an authentic transcendence of one's self. Fellow-feeling creates a "change of heart," a fundamental "change in the innermost nature of reality itself" (Scheler 1954, 59). With the intention of fellow-feeling, one is able to concentrate on cherished, intrinsic qualities in another as well as acknowledge suffering and pain. This form of empathy creates an expansion in our lives that enables us to transcend personal limitations and egocentrism. Fellow-feeling is a primary process of somatic empathy, one that fosters embodiment of the intersubjective field and the sense of shared truth and connection. Engaged in this empathic connection with Jim, Bret was able to stay curious and interested in Jim's decision to move into his small community. He also let Jim know that he now could feel the emotions Jim was trying to communicate, the rage and powerlessness that led to compliance. This made for a series of very rich and transformative sessions: Jim was deeply touched by Bret's honesty and humility to feel with him. No longer needing to communicate these feelings by moving into Bret's community, Jim withdrew his decision and found another neighborhood.

When enactments such as the one between Bret and Jim occur, practices of somatic empathy can clarify the breaches in relationship and contribute to the restoration of connection. The silent, receptive energy of somatic empathy allows the active wisdom of the body to regulate and access hidden dissociated traumatic memories. Through somatic empathy, a practiced clinician is able to perceive bodily cues regarding the presence of "not me" aspects of the self (Bromberg 2011), energies in the intersubjective field that indicate one's own inner trauma has been triggered and is contagious. The high emotional charge accompanying the sense of "not me" clues us into the emotional contagion in the relationship—such as Bret's rage. With attention to these cues, practitioners can pause, take time to ground, become embodied, consult, and humbly open to the neural states and emotions that are present in the intersubjective field. As Bret felt the sensations and emotions Jim was trying to communicate, he was able to reflect on their encounters and bring compassion and understanding to his relationship with Jim. This compassion emerged from an unconscious empathic connection where Bret felt a sense of invasion similar to

Jim's. Somatic awareness of the sensations beneath emotions allows us to read the cues within our own bodies that are unconsciously resonating in the bodies of the other. These cues can lead to creative repairs rather than the reinforcement of defensive postures. By acknowledging the barely perceptible arousal states and intense emotions present in a relationship, breaches caused by survival defenses can be repaired. When helping professionals acknowledge how they are experiencing an encounter rather than attempting to subtly blame the other or quickly regulate the other's feelings, repairs can begin and people are able to come into deeper affective connection with each other. In a moment of an authentic, transparent, and respectful repair, the expectations for relationship of both can open with hope and possibility.

The Art of Attunement: Engaging in Somatic Empathy with Oneself

Before practitioners can engage in somatic empathy with another, they must first be able to attune their own bodies, minds, and hearts, bringing them into coherence. Beebe & Lachmann (2014) describe research related to how a person's emotional facial expression is associated with a particular state of neural arousal and that an onlooker unconsciously matches the expression of the other and produces a similar physiological state within their own bodies. It is clear that the current state of neuroarousal and unconscious emotional facial expression of the helper profoundly influences people in trauma. Engaging in somatic empathy with ourselves can create a tangible sensation of being grounded with calmness and rising up with vitality, a state that is shared with the other.

The ability to attune to one's own internal state and self-regulate is a prerequisite for creating an emotionally healthy intersubjective field. For helping professionals, an internal somatic practice is necessary in order to prevent emotional infection, contagion, and identification, and assume responsibility for them when they occur. An example of a somatic practice includes somatic awareness of self-regulation before and during encounters with others; orienting to the environment, sensing the gravity of the ground through feet and legs, allowing the mind to rest in the heart and then, energetically, reaching out with attuned and resonant caring to invite the other into the shared space. The practice of somatic empathy for the self holds awareness of internal visceral states in each moment. As we enter into relational somatic encounters, the intersubjective field shifts from a dual awareness of self and other to a unified awareness, without merging or giving up a sense of subjective individuality.

This midspace of shared awareness then becomes a home that invites dissociated memories to slowly open, to be felt by both, and to be incorporated into lived experience. Dissociated memories from trauma are protected, like a cocoon, with survival self-care strategies that honor the soul within (Kalsched 2013). When the conditions are right, there is a natural unfolding of the survival self-care system, and what has been hidden emerges. Donnel Stern (2010) identifies perceptions as the opening of dissociated memories: "Phenomena may either be perceived or left unperceived, their potential untapped. When they are left undeveloped, we are making the 'choice' to leave them—in a word—unformulated. But if they are formulated, perceptions of oneself or the other may take either a verbally symbolized form that allows reflective consciousness, or a nonverbal form that then becomes part of the intuitively organized relating to come" (2010, 10). The task of the practitioner is to create the conditions for the perceptions to formulate, the natural process of connection and healing.

The first goal of this process is to create safety, a sense of "shelter from the storm." Knowing that the body senses safety well before the mind recognizes feelings of security, practitioners can begin with their own bodily-based awareness. Consciously intending to notice sensations and feelings throughout our own bodies and regulating for safety allows us to discern the sense of safety in the body of the other (Stanley 1994). This means to sense muscular tension and ease; discern movements of energy in the arms, legs, and viscera; feel our hearts beating, expanding, contracting, and pulsating; feel our guts gripping and releasing; and our cells vibrating with health and vitality. See Exercise 7.1: Practicing Bodily-Based Awareness, Attunement, Resonance, and Responsivity on page 204 of the appendix. Repeating this practice a number of times can deepen the somatic awareness necessary to enter into hidden emotional aspects of ourselves and another with an attitude of curiosity, wonder, and appreciation.

The Art of Attunement: Engaging in Somatic Empathy with Another

Somatic empathy begins by perceiving the subtle communications of the face, voice, and body and the feelings that motivate the distinct quality of these messages. Just as a sommelier learns to differentiate sensory details of wine, helpers can discern sensory-based elements of dissociated primitive emotions as they manifest in the intersubjective field. Jaak Panksepp and Lucy Biven (2010) identify brain circuits for primitive emotions including fear, caring, seeking (the urge to explore), play, grief, lust, and rage. Each of these emotions, and combination of emotions, has its own specific sensory quality or "taste" for an individual. This information flows from neural states in the body and can be felt and recognized through somatic awareness, empathy, and inquiry. When emotions stop flowing and processing is interrupted by trauma, the emotions are caught in fixed-action neurological patterns in the body. The face, heart, and viscera hold sensory-based emotions in fixed-action patterns (Llinas 2001). For example, we might feel the tight grip of anger and rage in the eyes and jaw, a light tingling, playfulness in the eyes and mouth, the heaviness of grief in our chest, the tightening of our guts with fear, the arousal of lust in our genitals, or the expansive warmth of caring love in our hearts. Through somatic empathy, we can recognize intense dissociated states in ourselves and others and bring them into the intersubjective field for processing.

"Identification with another happens at the level of bodily sensations rather than feelings" (Zanocco, De Marchi, and Pozzi 2006, 146) and is based on sharing eye gaze, verbal sounds, touch, and movement. Awareness of eye gaze helps to communicate inner intentions. It's important to consider whether you unconsciously frown, subtly avert, probe, or, rather, intentionally hold a soft, inviting gaze that allows people to emerge and unfold in their own time.

There is a direct link between the body sensations of empathy and imagination that allows us to enter into the distorted imagination of trauma and shift body sensations within the intersubjective field. By altering the sensory data based on the past, the distorted imagination can take a new form, one that is more accurate for present moment experience. For example, consider Denise. As she dropped into states of collapse and neural immobility, she was unconscious of the shame she felt. However, as she began to feel more vitality and interest in her sensory experience, she realized how numb she had been for years, yet suffering at the same time. With sensory awareness, she became conscious of shame as a contraction in her belly. When I was reluctant to feel with Denise, knowing on some level that I did not want to encounter my own shame, she felt abandoned and judged. By working through my own shame and increasing my caring intention toward Denise, we were able to enter into her disassociation from her trauma (Zanocco, De Marchi, and Pozzi 2006). Together we learned to attend to sensory experience and emerge out of numb suffering. With the intersubjective field to support us, we opened ourselves to the immobilized fear and brought it into present moment somatic awareness. Zanocco, De Marchi, and Pozzi (2006) critically affirms the power of an empathic encounter to break through the dissociated traumatic memories of the past, releasing the bedlam of dissociated affect into the intersubjective field for coregulation and then into a new order based on images, symbols, and archetypes.

Helping professional need to trust that, under the right conditions, the chaos of trauma can be reorganized with bodily-based wisdom. Once regulation is established contingent symbolic representations can reconsolidate the body with meaningful and current perceptions of reality. When fully processed, the right-hemispheric elements of trauma result in a new, elegant order of data and information, meaning that may go beyond the individual into archetypal and spiritual dimensions. In my clinical experience, it is the energy contained in the archetypal symbols that can offer essential vitality to sustain and expand the regulation of fragmented neural-emotional states. For example, let's consider Denise again. Following the establishment of a regulated intersubjective field through processing the sensory-based emotions generated by the brain stem and limbic system, we were able to process specific implicit and explicit memories with the boundaries of our shared optimal arousal. Her traumatic memories included both physical and sexual abuse at the hands of her brother and his friends. As we processed the dissociated memories, Denise recalled times she was held captive in the woods in the "game" of sexual abuse, and the forest around her came to life and comforted her. She could hear and see the trees take on a light, an essence that seemed to radiate a sense of wholeness to her, to help her know she was loved and valued in the midst of the brutality in the moment. As we brought our attention to the archetype of the tree and its light, we were able to sense its numinosity in the present moment and to incorporate that light into an expansion of our hearts and bellies, bringing our neural states beyond regulation and into synchronicity.

This synthesis of neural states and symbolic systems does not happen quickly; each element of a dissociated affect needs attention and transformation within the intersubjective field. Sensations, feelings, movements, emotions, and images all need phenomenological attention to discern and relieve the fear that has coupled with immobilization and to open up to the safety of processing lived experience. Practitioners are responsible for slowing down and offering mindful attention and compassion to the subtle phenomena of perceptual, sensory-based elements. With loving acceptance of chaotic, fused, and fragmented neural-based sensations and emotions, they begin to differentiate and create new neural connections that are in healthy relationship to each other. Reorganization is an intriguing aspect of the empathic process. This is a time where the practitioner intentionally lets go of trying to make sense out of the content and trusts in the innate energies of the mysteries of the embodied intersubjective field to create a new arrangement out of the previously disorganized energies.

A Caution against Bypassing Somatic Empathy—Case 7.3: Connor

Before the chaotic energies of hyper- and hypoarousal can be reorganized into creative meaningful patterns—they must first be regulated. When two people share a mutual visceral state through somatic empathy, coregulation entrains the two nervous systems so a traumatized person can enter into calm states of social engagement and begin reorganizing their inner world of sensation and primitive emotion. In these shifts, neural connections are gradually forged that eventually facilitate self-regulation, as a person implicitly learns to coregulate the bodily-based chaos with someone who is able to feel with them.

When clients experience intense arousal, it can be tempting for practitioners to try to coregulate without first feeling the sensory emotional dynamics of another's inner world. This approach will often backfire—a lesson I learned during an encounter with Connor, my eight-year-old grandson. The summer before kindergarten, Conner had experienced a traumatic anesthetic complication during a surgery that resulted in terrifying hallucinations. Eighteen months later, following a yoga class where he felt physically paralyzed when the teacher put weights on his body, Connor experienced flashbacks of being immobilized by an anesthetic while he was still conscious. Several days later, I asked Connor to paint the feelings he had inside, but he resisted. "They would scare you too much," he said. After some thought, Connor put his brush in black paint and made the sounds as he wrote the words, "BOOO" and "GRRR." He then said, "Sorry, Grandma . . . are you scared?" I was curious but not scared and told him so. I then suggested he choose some music from Pandora to help us regulate his feelings. He selected a soft, rhythmical tune with a feminine voice. I suggested we join hands and dance slowly. What I didn't realize was that Connor did not want me to regulate him in that moment; rather, he needed to know, more than anything, that I was feeling the specific sensations of his fear. In order to help me feel his intense subjective fear, Connor gripped my hands and turned the slow dance into a dizzying spin where I felt suddenly disoriented. When I was about to fall, he stopped and apologized. "Sorry, Grandma," he said with a bit of a gleam in his eye. He watched me carefully as I restored my balance, grounded myself, and then reoriented to the environment. I told Connor I had felt frightened, and I was glad that he helped me to understand his feelings. During the spinning dance, I had tasted and felt his intense disorientation and terror.

Somatic empathy relies on the physiology of sharing an energetic field based in sensory knowing, an interactive connection that allows for implicit unconscious processing of right-hemispheric phenomena. I had to feel Connor's energetic inner world in order to know his current experience of himself and the environment and what might help us. My momentary experience of panic, fear, and overwhelm let him know that his behavioral communication had been received, he had been felt by another, and he was no longer alone in his terror and horror of the hallucination. My self-regulation of physical terror triggered by spinning with Connor strengthened my resilience and solidified his trust that we could coregulate. By observing my ability to regulate overwhelming fear, Connor learned that his inner sensations could be managed.

Reflecting on this experience, I imagined how frustrating it would be to have someone try to regulate you without a shared visceral state. However, few clinicians have been taught how to perceive the subtle yet direct and visceral somatic communications from their own bodies in order to consciously self-regulate, much less intentionally feel communications from the body of a person suffering intense anguish. As clinicians, we can strengthen our resilience to adversity through coregulation of intense fear, pain, and dissociation in the moment of an interpersonal encounter and learn to self-regulate when necessary. As people struggle together to face

the demons within, they can consciously create a sacred ceremonial relational space—the intersubjective field—to regulate their distress, contingently process a trauma memory, and ultimately heal each other.

Using Somatic Empathy to Enter into Affective Experience

Practices of coregulation through somatic empathy allow the inner world
of the person suffering from trauma to reconnect sensory-based experiences
with healing symbols and images, restoring the split of innate processing
of the right hemisphere. Interruptions from trauma form survival-based
fixed-action patterns that inhibit right-hemispheric processing. There are
many different fixed-action patterns that come from trauma since they
are often dependent on the particular way trauma affected the body. For
example, Denise disconnected from her body in the moment of trauma,
an interruption that helped to keep her soul safe. This fixed-action pattern
of dissociation from sensation helped in the moment but left her vulnerable and unable to integrate lived experience.

It is important to recognize the developmental moment when dissociation was first used as a primary defense. In Denise's history, her pattern
of dissociation as indicated by Beebe et al. (2014) suggests that it was
very young, probably in the first four months of her life. Her pattern of
dissociation formed in early life may have made her more vulnerable to
sexual abuse in her later childhood development. Our work of regulating
in the intersubjective field before explicitly attending to abusive traumatic
memories was necessary to form the developmental foundations for integration of her lived experience.

To assist in the restoration of natural right-hemispheric processing of
lived experience, practitioners can enter into embodied affective experience
in any of its forms. The choice of where and how to enter into affective
experience is dependent on the knowledge gleaned through somatic empathy and the ability to coregulate intense affect within the optimal arousal
zone. For example, we may attend to sensation, or we might begin with the
development of symbolic images or reflective, right-hemispheric processes.
For people with little capacity to consciously feel sensations, it is helpful
to focus on images that generate vitality. People with a sense of anguish
or chaos in their bodies are able to enter into right-hemispheric processes
through reflection on lived experience, while people who are familiar with
sensation in their bodies and have learned to tolerate discomfort without
dissociation are more able to enter into the perception of sensation. When
people are able to feel pleasant sensation as well as formulate images, we
can phenomenologically explore the connections between the body and
the protective visual memories.

When I was working with Denise, we entered into affective processing
of her traumatic memories by attending to sensations of the protective elements that were at the periphery of the abuse. One day, she recalled a hike

she took in the woods, and she discussed being in the forest, near the river, with her faithful dogs. Together, we felt the trees, sensed the light and connection, saw and heard the river, and sensed its flow within our bodies. We were present to petting the dogs and feeling the protection they offered, all embodied affective experiences that linked sensations with images that had symbolic meaning for her healing.

Similar to my experience with Denise, practitioners need to strengthen a client's particular life-giving aspects of any affective experience to contain, metabolize, and reorganize the brutal aspects that have been separated— with the goal of bringing fragmented elements together. The intuition that is stimulated from somatic empathy guides our way in this labyrinth of differentiation and linkage of traumatic implicit memories. When accompanied by an empathic somatic witness, the neural states that hold traumatic memories can be transformed into more expansive and authentic perspectives. Exercise 7.2: Becoming a Participating Witness prepares practitioners to enter into traumatic memories with another while holding a participating witness perspective. See page 205 of the appendix.

Somatic empathy fuels the intersubjective field with caring and compassion so that practices of wonder, curiosity, and interest can be used to inquire into dissociated experiences. Somatic inquiry, which you will learn more about in Chapter 8, delves into the mutual felt sense in the moment, a portal that reveals implicit memories of earlier trauma. When practices of somatic empathy and inquiry are skillfully embedded into the therapeutic conversation, unconscious neural and emotional states come into awareness and are available for reorganization. As implicit traumatic memories emerge, the hidden suffering that has accompanied the trauma can be acknowledged on a bodily, emotional, imaginal, and cognitive level, a process that allows for gradual transformation of even the most devastating complex trauma.

References

Atleo, E. R. 2004. *Tsawalk: A Nuu-chah-nulth Worldview*. Vancouver: University of British Columbia Press.

Beebe, B., and F. M. Lachmann. 2014. *The Origins of Attachment: Infant Research and Adult Treatment*. New York: Routledge.

The Boston Change Process Study Group. 2010. *Change in Psychotherapy: A Unifying Paradigm*. New York: Norton.

Bromberg, P. M. 2011. *The Shadow of the Tsunami: and the Growth of the Relational Mind*. New York: Routledge.

Ginot, E. 2009. "The Empathic Power of Enactments: The Link between Neuropsychological Processes and an Expanded Definition of Empathy." *Psychoanalytic Psychology* 26(3): 290–309.

Kalsched, D. 2013. *Trauma and the Soul: A Psycho-spiritual Approach to Human Development and Its Interruption*. London: Routledge.

Kilpatrick, S. 2000. "Language Before Words: The Ignored Body." PhD. Diss., C.G. Jung Institute, Santa Fe.

Llinás, R. R. 2001. *I of the vortex: From neurons to self.* Cambridge: MIT Press.

Marks-Tarlow, T. 2012. *Clinical Intuition in Psychotherapy: The Neurobiology of Embodied Response.* New York: Norton.

Panksepp, J., and L. Biven. 2010. *The Archaeology of Mind: Neural Origins of Human Emotion.* New York: Norton.

Rogers, C. 1986. "Rogers, Kohut, and Erikson: A Personal Perspective on Some Similarities and Differences." *Person-Centered Review* 1(2): 125–140.

Scheler, M. 1954. *On the Nature of Sympathy.* Translated by P. Heath. London: Routledge.

Schore, A. N. 2010. "The Right Brain Implicit Self: A Central Mechanism of the Psychotherapy Change Process." In *Knowing, Not-knowing and Sort of Knowing: Psychoanalysis and the Experience of Uncertainty,* edited by J. Petrucelli, 177–202. London: Karnac.

Schore, A. N. 2012. *The Science of the Art of Psychotherapy.* New York: Norton.

Schore, J. R., and A. N. Schore. 2014. "Regulation Theory and Affect Regulation Psychotherapy: A Clinical Primer." *Smith College Studies in Social Work* 84: 2–3, 178–195.

Stanley, S. A. 1994. "The Process and Development of Empathy in Educators: A Phenomenological Inquiry." PhD diss., University of Victoria.

Stern, D. B. 2010. *Partners in Thought: Working with Unformulated Experience, Dissociation, and Enactment.* New York: Routledge.

Zanocco, G., A. De Marchi, and F. Pozzi. 2006. "Sensory Empathy and Enactment." *International Journal of Psychoanalysis* 87:145–158.

8   Somatic Inquiry
Exploring the Intersubjective World through Language

"The discipline of phenomenology is similar to Eastern mindfulness meditation practices in its goal of developing the untrained person's ability to experientially access his or her own conscious states. Both disciplines involve the development of an interested, open nonevaluative and receptive form of awareness."

(Lanius and Frewen 2015, 48)

Somatic Inquiry: A Phenomenological Method

How can we make meaning out of direct lived experience, the moment-to-moment phenomena of ordinary encounters? How do we know the precise interventions that can unwind the effects of trauma and open us to coexist in mutual acceptance and care, the neural state of social engagement? In the absence of ancestral traditions and ceremonies to guide us, in Western culture we can create shared states of ventral vagal engagement and restore the natural processing of the right hemisphere. An integral part of that process is phenomenological inquiry.

Phenomenological inquiry offers a methodological approach to the chaotic and random dynamics of trauma. Practitioners and clients can use this path of inquiry to slowly enter into the intersubjective world, discover obstacles and resistance to healing, and attend to unresolved trauma in the moment. Phenomenological inquiry offers a well-researched process and intersubjective language for discerning the truth of our lived experience and what it means to be human. As I discussed in Chapter 5, phenomenology, sparked by wonder, is rooted in the present moment, but seeks to unify the past, present, and future.

In a technological approach to phenomenology, Lanius and Frewen (2015) suggest that the concurrent neurological and phenomenological experience of the patient can be assessed with "neuroimaging, EEG, neuroendocrine, or peripheral psychophysiological measures. We suggest that neurophenomenology, in particular, proves an especially strong methodological paradigm for consciousness studies and psychotraumatology" (48). In this book, I suggest a similar methodology for therapy, a neuro-phenomenological approach in the context of an embodied intersubjective relationship rather than a technological laboratory, a human space where the practice of somatic ways of knowing, including somatic inquiry, reveals the neural state in the moment and the particular patterns of arousal between two or more people. This living knowledge then informs one's intuition as to the right moment for physiological, imaginal, or reflective interventions. Interpersonally, a neurophenomenological method of somatic inquiry is interested in revealing the true self by focusing on subtle bodily-based perceptions communicated through facial movement, eye gaze, tone, rhythm of voice, touch, and meaningful gesture, and maintaining a neural state of optimal arousal.

When applied to healing trauma, phenomenological processes of inquiry are useful to helping professionals because they value and explore the subjective lived experience of all individuals with a methodology that is free from fear, judgment, and presuppositions regarding pathology, dysregulation, and "appropriate" inner ways of being. Lived experience, sometimes known as the unconscious, is inner knowledge that is considered too intense to be explicitly and consciously known in the present moment, particularly without the support and assistance of another. It is a kind of knowing that has not yet been embodied, verbalized, or incorporated into a coherent sense of self. Phenomenological methods of inquiry gently reveal dissociated, subjective lived experience, including the implicit and truncated memories of trauma, and provide ways to explore the co-consciousness that is created in the intersubjective field. With an inquiry-based methodology versus a theoretical-analytical or cognitive-behavioral approach to assessing and influencing the inner world of another, practitioners are able to diminish bias and invite, with a fresh, open, and welcoming state of mind, the dissociated traumatic experience of both themselves and clients to come forward into the language of meaningful dialogue.

The dialogue of a somatic inquiry is a phenomenological approach to exploring lived experience that seeks to uncover and repair interruptions in the right hemisphere's innate processing system. Grounded in bodily-based awareness, somatic inquiry allows helping professionals to enter into the mystery of their clients' lives, grasp the interconnections of their experiences, and explore how underdeveloped and tangled neural-emotional states from hidden memories affect current reality. A somatic inquiry is interested in the unfolding of the disturbed neural states of the past and emerging primitive emotions while in contact with the innate bodily-based wisdom available in relationships of acceptance and care. Unresolved neural states and primitive emotions are then able to reconnect with higher levels of knowing, such as image, symbol, and archetype.

Within the context of an embodied, intersubjective field, a somatic inquiry begins with the trauma survivor's ability to slowly incorporate relational strength, trust, and vitality while expanding awareness and acceptance of their troubled inner world. When people have developed the ability to incorporate vitality and life-giving resources, the intersubjective field can integrate the stark terror, horror, and anguish of trauma including the subsequent suffering. Each step toward a synthesis of implicit traumatic memories and anguishing bodily-based symptoms is contingent on the interpersonal communication in the moment. A somatic inquiry is guided by attuned observation and the interactive nonverbal and verbal communication regarding moment-to-moment phenomena: the sensations, emotions, images, and reflections that emerge in the dialogical encounter. Through informed intuition, heartfelt interest, and curiosity, both people engage in the collaborative and reciprocal interactions that constitute an inquiry. Although an accurate sense of reality is essential, a somatic inquiry should not be reduced to fact finding and sophisticated explanations and theories. Rather the goal is to hold reverence for the natural yet mysterious healing processes of the body, brain, soul, and spirit. These invisible relational dynamics move both practitioner and client, in a systemic, nonlinear way, toward coherence and reconnection with the reality of life.

This descent through dialogue into the inner realms of subjectivity allows neural states to shift in the moment, emotions to reveal meaning, and new aspects of self-identity to integrate. Neural states provide the inner thrust that moves us away from or toward an experience. For example, the neural state of fear can warn us about a possible danger and the need for defense and protection; the neural state of life threat results in insensitivity and numbness as the death process begins while the neural state of social engagement provides safety. Primitive emotions move us toward the significance of the experience. For example, the primitive emotion of seeking, according to Panksepp and Biven (2011), motivates us to integrate our lived experience. The failure to attend to the arousal of dysregulated neural states and the primitive emotions they generate results in lives wasted in alienated states of disembodied dissociation. With the open-ended yet integrative methods of phenomenology, the natural process of transformation can take place, first reorganizing the relationships between subcortical neural states and primitive emotions, then, fully incorporating higher cortical aspects of lived experience of imagination and bodily-based reflection. A somatic inquiry with another is an "old/new" method of discerning the wounds of trauma and providing affective embodied experiences for healing.

The Potential of Dialogue

Part of what makes somatic inquiry an effective tool for healing trauma is its moment-to-moment dialogical approach. The word dialogue comes from the old Latin *dialogos*, with *dia* referring to a blessed or sacred relation between two people and *logos* signifying language, the word, or meaning. Romesin and Verden-Zoller (2008) claim that human beings in cultures with rich oral traditions lived in the present moment with languaging that brought coherence to emotions. *Languaging* refers to the spontaneous emergence of words congruent with immediate bodily-based lived experience. Trusting in the "goodness of a living cosmos that includes humans" as they went about their lives, many cultures with oral traditions honored the fundamental biology of human love and connection (2008, 125). Romesin and Verden-Zoller contend that the patriarchal view of Western culture lacks a sense of inclusion in the coherence of a systemic cosmos. With that perspective, people in Western culture often try to maintain control through aggression and competition, employing strategies that separate them from their own biological lives and loving connection with others. Languaging without attempts to control allows for trust and respect for the multidimensionality of each individual. People who live with the belief they need to control and dominate others negate the trust and love that holds human relations in coherence. For Romesin and Verden-Zoller, the biology of love is the fundamental bond between the mother and infant, and cultures that honor the optimal development of children respect this biological imperative. In a healing dialogue, a somatic inquiry attempts to recognize, respect, and language the biological sacredness of each individual's inner world, similar to the essential contingent, reciprocal communication between mother and child (Beebe and Lachmann 2014).

Building on Romesin and Verden-Zoller's concepts of inclusion and connection, scientist David Bohm (2004) describes dialogue as a process that creates shared meaning between people by allowing multiple points of view. For Bohm, finding a shared meaning or a "tacit ground" holds people together, while defending assumptions and opinions creates incoherence and distrust. Dialogue offers a way to seek truth together that is coherent and does not demand compliance, but instead searches for cues that signal new ways of perceiving, languaging, emotioning (skillful ways we perceive, interpret, and express the current neural states in our body), and thinking with authentic interconnection. Bohm (2004) quotes Humberto Romesin: "When one human being tells another human what is 'real,' what they are actually doing is making a demand for obedience. They are asserting that they have a privileged view of reality. Understanding through participation allows truth and meaning to continually unfold" (xi–xiv). Bohm explains a universal principle of human interaction. Communication through dialogue allows something new to be created—it opens a space where people are able to truly listen to each other and willingly question their fundamental assumptions. People become free to intuitively communicate in the moment without having to hold their ideas as permanent positions and later defend them. In an intersubjective field, the contingent interaction of a somatic dialogical inquiry allows awareness and knowledge to grow and expand, shifting perspectives in the moment while transforming the biological regulation of the relational system.

The Elements and Form of a Somatic Inquiry

Somatic inquiry begins in the knowledge gleaned through somatic empathy and the intersubjective field. Exploring the "wordless spaces" of lived experience, somatic inquiry circles around an issue in an ever closer spiral to gently open awareness to the deeper truth of existence. Truth in this sense stems from the etymology of the Greek word *aynoeia,* which means "forgotten," and can refer to those experiences that have been hidden from the mind in the struggle to survive trauma.

Oscillating attention between the polarities of "forgotten" experience and sources of vitality differentiates neural states that may be fused, then allows them to link as new neural connections. Oscillation can be expressed visually with the infinity symbol, the figure 8 on its side. See Figure 8.1. Differentiations of phenomena reveal the opposites contained within an experience, and linkage brings the opposites into a more expansive form, leading to perspectives that integrate polarities. Jung describes how the unconscious holds the unity of the self: "The essence of the conscious mind is discrimination; it must, if it is to be aware of things, separate the opposites, and it does this *contra naturam.* In nature the opposites seek one another—*les extremes se touchent*—and so it is in the unconscious, and particularly in the archetype of unity, the self" (Jung 1983, 275). Jung calls "the union of opposites 'the transcendent function'" (226)—a goal in therapy that is beyond the alleviation of symptoms. For Jung, "the conflict between two

OSCILLATION OF POLARITIES TO CREATE A MORE EXPANSIVE PERSPECTIVE

© 2015 Sharon Stanley, Ph.D.

Figure 8.1 Infinity Cycle

Oscillation of somatic awareness between differentiated phenomena and opposites creates a larger perspective with more complex knowledge.

fundamental psychic facts" the conscious and unconscious, was at the heart of human development, and the process of individuation (225).

To begin a somatic inquiry, we dialogically explore sensations, emotions, images, and lived experience to sense their innate coherence or polarities. We somatically feel the phenomena that is offered by the other in dialogue and allow the meaning and value of that communication to surface, then use that meaning to continue the inquiry. Wonder, interest, and curiosity allows a portal to open between you and the other, and between the lived experience and the meaning it contains.

More specifically, a somatic dialogical inquiry is characterized by an intention to feel, know, accept, and care for the other in the other's own terms. It requires a suspension of the past to be present in the moment, a "bracketing" that avoids arguments, explanations, and the kind of rationality that is devoid of emotion. It's important to note that assumptions should neither be suppressed nor carried out—the key is to suspend them, and then observe how those assumptions live inside the body through movements, feelings, and sensations. When two people have differing assumptions, and each person listens to the other, they can begin to see the other's point of view and imagine new, more complex ways to hold what seemed to be a polarity. Bohm (2004) believes we have not fully developed the art of suspension; with suspension we can resist impulsive reactions and recognize how the self produces thoughts and feelings. Suspension is similar to the phenomenological concept of "bracketing," in order to differentiate phenomena. In Exercise 8.1: A Somatic Dialogical Inquiry, you can practice suspending assumptions. See page 207 of the appendix.

Somatic inquiry into lived experience supports the differentiation of trauma states from vitality affects. As a state of vitality is freed from a traumatic memory, the state of ventral vagal social engagement can be strengthened, helping to balance the polarity. The innate wisdom of the body-mind is then able to create linkages that move awareness into a larger perspective.

When differentiation has created distinct polarities that can be felt in the body, the oscillation of the two distinct states initiates more complex states in which people can recall the trauma, yet are not physically and emotionally determined by it. The energy that has been locked in the fusion of neural states becomes available for more creative purposes than suffering. When a third, more complex, state emerges from a polarity, it can be amplified and fully embodied to integrate it into the body, the personality, and sense of spirituality.

In a somatic inquiry it is a challenge to hold the balance of the differentiated elements, to sense how they are each embodied, to gently shift attention between them, allowing them to oscillate with each other, and unconsciously link together in a higher, more complex way of being in relationship to each other. Practitioners can meet this challenge by considering the extremes of their own lived experience and imagining a larger perspective that can incorporate both. A personal practice of allowing fluid perception of reality and changing perspectives allows a practitioner to lead another in a similar processing of lived experience.

Conducting a Somatic Inquiry into Vitality—Case 8.1: Harold

The methodology of conducting a somatic inquiry with a person suffering from trauma involves several levels of right-hemispheric processing. Somatic inquiry employs what Panksepp and Biven (2011) call the "seeking system," a primitive emotional brain circuit that stimulates interest and curiosity. Using somatic awareness, practitioners first establish an embodied empathic connection and an intersubjective field. With this relational foundation, they then orient to the current moment, with a clear intention and attunement to self and other. A search for vitality affects, such as a sparkle in the eye, coloring in the skin, lightness in the tone of voice, or enhanced rhythm can initiate a somatic inquiry. These physical cues indicate experiences where the burden of suffering has lifted, even for a moment, and humor, hope, or caring has emerged. Vitality may appear as people talk about gardening, caring for a pet, being in nature, listening to music, creating or viewing art, or simply spending time with a friend or family member. Once practitioners have noticed the cues indicating vitality, they may enter into an exploration of the phenomena of the content. Below is an example of a contingent somatic dialogical inquiry into vitality affects with an 82-year-old man struggling with pain and sorrow in the last stages of cancer:

Sharon: Harold, when you talk about feeding the deer in your yard at sunrise, I noticed the sparkle in your eyes.

Harold: Yeah, some mornings I am up before the light comes, quietly sitting in my yard waiting for them.

Sharon: As you wait, I am wondering what it feels like for you.

Harold: Well, it feels like I am not stuck inside myself but am out ready to be with the deer.

Sharon: Harold, I wonder if you could tell me more about your interactions with these wild animals in the early morning.

Harold: Well, they can see me in my chair so they only come up to the edge of the grass. Each morning when it is still dark, I put a small amount of food on the flat rock out there, next to the one that fills with water. I pour a little hot water on that rock to thaw the ice and then I stay very still and watch the light and shadow in the woods.

Sharon: I'm wondering, Harold, if you can see in your mind's eye the light of the early morning and feel the movement of the animals as they come out of hiding.

Harold: When I first glimpse their movement, my heart opens up and I feel them coming.

Sharon: I'm wondering if you can feel that sensation in this moment as you are gesturing that upward movement near your chest.

Harold: Yes, it keeps moving up and out and the tears come.

Sharon: (*After a time of silence and nonverbal connection and communication*) And when you recall this daily experience with the deer, I wonder what you notice in your body?

Harold: (*After a time of silence*) Yeah, it's nice to know I can still feel this even if the rest of my body is in pain.

When conducting a somatic inquiry into vitality, it is best to first inquire into very simple experiences that have occurred recently, such as Harold's interaction with the deer, a morning walk in the sun, the smile of a baby, a glimpse of the sense of self, or the texture of a pleasing fabric. For example, a starter question might be, "When have you had a glimpse of your true self in the last several days?" This question then can be tracked into more authentic parts of the self, those aspects that are often obscured in daily life. Perhaps most importantly, the spoken language of a somatic inquiry should come directly out of the clinician's embodied wonder and interest and in the words best suited to that particular intersubjective field. A somatic inquiry is energized by authentic interest, wonder, love, and feeling felt. Focusing attention on inner dynamics that bring life and vitality strengthens the ventral vagal neural networks, even if the sense of vitality feels weak (Koch 2004). Somewhere, sometime, something has given this person the gift of life and enough resources to sustain that life. It is up to helping professionals to discover, appreciate, and amplify the phenomena of the life force, an ordinary daily spiritual energy that is necessary to process and reorganize traumatic memories.

Sometimes helping professionals are the only people in their clients' lives with whom they currently experience a sense of vitality. In this case, a somatic inquiry into vitality could explore the intersubjective field, for example, "I wonder if you have felt my care for you when we have worked together?" The phenomena of the response provides the next step of the inquiry. Alternatively, if therapists can catch these phenomenological moments as they spontaneously emerge in relationship, they can pause, inquire, amplify, and integrate the energy into the fabric of the intersubjective field.

In the early development of the intersubjective field, as regulation is being established, practitioners should inquire into vitality affects long *before* exploring the depth of traumatic memories. Vitality affects accumulate in the relationship and provide the necessary energy to coregulate terror, aggression, and immobility. When the dynamics of coregulation of vitality affects become part of the natural rhythm of the relationship, then practitioners can begin to inquire, little by little, into traumatic memories, incorporating the dissociated elements as they emerge. Without coregulation in the context of an intersubjective field, an individual may struggle for years to break the cycle of an active, yet hidden, implicit memory.

Inquiring into Traumatic Memories—Case 8.2: Denise

A somatic inquiry into lived experience is invitational and receptive, seeking to identify and embody small but essential fragments of phenomena related to a traumatic memory, a little bit at a time. These fragments are primarily implicit and may include neural states, anguishing sensations, intrusive sounds, voluntary and involuntary movement, emotional dynamics, disturbing images, and distorted cognitive processes. Each entry point can reveal a deeper truth. The invitational tone of the inquiry is important: it reduces the feelings of pressure, judgment, and premature interpretation. When regulation is established, both practitioners and clients are able to attend to the phenomena of traumatic memories from the perspective of an embodied witness.

A somatic inquiry begins on the periphery of the traumatic memory and gently spirals its way in as the dissociated fragments arise, are differentiated, oscillated, linked, and incorporated. Practitioners intuitively choose which phenomena to focus on and how intensely to enter into the phenomena, moving toward a state of optimal arousal. Directed attention toward frightening phenomena causes an increase in neural firing, raising activation and threatening regulation, for both practitioner and client. In order to know what to select for attention, therapists must have somatic awareness of the current arousal state of their own bodies as well as the bodies of their clients. During this process it's important for practitioners to attune to and regulate the pain, anguish, and suffering caused by the recall of traumatic memories. While unregulated suffering cannot be endured without some aggression, withdrawal, or dissociation, regulated relational suffering reveals redemptive meaning over time.

The goal of a somatic inquiry is to physically, emotionally, and spiritually participate in the distress, pain, grief, terror, and horror that lie at the core of a person's traumatic memories. As they arise, the intense emotions are brought into the intersubjective field and regulated. People suffering from trauma often experience loneliness and alienation and require a deeply felt companionship in order to reorganize the bodily-based remnants of complex trauma. In order to approach these protected memories, a therapist must contain the process within a state of optimal arousal, employing relational interventions to reduce hyperarousal and restore vitality to hypoaroused states so that highly charged traumatic memories can transform into meaning. In the following example with Denise, whose experiences of shame due to a history of sexual abuse were discussed in Chapter 7, we'll explore how a somatic inquiry can assist in the creation of meaning.

During one of our sessions, Denise revealed that she had received a subpoena to testify in court against her abuser. To explore her less visible inner feelings, conflicts, and thoughts about the issue, I initiated a dialogical somatic inquiry. As you will observe, a somatic inquiry begins in general terms and moves into the specific phenomena of lived experience, bringing awareness and possibility to the unformulated experience (Stern 2010).

Sharon: Denise, I'm wondering what happened for you when you received the subpoena.

Denise: Well, I was doing the dishes when the doorbell rang and I was handed some papers. I just stood there and looked and saw his name (*her abuser*) and my name. It was like I was frozen to the carpet. Everything felt like it was swimming around me.

As she talked about her experience, the color in her face shifted to a whitish gray, she became quite still, her head was rigid, and her voice lost its prosody and became monotone. Being "frozen" and "swimming" indicated that the vestibular system, the sensory organizing system of incoming information from the body, was overwhelmed at the moment of receiving the papers—indicating to me that Denise had experienced a shock reaction of "immobility with fear." I wanted to regulate this hypoaroused state into a more optimal neural state by oscillating it with the present moment experience of our relationship. If we had waited to hear the rest of the story, we would have missed an opportunity to coregulate and open at a deeper level. Our goal was to differentiate the sympathetic arousal of the past from our social engagement of the ventral vagal system in the present, allowing the feeling of being "frozen" to be past and the present to be animated with vitality.

Sharon: When you remember holding the papers at your door, what do you notice right now?

Denise: I'm feeling a little cold, but it's like I'm really angry at the same time.

My intuition told me that Denise's feelings of coldness could be related to the immobility of shock, while her anger felt like a form of self-protection, an energy that can be mobilizing for moving people out of shock. People who begin to dissociate at a very early age often repeat that pattern in moments of shock and miss the development of skills to relationally, justly, and effectively protect themselves; instead they use withdrawal through dissociation as a primary defense in moments of stress. In this moment, I wanted to help Denise differentiate between her anger that protects her and the aggressive anger her abuser had used against her.

Sharon: Denise, I'm wondering when you feel this anger, if you notice how it moves in your body?

Denise: The anger starts in my gut and moves up my chest and it feels like it comes out of my eyes.

This was great news—her anger was acting as a healthy transition out of the immobilization of shame and did not seem to face any obstacles. Obstacles to the innate energy of anger include physiological fixed-action patterns with psychological fragments of implicit memories where guilt, fear of the potency of anger to hurt self and others, and fear that refusing to comply might alienate the people someone is dependent upon. If these obstacles had emerged, I would have noted it and moved to a more ventral vagal focus. As it turned out, I did shift the sympathetic arousal swiftly into a shared vagal state, activating her vagal brake on sympathetic arousal so that we would not have the interference of adrenaline and cortisols to contend with.

Continuing with the inquiry, I engaged Denise in the mystery of her own internal emotions and their subtle movement within her body. Within my own body, I had noticed a sense of waves of energy. I could feel the potential of the anger to become vitality rather than high arousal outside her optimal state.

Sharon: Denise, as you observe and feel that anger move up your body, does it come in a steady flow, in waves, or in some other form?

Denise: (*Her eyes closed*) Well, I think it has these waves, like dark smoke rising up from inside.

As she spoke, I sensed a pulse in my gut, with energy rising into my head.

Sharon: I'm wondering if we could take a moment and ground this energy. There is a lot of power here and I would love to see it really grounded for your use.

The rising up of the intense energy that I felt through the intersubjective field seemed to be the arousal of dissociated emotions in the gut releasing into the body and head. I was cautious of too much, too fast and wanted to slow it down to an optimal arousal, so it could be incorporated. When energy of released dissociated affect comes too fast, people become frightened and may drop into states of hypoarousal to cope with the intensity. This fuels the cycle of hyper- and hypoarousal and is potentially retraumatizing. Simple grounding exercises help the energy of self-protection to begin to move through the soles of the feet and down into the earth.

Denise: I can feel my feet on the ground . . . and oops, the energy just started going down into the ground. That feels better than in my head and eyes. My head was starting to hurt.

Early in our work together, Denise had learned to ground, developing a stable center that allowed us to coregulate and process both explicit and implicit memories of abuse and allow excess energy to move down into the ground. In that moment, it was important to reorganize some of the energy from her anger into a strength that could be useful. Grounding rhythmical movement and dropping into gravity allows intense energies to stabilize as strength.

Sharon: Let's take a few moments to rest and ground. Sometimes when we move our ankles like when we are walking, it helps to ground the energy of anger and keep us mobilized. Let's just lift one heel at a time and then let it drop. (*After a few minutes of this intervention, I returned to the inquiry.*) Denise, when you sense the ground and drop down into gravity, I'm wondering if you notice any images?

Opening to sensory-based images allows protective spiritual resources to arise in awareness. A primary symptom of trauma is the disruption of the innate processing system of the right hemisphere, including the severing of the higher cortical structures of the brain from the bodily-based activation of the autonomic nervous system and the brain stem. By inviting images into the intersubjective field, we are building a bridge between the disconnected fragments of right-hemispheric processing. This is most effective when a person can stay on the edge of optimal arousal, yet remain grounded and regulated. The images that emerge contain the neural-emotional arousal in a more complex and meaningful form.

Denise: I'm walking along the path I used to travel back and forth from school, I loved it. It was near the beach and in the woods. My neighbors' dog is right next to me; he used to walk me back and forth. I feel like he is watching out for me.

People from traditional societies may recognize the presence of the dog as a spiritual guide, one that transcends ordinary reality to provide support and relationship in moments of danger and life threat. This image allowed the resources of the beach, the woods, and the dog to become fully embodied. I told her to take her time and enjoy the beach and the woods as she felt the presence of the dog. Denise and I spent approximately five minutes engaging in nonverbal exchanges, eye gaze, sounds of prosody, and subtle rocking of both of our bodies. A familiar sensation to us, the rocking became more intense as her experience was integrating. Often this circular rocking movement, an inner spiral, had occurred as we processed her early abuse. When the rocking settled, I continued the verbal dialogue to integrate our experience with language.

Sharon: Denise, when you recall receiving the papers from the court, what do you now notice in your body?
Denise: I'm feeling stronger on the inside, like I can say what is true, and I can stand up for myself. I feel like I'm connected inside.

The integration of the bodily-based optimal arousal with imaginal phenomena allowed Denise's energy for self-protection to mature into strength rather than remain in a primitive state of power and mastery. The instinctive power of a thwarted defense can be connected to higher cortical processes through imaginal links and then mature into a more relational wisdom. I was then interested in helping Denise know that she could stand up for herself, yet she did not need to stand alone. I wanted her to have a felt sense of the intersubjective field, as she stood up for herself.

Sharon: Denise, what if we stand together, and I take a stand with you in this moment, would that be ok?

She expressed that she would like that, so we stood next to one another, shoulder to shoulder. Then I asked Denise if there was anything she would like to say. Quietly and with a tone of voice that indicated confidence and trust of her inner world, she made a break through. As she spoke, I could feel my heart pounding and tears rose up behind my eyes.

Denise: What happened to me was very wrong and it changed my whole life from what it could have been. I want to make sure this stuff doesn't happen to other kids. I need to take a stand and say that it was wrong and it was not my fault. It was his. He was older and stronger and very mean. I was just a scared little kid.

We quietly stood together for a time. The silence was filled with changing energies; the pounding of my heart quieted, I began to feel more settled, and Denise reached out for my hand. Wordlessly, we softly held hands, then after a few moments, Denise sat in her chair and rested with her eyes closed before we reflected on the inquiry.

Sharon: In the last twenty minutes, we have been talking about some pretty intense experiences. I'm wondering what felt most helpful for you?
Denise: It was remembering that dog from next door. I haven't thought of him in a long time, but I felt really warm and safe when I remembered how he would be there walking with me every day. He really helped me get through those years.

Following our session, Denise testified against her abuser. I was able to be in the courtroom that day to silently support Denise while the abuser was held accountable for his actions. For the next few months, Denise and I processed the day in court and its consequences to the family and community until it was no longer activating or highly arousing.

Somatic Inquiry in a Group Setting—Case 8.3: Eileen

While Denise and I worked together one on one, a somatic inquiry can also be effective in the context of a caring, supportive group. Drawing from her vast store of experiences as a physical therapist, Eileen frequently served as a coordinator and impromptu teacher in Somatic Transformation trainings. One day, while Eileen described to the group how she had used somatic practices to support a patient, she suddenly began to experience flashbacks and hyperarousal connected to a violent assault she had endured many years ago. She asked if I could help her regulate in a demonstration. The relational processes of somatic empathy had been developed in the group over the year we had been training together and was immediately available to support Eileen, so I agreed.

Sharon: Eileen, as you sit with me now and feel the presence of the group, what do you notice happening for you?
Eileen: I feel like I am back on the beach where it happened and I keep seeing that man coming toward me with the club that had the nails in it.

It felt important to stay oriented to the present moment and the love and support of the group, so I continued with an intervention that would call upon her natural instinct to turn toward sound.

Sharon: I'm wondering when you hear my voice, if you can listen to me and use my voice to find where I am in the room.

Eileen slowly oriented her face toward mine and we connected with a gaze. Her eyes were hyperalert with terror and horror. I invited her to look into my eyes. With that invitation, Eileen began to drop the extreme arousal and soften her gaze. She held my gaze for a few moments and I watched her body begin to softly shake from the inside. After many years of enduring this trauma, the shaking indicated that her bracing was releasing. I then invited her to gaze around the room to see the faces of people who cared for her and were supporting her. With a deep breath, she began to settle, the shaking stopped, and she was now in a state of high arousal, but open to connect with the group. With this containment of a relational ventral vagal state, I asked if she wanted to continue exploring the trauma. She thought for a moment, slowly looked around the room, and said that she was ready to try.

Vocalizing her agreement empowered her and was a step toward unlocking the neural fusion of intense sympathetic arousal with her immobility response—a chronic hypoaroused state that had severely affected her physical and emotional health for many years. In the moment, the trauma was no longer controlling her, so we could collaborate to restore her power and strength. At the time, I already knew that her first encounter with her assailant had been casual. I chose to intervene there to explore unconscious feelings she may have had warning her of danger. In the processing of a life threat, it is important to detect the early inner warnings of danger and activate the sympathetic arousal before the moment of trauma.

Sharon: Eileen, I am wondering what you notice in your body as you recall the moment you saw that man.
Eileen: I first saw him walking down the path to the beach and he seemed sad and said, "Isn't it a lousy day?"
Sharon: When you remember seeing him coming down the path and hear his voice, what do you notice right now?
Eileen: He looks really sad but he looks kind of scary also.
Sharon: And when you sense that he is scary what does your body want to do?
Eileen: I want to run away, really fast.

Now, we had established the phenomenological moment as one that she was able to respond to with mobilization. Our task was to begin the processing before the perception shifted from danger to life threat. With life threat, she could have gone back into immobilization.

Sharon: I'm wondering if you can begin to run really fast in your imagination, and right now we can both feel that running while we make micromovements with our feet.

Together, we began to simulate the experience of running together. I invited Eileen to find a rhythm in her running that she enjoyed. For about three minutes, we ran together. In order to differentiate her ability to run from her attacker from running for pleasure, I inquired next:

Sharon: What is the most beautiful place you have ever run?
Eileen: I remember running on the track in college, in a cross-country event where I came in third. It felt so good and I felt strong.

Although she did not reply directly to my question, she was reminded of her strength and accomplishment, so I continued to inquire as her feet slowed down.

Sharon: I'm wondering where you feel that strength in your body right now.
Eileen: I feel it in my lower back, like it has a lot of power.
Sharon: And as you feel that power, I am wondering if we can go back to the moment when you saw that man with a club. What does your body want to do now?

Eileen: It wants to run, to run very fast. (*The differentiation has helped us to come to a place where we could create a new link.*)
Sharon: I'm wondering where you can run in your picture.
Eileen: I'm running to the water, he can't swim and I can.

Eileen went into her imagination to complete her run, and I saw her small movements shift from running to swimming.

Sharon: And when you swim what do you notice in your upper body?

Eileen began to make larger movements in her shoulders, arms and hands: rising, lowering, opening, closing. After a few moments, the movements slowed and then stopped.

Eileen: I made it to the beach on the other side of the bay. I'm safe.

Voices in the room cheered at the quiet strength of her words. In that moment, Eileen looked around the room like a swimmer fresh out of water, surprised by an audience. The facilitators took over group reflection, so I could sit with Eileen while she rested and her changes could integrate. After about ten minutes of rest and silence, she opened her eyes and wordlessly communicated her appreciation for our work together.

The somatic inquiry into the effect of Eileen's imagination and micro-movements helped her to embody the power and strength to escape from her internal prison of immobility and allow the neural perception of life threat to transform into a manageable danger, one that she was finally able to negotiate and find safety. It's important to note that the focus of the inquiry was always the present moment—how the memory currently lived in the body and the imagination. This allowed the neural networks associated with the trauma to shift, grow, and reorganize, the first step toward reconsolidation.

In addition to somatic inquiry of vitality affects and traumatic memories, knowledge of somatic interventions to regulate arousal—as I conducted with Eileen when I asked her to follow my voice—are essential for healing trauma. Somatic interventions reflect the two levels of brain-body-mind processing; the subcortical with brain stem and innate autonomic reactions and the limbic brain with the amygdala and emotional responses, and then the higher cortical structures that organize phenomena through images, symbols, metaphors, archetypes, and reflection. The following chapter will explore somatic interventions, which have been drawn from a wealth of body work, emotional processing, and imaginal resources.

References

Beebe, B., and F. M. Lachmann. 2014. *The Origins of Attachment: Infant Research and Adult Treatment.* New York: Routledge.
Bohm, D. 2004. *On Dialogue.* Edited by L. Nichol. London: Routledge.

Jung, C. J. 1983. *The Essential Jung: Selected and Introduced by Anthony Storr.* Princeton: University Press.

Koch, C. (2004). *The Quest for Consciousness: A Neurobiological Approach.* Englewood: Roberts & Company.

Lanius, R., and P. Frewen. 2015. *Healing the Traumatized Self: Consciousness, Neuroscience, Treatment.* New York: Norton

Panksepp, J., and L. Biven. 2011. *The Archaeology of Mind: Neuroevolutionary Origins of Human Emotion.* New York: Norton.

Romesin, H. M., and G. Verden-Zöller. 2008. "Virtual Realities and the Nervous System." In *The Origin of Humanness in the Biology of Love,* edited by P. Bunnell, 190–194. Exeter: Imprint Academic.

Stern, D. B. 2010. *Partners in Thought: Working with Unformulated Experience, Dissociation, and Enactment.* New York: Routledge.

9 Somatic Interventions for Regulating Neural-Emotional States

"Whether we like it or not, one of our tasks on this earth is to work with the opposites through different levels of consciousness until body, soul and spirit resonate together."
(Woodman 1985, 26)

Subcortical-Based Change in the Brain

Somatic interventions include embodied affective experiences to stimulate and reorganize the deeply unconscious bodily-based subcortical parts of the brain—the invisible matrix for our fluctuating moods, thoughts, and behaviors. Subcortical interventions differentiate overcoupled circuits of trauma that interfere with an accurate perception of reality by inhibiting clarity of vision, hearing, and feeling. Differentiating fused brain circuits and their neural networks allows linkage, a natural process of growth and development, to utilize the most adaptive brain circuits and create new neural networks. Practitioners can initiate this differentiation by bringing sensory-based attention to the face-heart-brain circuit and inviting spontaneous movement to the voluntary facial muscles of perception and social communication, such as the eyes, ears, mouth, larynx, and pharynx.

Playful in nature, like the spontaneous "chatting" between parents and infants, subcortical interventions inquire into the wordless spaces, the areas of "unformulated" lived experience that are inaccessible to left-hemisphere-driven conversation, logic, and control. I have found these somatic interventions open the intersubjective field to coregulate implicit traumatic memories through entrainment. A physics concept, *entrainment* occurs in relationships when two oscillating systems couple together to create a shared tempo, where one slows down and the other speeds up to find a common meeting point. How does this translate to the intersubjective relationship?

Helping professionals draw the other into a rhythm and pace through empathically chosen interventions to down-regulate hyperarousal or up-regulate hypoarousal, so they can enter the optimal arousal zone of the ventral vagal circuit for present-moment social engagement. Unlike therapeutic tools, strategies, and techniques, somatic interventions effect change through a two-person entrainment, characterized by shared rhythm and intentional, voluntary choices for selecting attention and initiating movement.

Entrainment between client and therapist can occur because somatic interventions support the regulation of the autonomic nervous system—by strengthening the ventral vagal brain circuit and decreasing the activation of sympathetic arousal. The ventral vagal brain circuit, as you will recall, refers to the myelinated brain circuit of interconnection between the eyes, ears, facial muscles, neck, larynx, pharynx, heart, and lungs (Porges 2011). This myelinated vagal circuit is fast-acting, stimulating spontaneous connections that hold people in relationship as they encounter stress and adversity.

Subcortical Interventions and the Vestibular System

Just as each intersubjective relationship is distinct, different categories of trauma require diverse interventions. For example, in most cases, a single-incident overwhelming event, such as a car accident or fall, for an individual with a history of secure attachment, results in a temporary state of dysregulation. The residue of such an event can be resolved in a relatively short period of time with somatic interventions that restore thwarted defenses and reorganize the sensory-based vestibular system. However, complex trauma results in deeply ingrained patterns of neural reactivity and emotional disorders, underdeveloped connections between the subcortical structures of the brain and higher cortical structures, and presents with chronic states of hypoarousal, depression, dissociation, and powerlessness.

Hypoarousal can occur with an overstimulated vestibular system. Composed of interconnected chambers located in the temporal bones of the inner ear, this system organizes visual, auditory, and kinesthetic data from the inner world and the environment to create maps in the brain. Many vestibular system disorders are stimulated from perceptions of danger and life threat that may begin as prenatal injuries, develop through insecure and disorganized attachment, or from adverse life events such as falls, motor vehicle accidents, stress, fatigue, depression, anxiety, illness, strokes, assaults, accidents from sports, conflict and war, loud or frightening sounds, and other serious losses or intrusions. These injuries are biological, psychological, and spiritual, requiring bodily-based interventions and relational attention. How can helping professionals repair the overstimulated vestibular system and assist in the restoration of developmental growth?

First, it's important to discern the difference between hypoarousal versus hyperarousal. Lethargy, fatigue, a sense of being victimized, a withdrawal of eye gaze, flaccid facial muscles, an inability to hear emotional nuances in the voice of others, and dissociation all indicate chronic hypoarousal. States of hyperarousal, stimulated by perceptions of intense danger, include frenetic high energy, aggression, and rage visible in fixed-action patterns of facial tension, narrowing of the eyes, thrusting of the jaw, low frequency vocal tones, and physical bracing throughout the body, like a fighter about to enter the ring. The entire body prepares to fight or flee from the danger. However, in a relatively short period of time, hyperarousal can shift into hypoarousal and vice versa, confusing helping professionals.

When emotions are blocked in the lower right hemisphere, the left hemisphere may respond with hyperarousal. In other words, helping professionals may feel the hyperarousal of a person engaged in frenetic left-hemispheric activity, however, hypoarousal can hold the person's dys-regulated neurological system hostage to problem solving of the left. As I have said earlier, hypoarousal occurs when intense sympathetic arousal is interrupted by dorsal vagal immobility. Clinically, hypoaroused states gradually up-regulate with interventions that create a stable perception of safety and belonging in relationship with self, others, and the environment, including nature. When innate vitality has been crushed by traumatic experiences, therapeutic interactions awaken the innate life force.

Before choosing an intervention, it is important to discern whether a client's current neural state stems from a neuroception of danger that needs support for defenses or if it is a left-hemispheric reaction to the hypoarousal of the right hemisphere, where vitality needs to be welcomed back into one's life. This is a critical aspect that is often overlooked in many trauma treatments—helping professionals cannot help clients achieve long-term change unless they address the effect of immobilization with fear and the gentle return to social engagement through vitality affects. If hyperarousal continues despite relational safety over time, it is fair to wonder if there is real danger in the environment of the individual or if it is a response to the helpless, powerless inner world of hypoarousal. This is usually unconscious knowledge and will be revealed in an embodied intersubjective relationship.

In the context of a nurturing intersubjective relationship, regulation of the autonomic nervous system can be stimulated on a subcortical level with somatic empathic awareness of sensations and the initiation of micromovements of the face, neck, and body positions. When a destabilized vestibular system is involved in trauma, it is critical to maintain an optimal tempo and pace when using somatic interventions. Reorganization of the vestibular system can be subtly addressed in the ordinary modes of emotional communication including eye gaze, voice, and connection through gesture, touch, and subtle movements as the neuroceptions of safety, danger, and life threat shift.

The prosocial interventions in this book begin with orienting, an activity that brings awareness to movements of the face and neck while in direct contact with the present moment environment. Interventions that invite people to slowly surrender to the pull of gravity reduce the chaos of the vestibular system, allowing sensory-based data to organize. When the safety of a stable ground is embodied, people begin to regulate and become interested in relationship. When working with clients who suffer from both hyperarousal and hypoarousal, the first somatic intervention I often use focuses on the gravitational pull of the earth. A surrender to the pull of the earth, yielding into gravity, allows us to begin to feel and trust the support of the universe in our bodies.

A Series of Prosocial Somatic Interventions

Orienting to the Present Moment

Orienting interventions involve somatic attention to the felt sense, the eyes, ears, spine, and subtle body movements, increasing a person's ability to assess the current reality of perceptions of safety, danger, or life threat. These interventions are effective because they help trauma survivors begin to embody their sensory emotional experience and connect with the earth, the environment, and other people by noticing sensory activation in the present moment and engaging in playful, rhythmical micromovements to ease tension and contraction and awaken vitality.

Orienting to the Present Moment includes a series of interventions that can be done together, in small steps, or in a larger sequence, depending on a client's state of hypo- or hyperarousal. These interventions should be entered into by both client and therapist, in the playful, safe—but not too safe—context of the intersubjective field. When orienting with people that are emotionally hyperaroused, we can create activities that offer a calming, regulating rhythm; however, people experiencing hypoarousal need far slower orienting activities to mediate the intense effects of the perception of life threat. Porges (2009) confirms that calming hyperarousal originating from perceptions of danger is relatively easy compared to helping a person with hypoarousal to trust their own body and relate to empathic others.

Orienting interventions are powerful because they invite people out of rumination and analysis and into the somatic felt sense in the moment. However, it's important to keep in mind that a felt sense may be terrifying for a person experiencing hypoarousal. For example, I began working with a client named Jack who awoke to feelings of stark terror and immobility every day. Together, we practiced his ability to orient a little at a time to his little finger, an activity that brought awareness to the sensation. Feeling the immobility and making very small movements, we were able to thaw the sensations of frozenness, little by little, and over time Jack was able to gradually become embodied. Slow movement while orienting to the felt sense helped Jack to perceive and organize sensory stimulation in just the right rhythm in a particular moment. Orienting to present moment lived experience with another can break the unconscious trance of implicit traumatic memories and move people into a more complex consciousness where they can notice and regulate their current level of arousal. Coregulating by orienting to the present moment organizes the vestibular system to discern the difference between implicit memories of danger and threat and present-moment lived experience.

I suggest practicing these somatic interventions a number of times with colleagues or volunteers, to fine-tune your approach and to learn how to creatively adapt them to different relational moments in somatic therapy. Before beginning any somatic intervention, it is important to prepare for what each of you will each do, review why it might be helpful, and assure the other person that you will join in the activity and help make sense of the intervention.

Orienting to the Earth

In the beginning of a clinical session or a class, I often invite people with high anxiety (hyperaroused) and dissociation (hypoaroused) to enter into an intervention like Orienting to the Earth, where I invite them to notice the pull of gravity on their body. This safe sensation is usually felt through the feet, arms, hands, sitz bones, and shoulders and helps the body release tension. This simple practice of coregulation, in the context of a caring relationship, allows people to feel a sense safety and helps restore innate ways of knowing. Below is an example of how to lead the Orienting to the Earth intervention with a client. The process can be similarly applied to other interventions.

Martha, a successful financial advisor, was plagued with symptoms of hypoarousal in her relationships with her husband and children. The invitation for this intervention was issued halfway through a ninety-minute session, after we had already met four times. Martha had been describing her exhaustion and attempts to problem-solve her emotional issues, particularly her grief, with analytic strategies. Martha often dissociated in moments of grief, and I was interested in helping her access her strength to stay present with this intervention.

Sharon: Martha, I'm noticing how difficult the tiredness and fatigue is for you. I'm wondering if you would like to join with me in a short exercise to help restore your energy?

Martha: Sure, I keep trying to figure all this out and sometimes I want to give up. What do you want me to do?

I was concerned that Martha would drop into hypoarousal, so I suggested that she choose whether she would like to sit up or recline in the chair. By offering a choice, I engaged her empowerment in this intervention.

Sharon: Martha, I wonder if we could begin by just noticing our bodies . . . sensing where your body makes contact with the chair, and noticing the places where the contact is not there.

Martha: I never thought about contact with the chair. It feels supportive, maybe I could take this chair home.

Sharon: What you can take home is a different awareness of the pull of gravity on your body. The contact with the chair helps you feel it. *(A moment of silence as Martha and I internally explored the sensations of gravity.)* I'm wondering if you could direct your attention to the earth and its pull of gravity.

Martha: You mean bring my mind to the earth?

Sharon: Yes, that's right, and I will do this with you. *(Another moment of silence.)* As you bring your mind to the space below this room, I'm wondering what you sense in your body?

Here I linked Martha's attention to present moment sensations in her own body, using her own words to encourage embodiment.

Martha: *(Silent for a while)* I feel a lot of buzzing in my body and I'm starting to relax. It feels good.

This marked a shift into embodiment, with a neural state of optimal arousal.

Sharon: As you notice this relaxation, take some time to enjoy how it feels when we sense it together.

The goal here was to lower sympathetic arousal and concurrently strengthen Martha's vagal brake in the intersubjective field.

Sharon: *(After a few moments of silence)* I'm wondering, Martha, if we could bring our attention back to the earth, perhaps look down into it.

The goal of this suggestion was to help strengthen the rhythm of oscillation and the ventral vagal system of social engagement. If someone with hypoarousal stays too long in bodily-based awareness, arousal can suddenly occur. I introduced the rhythm of oscillation to deepen embodiment of gravity. When I observed that Martha's breath had deepened and had become rhythmical—an indicator of heart-rate variability that strengthens the vagal state—I continued.

Sharon: I'm wondering if you could shift your attention from the earth to the sensations on your skin right now.

Martha: My skin is tingly.

It's important to note that the sensation of tingly skin can be very disturbing when frightened.

Sharon: Let's take time to notice that tingling sensation on the skin for a while and see what might happen.

After spending a little more time in the ventral vagal state, I wanted to replace her habit of analyzing with the curiosity of a somatic inquiry.

Sharon: I'm wondering if you could bring your attention back to the earth and just notice whatever you might imagine?
Martha: I can see the way the earth goes down into the core.

Here Martha's embodied imagination kicked in and higher cortical processes began to fire—telling me it was possible to engage her somatic observing witness in a more expansive awareness.

Sharon: As you notice the earth beneath us, I'm wondering if you would like to bring your attention to the tissue under your skin?

Martha's breath became deeper and more rhythmical indicating the intervention was linking our bodies to each other and the earth. After a few moments, I oscillated the focus.

Sharon: Now, I'm wondering if you might want to bring your awareness as deep into the earth as you would like.

Again, I infused the intervention with consciousness and choice.

Martha: I feel really plastered to the chair with gravity.

Martha described the neural state where immobility was differentiating from its fusion with fear.

Sharon: Thanks for letting me know how gravity feels right now. This can really help us restore energy as we continue.
Martha: Ok . . . I've needed this for a long time.

Martha is enjoying the drop into immobility—a bliss state when uncoupled from fear.

Sharon: As you notice your own body, notice your muscles in your legs and arms and then notice the depth of the earth and gravity, and after a few minutes move your attention back to your muscles and notice how they are connected to gravity.

Here I linked the pleasurable sensations in the body with a sense of feeling "really plastered to the chair," a surrender to the immobility response that releases the fusion of fear with immobility.

Sharon: As you feel gravity, notice the heaviness of your bones and the nerves and fluid that runs through them.

We were both in a meditative state, allowing intuition to guide the dorsal vagal immobility system to release its chronic holding of fear. Martha goes on to describe the feeling of immobility being differentiated from fear.

Martha: I feel really heavy.
Sharon: Martha, take as long as you like to enjoy this feeling of heaviness.

When fear is differentiated from immobility, it is important to rest for a while so that the natural sources of vitality and life force can return. Below you will see Martha reorienting after enjoying the descent into sensation, oscillation, imagery, and dorsal vagal immobility separating from fear.

Martha: *(After a silence of about three minutes, she began to sit up)* Wow, I came in exhausted and I feel more relaxed and hopeful. How long did that take?
Sharon: Well, from start to finish, it has been nine minutes.
Martha: Wow, it felt like an hour or so. I could do that in my office before I go home at night and I bet I could cope better with the chaos.

Following this somatic intervention we each reflected on our own vivid moments in the meditation and the changes in our intersubjective field. As we did so, Martha expressed a new hope that she could help herself and her family when they were overwhelmed, a hope that reflected a shift out of immobility with fear into more social engagement.

Interventions of the Face and Body

Subcortical somatic interventions of the face, eyes, and ears include invitations to touch the face, especially when a person is experiencing a visceral gut level numbness or distress. I will also invite people gripped by visceral distress to communicate the pain to me through nonverbal expressions of the face. With a "still face"—immobilized muscles of the face—I will invite animation of those muscles with interventions of lifting the eyebrows, allowing gravity to pull the lower jaw down slowly, opening and closing the mouth. Sometimes, the invitation to physically touch their own face and sense with their hands the skin, muscles, and bones helps to make contact with dissociated emotions. Once someone has begun to embody the face, we can invite somatic interventions with subtle eye movement, vocalizations, and facial movements.

Orienting to Present Moment with the Eyes

The muscles that control the movement of the eye are the most fast-acting in the body, as quick as 1/100 of second, in their effort to organize images that come in with light. Somatic interventions of the eye invite a person *to look* more closely. When conscious of perception, patterns of volitional consciousness replace unconscious fixed-action patterns. When interrupted, the fixed-action patterns spontaneously release the energy from the trauma in the form of vibration, pulsation, shaking, heat, movements up and down the central core or spine, and other spontaneous internal sensations. When people are unfamiliar with the natural releases from trauma, they may need assistance to guide this energy to the ground by oscillating attention between the feet, sitz bones, and eyes, similar to the way that I helped Martha surrender to the sensations of her own body through the support of gravity.

This particular intervention helps to restore embodiment in the present moment and fluidity in the muscles of the eyes. It also serves to deepen the intersubjective connection. The following script can guide you through the process, but adapt it to fit your needs.

Therapist: I'm wondering if we can take a few minutes to orient to this room.

Your tone of voice should clearly offer an invitation that can be refused.

Therapist: Orienting in the present moment can help us shift the effects of trauma on our bodies.

A brief explanation of the intervention can open interest in mechanisms of change. Notice the emphasis on joining together—rather than commanding the other to do something, an approach that fosters a sense of safety and empowerment.

Therapist: Together, let's turn our heads very slowly to the right, then back to center. As you turn your head, allow your ears to lead, and slowly move your eyes, jaw, neck, and shoulders at the same time. Allow your eyes to softly gaze at the environment.

Describing the activity allows people to prepare in their imagination.

Therapist: When you come to a place on the right where you begin to feel some strain, stop and rest. Slowly we will bring our ears, eyes, jaw, head, and shoulders back to the center. As we come back to the center, let's take a moment to check in with each other.

In this moment of checking in, observe the mutual eye gaze. I like to repeat this exercise three times. As you make eye contact with each other following each segment, allow your eye gaze to meet with the other at an optimal level of arousal—taking care not to intrude nor avoid. Allow yourself to feel the sensations that arise in the intersubjective field as gaze is explored.

At this time, you might continue by exploring the opportunity for somatic dialogue and further somatic inquiry—something like, "I'm interested in what you might notice as you explore this movement." When and if both of you are ready, continue the same exercise on the left side, observe the mutual eye gaze, and create space for a phenomenological somatic dialogue.

Next, as you prepare to continue the exercise on the right side again, add more focus to eye gaze, a step that encourages the choice to look at details and strengthen somatic awareness.

Therapist: As we slowly orient again to the right, I would like to invite you to notice the quality of light as you look at the space around you. Notice where there is more brightness, shadow, darkness. You might want to take your time and be curious about how your body responds to light and to darkness. When you come to the edge of strain, we can rest and then slowly come back together.

This time, when you gaze at each other, notice if there are any shifts. Simply note the shift, feel the effect of it on you, and adapt as you go.

Therapist: Now we are going to explore the left again, paying attention to light, shadow, darkness, and your own inner reaction. When we come to a place of strain, we can rest again, then slowly bring our ears, eyes, jaw, neck, head, and shoulders back to the center.

When you come back to center, take time to connect in ways that are congruent for the relationship in the moment. You might inquire, "I'm wondering if you would like to take a few moments to simply close your eyes and rest. I will be here with you." After focused attention on a change mechanism, rest allows the neural system time to reorganize on its own. As the person rests, you might notice any activity in the eyes, spontaneous blinking or other movement that indicates neural activity. When you are both ready, continue:

Therapist: I'm wondering what it might be like if we smiled to our eyes, bringing care and gratitude to any tension you might feel.

This invitation introduces the choice of self-compassion through somatic awareness and awakens ventral vagal innervation of facial muscles.

I usually wait for the person to spontaneously open his eyes and indicate he is ready to move on. A reflective inquiry helps to close the exercise.

Therapist: I'm wondering what parts of this exercise seemed interesting or intriguing for you.

A somatic reflection on the lived experience follows.

Therapist: What did you notice during this exercise? Were there any intriguing sensations on the right or the left as we looked at each other? What did you notice as we rested?

Continue to follow the phenomena that emerge from the subjective experience in a somatic dialogue that strengthens the intersubjective field.

Stretching the Muscles of the Eyes

This exercise encourages fluid movement of the eyes through a conscious, contracted focus on a small, specific detail and then expansion of the eye muscles with a focus on the periphery. The goal is to bring awareness to the sensations in the eyes by paying attention to the polarities of the neural states of hypervigilance or hypovigilance. The following script can guide you through the process, but you can adapt it to fit your needs.

Therapist: Take a few moments to close your eyes, rest, and when things feel settled, slowly let light into your eyes.

Allow the other to voluntarily open his eyes before you move on.

Therapist: As you open your eyes, select a point or object in the center of your vision and focus on a very small part of what your see. Notice the current sensations in your body.

This moves the eye muscles into a contraction that may be uncomfortable.

Therapist: Let's let the contraction of the eyes release, and slowly allow your vision to expand out in a circle to the periphery of what we can see without moving your head and hold your gaze for a few moments. As you do this, notice any sensations in your body.

Oscillate this contraction and expansion three times.

Therapist: Take a few moments to rest and open your eyes when they feel settled.

Nonverbally invite eye gaze with your client, and when you feel connected, invite a somatic inquiry with questions such as, "I'm wondering what you notice now in your body?" or "What was intriguing in that activity?" or "Has anything shifted or stayed the same in this exercise?" Bringing interest and curiosity to the felt sense of the experience helps people stay focused and resist judgment. You might continue with questions that explore emotional patterns: "What was difficult?" and "What felt easy?"

Coordinating the Inner and Outer Eye

Once rhythm has begun to return to the muscles in the eyes, they are more able to stimulate neural connectivity and form spontaneous images in the higher cortical levels of the brain. Linking subcortical bodily-based sensations with the higher cortical process of images is the critical work of trauma therapy (Kalsched 2013). As we link the environment with our perceptions, we are developing coherence in the processing systems of the right hemisphere of the brain. The following script can guide you through the process of this intervention, but you can adapt it to fit your needs.

Therapist: I'm wondering if you like to explore an exercise in creativity?

With agreement and interest, begin describing the exercise, explaining that trauma often causes people to disconnect their sensory experience from the creative images of the mind.

Therapist: Take a few moments to close your eyes and rest, and when you feel ready open your eyes and we will begin.

When the person opens her eyes, enjoy mutual eye gaze until you can see she is ready to move on.

Therapist: Let's begin by simply noticing what we see, as we gaze into the space in front of us. When you have a sense of what you see, close your eyes, rest, and replicate the scene in your inner vision. I will do this with you.

I demonstrate by looking to the side, usually out the window and observing the environment and then closing my eyes.

Therapist: Take your time. Then we will open our eyes and compare the image in your inner world with the scene in front of you. Take time to let the details in, and when you are ready, close your eyes again and replicate the scene in your inner vision again.

If the person is regulated, continue with a third oscillation of the inner and outer ability to form image. In this exercise, we are developing the art of active seeing and moving away from perceptual fixed-action patterns. The gradual increase of mindfulness in the habits of seeing are critical to the dissipation of the fixed-action patterns of the trauma. When finished, engage in a somatic inquiry, dialogue, and reflection on the experience, asking questions like "What do you notice now in your body?" "What happened for you in the exercise?" "What was difficult?" "What was easy?" "What seemed to be intriguing in the exercise?"

Massaging the Eyes

Particular energetic symbols, such as the infinity sign with the figure 8 on its side, a spiral, a fern, or a tree branch can be valuable in supporting the reorganization of dysregulated neural-emotional states. In this intervention, helping professionals trace a circle in the air around each eye. This somatic intervention is best offered when there is considerable trust in the intersubjective field and memories from trauma can be incorporated into the optimal arousal zone. The following script can guide you through this intervention, but you can adapt it to fit your needs.

Therapist: I've noticed that we seem to loop around this issue over and over. I'm wondering if we might take a few moments to see if this pattern might need a little more support for healing? As you probably know, the eyes connect directly with the brain, and sometimes the muscles in the eyes hold on to traumatic memories and need an inner massage to release. I will invite you to watch my finger as it moves and then notice any sensations, emotions, images, or thoughts.

With consent and interest from the other, begin very slowly from the center to draw with your index finger, from about eighteen inches away, an imaginary circle around each eye, using the template of a figure eight on its side. When you return to the center of the figure eight, invite the person to close his eyes and notice any sensations, emotions, images, or thoughts. Do one oscillation at a time, waiting to see how fixed-action patterns in the eye muscles are formed and if they release energy. Watch for little jerks or changes in the iris, whites of the eyes, or pupils. Take time to dialogue and process any responses, embodying the unresolved bits of trauma that might emerge. Once the residue from the fixed-action pattern is fully embodied, you may want to continue with more oscillations. Exercise 9.1: Directed Eye Movements for Integration of Opposites focuses on stimulating the integration of polarities. See page 209 of the appendix.

Spiraling around the Body

This somatic intervention utilizes the spiral to reorganize energy in a down-regulating movement. It is usually introduced midsession when a client is experiencing hyperarousal from the release of fixed-action patterns. However, it can also be used to up-regulate hypoaroused states. The following script can guide you through the process of this intervention, but you can adapt it to fit your needs. First, we'll begin with using the spiral to down-regulate hyperarousal.

Therapist: I'm aware there is a lot of energy rushing up to your chest [or head]. I'm wondering if you might want to use the image of a spiral to help it move down into the ground? *(If there is interest, continue.)* If you imagine a spiral wrapping around your body, it may be helpful to contain this energy and move it in any direction you choose. Slowly moving your torso in a spiral energy can help the intensity to move from chaos into order and direction.

As a facilitator, I like to imagine a spiral around my body and the body of the other, gently and subtly moving my torso in a spiral toward the earth.

Therapist: As you notice the release of energy in your body, with this heat and shaking, I'm wondering if you can imagine a spiral forming around your body to take this energy back down to the earth.

To up-regulate hypoarousal, you might invite the person to participate in the following way.

Therapist: When you ponder the feeling of sadness and the sense of relief that this suffering is now over, I'm wondering if it would be helpful to imagine a spiral lifting you up. When you notice this energy moving up through your body, I'm wondering if you can sense how it could then move into your heart and your eyes.

The muscles around the eyes help us to fluidly gaze at one another and express our deepest emotions (Porges 2009). However, the eyes of someone experiencing hyperarousal can be very tiring to hold in contact because they are probing, appear tight and constricted, and may dart around in hypervigilance. Exercise 9.2: Oscillating Eye Movements to Deepen the Intersubjective Field is an exercise that will help you hold a person's eye gaze with fluidity, without locking into the hypervigalence of the other—a skill that is essential in down-regulating hyperarousal. See page 210 of the appendix.

Interventions of the Voice and Ears

The temporal regions of the right hemisphere of the adult brain are highly sensitive to emotional prosody in social communication (Grossman et. al, 2010). Prosody is the rhythmical language of sound and vocalizations that communicate emotion. Porges and Furman (2010) found that the way we react to specific sounds and frequencies is determined by neural circuits that detect safety, danger, and life threat. Low frequencies are associated with danger while higher frequencies elicit empathy. Specific frequencies elicit adaptive physiological and emotional states. People who have experienced trauma may no longer be able detect some frequencies due to the muscular fixed-action patterns of the small voluntary muscles in the ear (Porges and Furman 2010). Allan Schore referred to this phenomena as "sound blindness" (personal communication). Stimulation of the fixed-action patterns of the ears allows for restoration of fluidity and tone in muscles of the ear and ventral vagal circuit, releasing the chronic effects of trauma and facilitating reconsolidation of unresolved emotions.

Clinically, I have found somatic interventions based on communicative musicality, prosody, sounds, poetry, vocalizations, and Tomatis-based listening strategies valuable in strengthening the vagal brake and opening authentic emotional communication between people. For those suffering from complex trauma, I often use voice and hearing interventions before working with the eyes, especially if the trauma came in through the ears rather than through vision. Direct work with eye gaze may be overstimulating for people who have experienced life threat from other human beings while subtle interventions associated with the voice, hearing, and listening opens up vitality and life force for people experiencing hypoarousal.

To successfully use these interventions, helping professionals must be sensitive to the sound of their own voice as an instrument of prosody, rhythm, tone, and cadence. Singing, playing a wind instrument, toning, and chanting can shift patterns of inhalation and exhalation to enhance prosody. When we inhale in short intakes followed by an extended exhalation, the mylinated vagus is enhanced and heart rate decreases (Porges and Furman 2010). The following vocalizations can assist by using the short inhalation and extended exhalation to carry the sound.

Developing Prosody in the Voice

A somatic intervention for prosody in the voice is to read your favorite poetry or prose aloud and invite images to spontaneously form. As you read, take time to feel the authentic emotions of your gut and heart and express those feelings in your voice. To practice, you can record your voice and listen to how your own body reacts as you listen. Singing, chanting, and humming can also stimulate prosody and strengthen the vagal brake. Pat Cook, PhD, director of the Open Ear Center, describes how the ears and the voice work in a coordinated way, where we cannot make the sounds we cannot hear (personal communication). Sounds with a wide variety of frequencies open the fixed-action patterns of the ventral vagal brain circuit.

Toning Vowels

Toning can be a valuable intervention for releasing "stuck" trauma, particularly intense emotions in the viscera. I was conducting a somatic inquiry with a client who felt her emotions stuck in her throat. When I asked Anne if she could tell me the sound that seemed connected to this sensation in her throat, she spontaneously said "ahhh." I asked if I could join her, as together we toned the sound "ahhhhhhhhhh." Between toning, we each inhaled slowly, then resumed our toning with the longer outbreath. The entrainment was immediate, and I could feel in my body how the vibration was moving in her body. After a few minutes of toning together, I invited Anne to rest and observe what she might notice in her body. As she settled, I noticed her face was softer, the lump in her throat seemed smooth, and her hands rested in her lap in a mudra position of holding. I asked Anne what she was holding and she described it as a "blue energy" that was coming out of her palms. I then suggested she place her hands on her jaw and simply notice what was happening. In a few minutes, Anne's chronically held jaw softened and her facial muscles relaxed into a soft, warm youthful expression. For the rest of the session, Anne and I co-regulated the "inner movement of her tissues" into a softening of the fascia of her muscles and viscera.

When engaging in toning, it's important to note that sounds have different frequencies ranging from high to low. It's best to begin with high frequencies, such as toning the sound of *aaaaa*, then *iiiii*, *ooooo*, *uuuuu* together, engaging the ventral vagal circuits and slowly move to lower frequencies that access the dorsal vagal circuit in the abdomen.

Toning Consonants

Very low frequencies of some consonant sounds such as *vooo* can stimulate fixed-action patterns that were formed in moments of life threat, but may be difficult to integrate immediately. Experiment with other less threatening consonant sounds such as *oooommm*, *ggggrrrrr*, and *rrrrrroooaaar* to elicit vibration in different parts of the viscera and dissolve fixed-action patterns in the larynx, pharynx, and ears.

Interventions of the Felt Sense with Gesture and Touch

Gestures express unconscious bodily states and are early forms of language (Ramachandran and Blakeslee 2009). These signals communicate bodily-based experience. As somatic practitioners notice the subtle gestures of hands, feet, legs, face, neck, and other parts of the body, and read these cues; they can bring the unconscious communication into the intersubjective field. For example, perhaps you are in the midst of a somatic inquiry and have asked the other what he notices in his body in this moment. His response may include an unconscious gesture with his hand indicating a fast-moving spiral in his guts. At this moment you might suggest a gentle somatic intervention to work with the spiral. For example, you might both move your hands in the same gesture at a speed that feels just right. The entrainment between your bodies helps support the sensations of this gesture. Almost any gesture can be explored in the intersubjective field and brought into conscious volition, intervening with the autonomic response in the body.

Other gestural interventions bring attention to the spontaneous movement of arms, legs, and feet. As you notice unconscious movements in the arms and legs, you might wonder about the intention of that part of the body and form a somatic inquiry, asking, "I'm wondering what your legs would like to do in this moment?" The intervention would follow contingently on the client's response. If there was a response that the legs wanted to run, you might suggest, "Perhaps, you could imagine running and we could simulate it with micromovements of our legs and feet?" Exercise 9.3: Balancing on an Exercise Ball utilizes micromovements. See page 210 of the appendix.

Subtle, unconscious intentional gestures in the shoulders, arms, and hands may communicate a need for boundaries and protection or reaching out for connection. For example, you might ask, "When you raise your hand, I'm wondering what your hand would like to do?" Gestures that describe the need for boundaries can be subtle, but highly potent in their ability to express the need for safety, integrity, and autonomy. They can look like a hand rising up, a fist to protect and defend, or a withdrawal movement of the face, neck, or spine. The fixed-action patterns of these gestures may reveal intense energies that can then be incorporated into the intersubjective field. For children with insecure and disorganized attachment, unconscious gestures of reaching out may have been thwarted, however, an alert somatic practitioner may see the fixed-action pattern that is interfering with the intention to reach out to another—a small jerk of the shoulder, a brief movement of the arm or hand, or a subtle leaning forward. Relationally attuned clinicians might respond by contingently reaching out with their own hands and arms in a subtle gesture to the other, or perhaps, with permission, moving their chair a bit closer.

Touch, an emotional form of communication, can be physical, emotional, mental, and spiritual. Early relational trauma usually includes a deprivation of nurturing touch from caregivers. People suffering from trauma have widely divergent reactions to giving and receiving touch. I have observed that people who have been systematically oppressed and traditionally have held a subordinate role may crave the touch they have never felt, yet dissociate to comply with available forms of touch. This conflict is usually unconscious and can lead to destructive power differentials and abusive encounters for men and women. Professional helpers hold the fiduciary trust and responsibility and must be clear about when, how, and where they touch another, watching for subtle cues of craving touch, compliance, dissociation, and emotional transference. Gestures of holding and embracing can be supported with pillows, stuffed animals, and blankets. For example, one of my clients loves to have me wrap her tightly in a large blanket, move my chair close and maintain physical contact through her feet and knees. When in this position, she is able to coregulate and maintain social engagement as we process her lived experience of stress and memories of childhood adversity.

It is important for professional helpers to remember when they ask a person to engage in a subcortical somatic intervention, the request may be felt as a "fix-it" power-over technique that can cause a breach in a developing relationship, adding to the client's burden of shame. Shame holds our crushed vitality, formed in moments of aliveness and a concurrent breach in relationship. Healing from shame begins with embodied intersubjective relationships that regulate and empower people, restoring the depleted vitality and opening the person to the imaginal and reflective processes of integration.

References

Grossmann, T., R. Oberecker, S. P. Koch, and A. D. Friederici. 2010. "The Developmental Origins of Voice Processing in the Human Brain." *Neuron* 65, 852–858.

Kalsched, D. 2013. *Trauma and the Soul: A Psycho-spiritual Approach to Human Development and Its Interruption.* London: Routledge.

Porges, S.W. 2009. "Music Therapy & Trauma: Insights from the Polyvagal Theory." In *Music Therapy & Trauma: Bridging Theory and Clinical Practice*, edited by K. Stewart. New York: Satchnote Press.

Porges, S.W. 2011. *The Polyvagal Theory: Neurophysiological Foundations of Emotions, Attachment, Communication, and Self-Regulation.* New York: Norton.

Porges, S.W., and S.A. Furman. 2010. "The Early Development of the Autonomic Nervous System Provides a Neural Platform for Social Behavior: A Polyvagal Perspective." *Infant and Child Development* 20(1): 106–118.

Ramachandran, V. S., and S. Blakeslee. 2009. *Phantoms in the Brain: Probing the Mysteries of the Human Mind.* New York: HarperCollins.

Woodman, M. 1985. *The Pregnant Virgin: A Process of Psychological Transformation.* Toronto: Inner City Books.

10 Somatic Interventions with Imagination and Dreams

"I saw the angel in the marble and carved until I set him free."

(Michelangelo)

Healing Trauma through Imagination

The human imagination has the power to bridge the gaps between people and between the body and the mind by integrating the unconscious, lived experience of the past and present, releasing tension from unknown fears and offering new perceptions of the future. When people can imagine a future that emerges from bodily-based integration, they can break the tyranny of trauma and awaken to a more dynamic sense of connection with the world. Through day and night dreams, the imagination reveals fear-filled dissociative experiences as well as moments of vitality and protection that, in the absence of relational support, helps people survive trauma (Kalsched 2013). Dreams clarify our subjective participation in life and support the realization that we each have our own lives to live in the context of our relationships. When we embody perceptions from images and dreams, we can detect the emergence of the unknown future that is already in progress.

In times of trauma, adversity, or loss, dream states provide embodied imaginal perceptions that reveal previously invisible knowledge, assisting people in coming to terms with life change. Embodied imaginal perceptions are transitory glimpses moving through the mind and body that remain unconscious and vague, yet when attended to, offer intrinsic meaning of the past and openings to a new future. As embodied imaginal perceptions accumulate, people can experience radical shifts in perspective, leading to change and transformation. These changes occur in the right hemisphere of the brain and are then available for left-hemispheric ways of knowing. Traditionally, many therapists immediately interpret imaginal experiences for meaning, as soon as they emerge. However, by bracketing the interpretation, and entering into a phenomenological somatic inquiry with the dreamer, imaginal experiences can be invited, amplified, differentiated, oscillated, and woven into more complex ways of knowing.

Embodied Imaginal Perceptions

Imagination functions on a higher cortical level than sensation, movement, and emotion, offering an organizing symbolic mode of discerning the truth of lived experience. Imagination rises to consciousness from sensory-based awareness, yet this natural emergence can be interrupted by the perception that one's life is endangered or threatened. With trauma, the flow of information from somatic awareness to creative imagination is overtaken by the urgency of survival, resulting in distortions of the imagination, such as illusions, hallucinations, and fantasies spawned in dissociation. Trauma can hijack subcortical neural states that feed the imagination, resulting in distorted perceptions of reality.

Hecht (2014) reminds us that when the emotions of the right hemisphere are blocked, a primary symptom of aversive events and relational-developmental trauma, the left hemisphere tends to adapt with goals toward personal power rather than affiliation, a dynamic clinicians see in people experiencing avoidance and disorganized attachment. An alternative reaction to blocked intense emotions is over-dependency, a factor in ambivalent attachment, creating a breach in the development of personal autonomy and mutual relationships. With a power motive, the imagination strategizes, organizes, and rationalizes advantages in relationships. With the goal of dependency, the imagination fantasizes about others saving, protecting, and defending, rather than risking the messy development of autonomy and interdependence in community. In either case, vitality in the body is diminished, depressed, and, at times, immobilized following traumatic experiences to unconsciously avoid past intense sensations and emotions (Porges 2011).

This vitality "hidden in plain view" (D. N. Stern 2010) can be awakened with embodied imaginal perceptions—visual, auditory, and kinesthetic representations that appear in states of right-hemispheric processing through intuitive images and dreams. These symbols represent unconscious lived experience and synthesize bodily-based sensations with higher cortical ways of knowing. When brought into consciousness in intersubjective relationship, embodied imaginal perceptions provide fresh, holistic ways of perceiving reality and empower people to navigate the intense frozen emotions through differentiation of immobility and fear. For example, recall Jack, the client from Chapter 9 who awoke to feelings of terror and immobility every morning. One day, as we were attending to the sensations of depression that followed his divorce, he noticed a spontaneous image of a hummingbird moving above a garden he had shared with his former wife. As we inquired into the imaginal perception of the hummingbird and garden, Jack recalled the grace and fruitful life the couple had once enjoyed. Embodiment of the vibration of the hummingbird and the peaceful abundance of the garden allowed Jack to, first, delight in sensory awareness as he internalized the garden and the vibration of the bird and as he came alive within, opening spontaneously to his authentic sadness. Genuine sorrow, from the loss of love, is clarified with embodiment revealing the "hidden" vitality that restores the ability to love again. Jack became aware of the true, vibrant feeling of love in his past relationship—a contrast to the current numbness of his depression.

The initial embodiment of his images were stimulated by my curiosity: "Jack, I am wondering what you notice in your body when we hold the image of the hummingbird and garden." The phrasing of the question, "I am wondering . . ." invites another to share imaginal experience. It does not direct the other but suggests wonder about the body in this new experience—a more respectful approach than directives. As we felt the vibrations around his heart, Jack described how his chest expanded for the first time in months and he felt lighter and more hopeful. Following these shared embodied imaginal perceptions, Jack and I discovered more energy and vitality in our relationship, which over time, was transferred into his current relationships.

When working with embodied imaginal perceptions, it's important to remember that implicit memories of the right hemisphere are not bound to actual events; they reflect the way unconscious memory systems cobble together a story to serve current needs. Skillful changes to the implicit memory with life-enhancing embodied imaginal perceptions allows the trauma to reconsolidate in the optimal arousal zone. Survival in times of war or oppression may require high intensity fear-based perceptions and images while life in a caring, relationally based community needs vitality-based embodied imaginal perceptions that weave connections between bodies, brains, and spirits. How can we discern the difference between prosocial imaginal perceptions and survival-based images?

When we embody an imaginal perception, we learn its motive by noticing the effect it has on the body. Healthy imaginal perceptions bring us closer to mutual relationships while destructive imaginal perceptions separate us. From the perspective of the polyvagal nervous system, embodied imaginal perceptions can strengthen the ventral vagal system of mutual social engagement and put the vagal brake on chronic sympathetic arousal from fear and anger (Porges 2011). When the imagination is freed from fear, prosocial, symbolic, and embodied imaginal perceptions can be recalled and amplified to guide regulation and healing for individuals as well as communities. For example, I had an unusual dream while I was teaching First Nations people to remember the somatic ways to heal trauma. In the first part of my dream, my daughter was lonely, pregnant, emaciated, and dying, while in the second part of the dream my daughter was in a nurturing community, pregnant and blooming with life while I cried milky tears of gratitude. The next morning, an elder asked me to share my dream with the group. I had given them no clue that I had had a dream the night before, however, the elder insisted that the community already knew I had dreamed. It was *their* dream and they needed me to tell it to them. The group had prepared beaded deerskin booties filled with eagle down to give to me to celebrate the new life we shared. Our dreams and the creative embodied imagination can serve as a portal to wisdom for others as well as for ourselves.

Archetypes and the Embodied Imagination

Embodied dreams and other imaginal perceptions can weave together physical, emotional, mental, and spiritual experience, providing a way through traumatic events and changing distortions of perception. For example, the embodied imagination in dreams activates the unconscious mind to mend the wounds of grief, loss, and trauma by providing unusual and surprising images, such as tears of milk. How does this happen? In dreams, hidden distortions from trauma take the form of unique yet familiar environments, startling dream figures and mysterious events—*waking up* the dissociated affect of traumatic experiences. Even when frightening, these apparitions may open unrecognized spiritual energies that lead to wholeness. For example, people become wise animals, homes expand with new rooms, the deceased visit, glimpses of wildness occur, and lost loves return to assure us all is well. The inner world of dreams is a parallel stream of consciousness to the fixity of trauma that can awaken vitality, creativity, and healing. When explored in a somatic intersubjective field, dreams provide a context for gradually incorporating the dissociated affect from trauma into the body—the synthesis of unbearable anguish and innate vitality, restoring neurological and emotional regulation.

When adverse experiences have severed the healthy imagination from the body, a survival strategy, the imagination can become a source of further trauma. Kalsched (2013) speaks about archetypes of destruction and creation in dream states. When trauma occurs, archetypes of destruction can replace imaginal archetypes of creation. Archetypal images have a quality of universal experience and those of destruction may emerge in dreams as volcanoes, Satan, hurricanes, tsunamis, and other massive and uncontrollable phenomena, while archetypes of creation can include creative phenomena from the natural world and divine feminine and masculine entities, including Mary, Quan Yin, Yahweh, Christ, and other loving entities. According to Robert Bosnak (2007), the imagination in dreams requires a body and the images that emerge have their own intelligence and mind. Bosnak believes that embodied images in dreams are self-organizing divine beings. In a similar psychodynamic tradition Robert Sardello (2008) claims that the act of sensing opens awareness of the body and imagination as an expression of love. Archetypes in this sense are represented as Sophia for Sardello, the imagined expression of divine love known through compassion and wisdom. Seeing the body, soul, spirit, and world as one sacred interwoven dynamic of love leads us into a sense of the imagination as that which forges interconnection. In this view, the heart is not just a pump but an organ that senses and synthesizes opposing sensations of inner conflict, a psychodynamic theory that reflects Porges's (2011) view of the social engagement neural system and vagal brake as the result of optimal heart rate variability and respiratory sinus arrhythmia.

The embodied imagination is grounded in bodily-based sensations, movements, and primitive emotions, offering a constructive way to represent both intense anguishing affect and the vitality of the life force. Once chaotic, subcortical affective dynamics from trauma are reorganized, people can integrate the incoming sensory data of the body with the embodied imagination revealing the meaning of lived experience. Using somatic awareness to bring selective attention to one's sensations, movements, and primitive emotions stimulates images that express this data in more complex and meaningful forms. Often, these images come from the natural world as well as the underlying organic forms found in nature. Symbols of the natural world remind us of our own physiologically based lives, such as the tree of life depicted in many cultures, the feminine images of maternal love, the stability of a mountain, the vast spaciousness of the sky, the power of the ocean, the solidity and fluidity of a stone, the fierceness of a bat, and the gentle wildness of a deer.

Organizing Symbols in the Natural World

The natural world offers animated symbols that can transform chaotic affective experience into vitality-based forms that reorganize one's inner world. As we discussed earlier, a fundamental energetic form in nature is the circle and spiral, an ancient organizing structure of the body-mind. Another organizing energy, the infinity symbol, integrates opposing polarities. A third, more complex symbol, is a parabola, an arch that comes with a thrown object that then returns to the starting place. A parabola represents a journey where the direction is transformed and the seeker returns home (Parabola 2014). These symbols and many others can organize the chaotic energy of trauma into natural evolving states of integration and new complexity. The parabola is a particularly appropriate symbol for the transformation of trauma, a returning home to the embodied self. Each of these more abstract symbols guide us in natural ways of change and transformation.

Observing and participating in the images of nature remind us of our own ecological needs for relationship. Dreams contain images of the natural world that can be incorporated for healing trauma: mammals such as horses, deer, bears, or dogs offer guidance, connectivity, and relational support. Rocks, water, light, vegetation, stars, the sun, and the quality of the air offer continuity and connection with the universe, affirming a sense of safety, connection and belonging. More abstract, archetypal symbols of connection and love such as the heart, a circle, a cross, or an extended hand are universal energies that can be incorporated into the body with profound meaning. Attention to the archetypal symbols that emerge in the imagination move us beyond the isolation of trauma into an expanded perception of interconnection with the fabric of mutual existence.

To embody the imagination and to fully incorporate healing images and symbols from nature into consciousness, one must first bracket the logical mind's compulsive attempts to interpret, analyze, and problem solve and then enter into the mystery of the inner world with curiosity, interest, and wonder. *We need to differentiate embodied imagination from disembodied imagination and relink the sensory-based imagination with the felt sense of self.* The disembodied imagination, often based on dissociated neural-emotional states, gives rise to distorted fantasy, grandiosity, addiction, and obsessive fears and thoughts. When we are embodied, the imagination naturally arises from sensory motor experience. Products of the disembodied and distorted imagination can fuel illness and breaches in relationship.

Dangers of a Disembodied Imagination—Case 10.1: Stephen

A disembodied, frightening imagination reflects the split of trauma, the disconnection between the subcortical and the higher cortical structures of the brain. With this split, the truth of lived experience is amiss and a person becomes ensnared in a survival thrust toward isolation, at times entering into alternate realms, imagining a reality to blame and demonize others or, in reverse, to rationalize and idealize one's own life. The latter was the case with Stephen, a man who was forced out of his ministry due to his inappropriate sexual behavior. When he first came to see me, Stephen was angry, confused, and intent on finding someone to blame for the rejection he suffered. Underneath his defenses, I believe Stephen wanted to forgive himself, accept humility, and release his shame and guilt for the harm he had caused.

As a young child, Stephen contracted a severe illness and was hospitalized for months. Lacking secure attachment and undergoing numerous, painful medical procedures, he turned to his radio for companionship and disassociated with vivid imagined fantasies. According to attachment research (Main 2010), when the inner subjective world of a lonely child like Stephen becomes disconnected from secure attachments with others, there is a thrust to find inner organization outside of relationships with others. This may take the form of disembodiment and depersonalization where one becomes numb, self-sufficient, one's own best companion and judge of self and others.

When Stephen was released from the hospital, his devout family believed it was a miracle and that God had chosen Stephen to survive and serve. He went on to prepare for life as a minister. While publically becoming a charismatic spiritual leader, privately Stephen engaged in secret sexual liaisons and partnerships with highly vulnerable people that had come to him for help. This relational pattern repeated itself over years, reenacting his deep yearning for human connection. When he was exposed publically, Stephen began to recognize his talent for rationalizing his behavior and arguing for his imaginal, "Godly" perspective. His disembodied imaginative life had created a protective shield for Stephen, one that kept him from authentic embodied emotional and empathic connections with others.

We all share in the imaginary illusions that protect us from the truth of our lived experience, at times disregarding the body-centered cues, the "vibes," that inform us about safety, danger, and life threat for ourselves and others. In our disembodiment, we dismiss these cues, fail to empathically imagine the suffering of others, and become more capable of hurting others. For some, the imaginary distortion is in reverse—traumatized men and women, often the powerless victims of perpetrators such as Stephen, who carry the shame and blame and unconsciously imagine themselves as victims or scapegoats. At the core of these illusions is the perceived insignificance of their own lives when they have not been held in securely attached relationships and have been vulnerable to adverse experiences, injury, and illness. Our imaginary illusions are constructed to protect us from further suffering, yet the trauma is deeply embedded in the body and manifests in physical, emotional, mental, and spiritual symptoms if it is not resolved. How do we face the truth of disembodied suffering, the despair, the helplessness without defaulting into imagined illusions? How can we find a way to embody our suffering and thus live out its meaning? In order to sort out the illusions from the very real possibilities offered by the imagination we must consult the body. What might seem to be an illusion to one person might for another be the imaginal opening into the future.

Using the Embodied Imagination to Restore Right-Hemispheric Processing

Embodied relationships provide a context for restoring the natural processing systems of the right hemisphere with a variety of imagined experiences, ranging from unconscious, spontaneous day and night dreams to conscious imagined constructions of lived experience, like storytelling, art, music, dance, and other forms of community-based affective creative expression. When people express their embodied imaginations within the safety and support of an intersubjective field and an interconnected community, they slowly reweave the natural unity of the body, mind, and brain. Slowly describing an image while attending to sensory-based internal dynamics with the guidance of an embodied other stimulates the felt sense, a foundational way of knowing that can be incorporated into bodily-based awareness.

Accessing the imagination through embodied imaginal perceptions was an important part of my work with Ellen. She had been coming to see me for about two months when she said that there was something at the source of her anxiety issues, but she couldn't tell me about it. I sensed that her shame and horror at what she carried inside was intense, and she needed to gradually open up her secret, so that it could be safely embodied. I invited her to wrap it up, whatever it was, in her imagination and place it between us, so we could hold it and she wouldn't have to talk about it.

As she mentally wrapped it up, she told me she was wrapping it as a gift, that she didn't want to go into it now, but that what had happened was teaching her what was important in her life. I intuitively knew a little at that time about the "gift" and did not probe. I trusted it would be revealed when she was ready.

Over time, I learned that Ellen's imaginary package held an overwhelming sense of shame from unacknowledged abuse she had endured in childhood. After establishing a rhythm of healing, a practice of coregulation in our dialogue, we were able to open this package together with gentleness and care, allowing her aversive childhood experiences to come into new meaning. The shared imaginal experience of wrapping up her overwhelming sense of shame to hold it between us, allowed us to gently unwrap the emotional anguish over time and face it together. Acknowledging, holding, and slowly unwrapping Ellen's "gift" eventually replaced the distorted images of "self as bad" that had plagued her for over fifty years.

The imaginal action of wrapping up the source of her anguish as a gift symbolized that she wanted to share the horror of the abuse, an experience that could only be truly known and incorporated if it could remain partially hidden and unwrapped over time. She knew that to reveal the abuse and shame all at once would be "too much, too fast" to regulate in the moment. The hidden shame of unacknowledged abuse amplifies a helpless sense of immobility with fear. The tremulous space of the intersubjective field can hold many mysteries that have been unbearable to face alone. As helping professionals become somatically attentive to the imaginative intersubjective space, they can hold curiosity, interest, and hope for both themselves and their clients.

Exploring Imaginal Perceptions with Clients

When a person brings a dream or imaginal perception into the intersubjective field, the first step is to honor it as a synthesis of current neural states, complex emotions, and knowledge within the inner world of the dreamer. Refraining from premature interpretation or assignment of meaning opens the space for helping professionals to somatically explore the dream or image with phenomenological methodology. When the truth and vitality of the image has been clarified, it is important to reflect upon it and embody it in the intersubjective field, resisting the temptation to jump to interpretation. "Interpretation is actually a defense against the dream. With the dream we come up against a different sense of reality. This reality is at the same time compelling and frightening" (Sardello 2008, 114). The richness and emerging unknown aspects of the self can be distorted by a premature interpretation, so it's important to allow the unfamiliar reality to slowly evolve from sensory-based data, movement, emotions, and images that move along in time.

Sardello suggests that "dream work can be a significant way of strengthening the creative force of the I. Strengthening the sense of creating . . . brings about a more vivid experience of the world as every movement coming into being rather than as already completed" (2008, 110–111). If we are not going to ease the tension of unsettling realities in the dream with an interpretation, how can we approach dreams in the intersubjective field? Sardello invites us to "step into" the images of a dream. This allows us to come back into the active experience of the dream rather than being the distant observer of an image. Stepping into the dream is similar to "feeling felt" (Scheler 1954), the process of embodied empathy. Entering the active energy of the image requires us to encounter this energy in a shared, creative form; it may be in a dialogue, colors on paper, or movement and gestures of the hands or a spontaneous full body dance, such as authentic movement (Stromsted and Seiff 2015).

The practice of entering into images and dreams and exploring the perceptions, sensations, and feelings they stimulate allows us to directly assess the current neural-emotional state of the dreamer in that moment of perception. As you creatively explore imaginal perceptions together, notice where you sense fear with sympathetic arousal, the powerlessness of life threat, the confusion of vagal and sympathetic arousal, and the warmth and expansion of social engagement and ventral vagal connection. With physical entry into imaginal realms from dreams, distorted neural states are available in the moment, capable of firing and wiring into new patterns. In other words, we can access deeply buried implicit traumatic memories by entering into these imaginal realms and transforming them on the neural-emotional level without having to fabricate explicit left-hemispheric ways of understanding the logic of the dream.

To access the rich, dark, and sometimes frightening energies of dreams, we first phenomenologically identify and explore perceptions of safety, protection, and connection that have emerged in the dream and offer vitality for transformation. For example, consider which elements of the earth provide safety and grounding in the dream: stones, mountains, trees, plants, or people? What elements in the dream offer protection: friends, family, older or younger versions of the self, ancestors, spiritual entities, or other guides such as animals and birds? What images are providing perceptual connection, such as light that enables us to see differently, or different powers of hearing, feeling, and tasting? What images may be encouraging fluidity and change, such as water and wind?

To embody and incorporate the safety and protection of sensation-based images, we first differentiate images from sensations and emotions, holding the different elements in their specific phenomenological identity. We then explore the images, one at a time, attending to the details of the image and intensifying the sensations that accompany each image. The subtle oscillation of images and sensations allows the images to be fully incorporated into the body's ways of knowing and with the mind's way of knowing. The intense emotion that was once coupled with the sensation can then shift.

Primitive emotions rising up from aroused neural states (Panksepp and Biven 2011) in response to perceptions of safety, danger, and life threat are felt in a number of sensory ways in dream images. For example anger can be felt as heat, tension, or cold. Fear can be experienced as a gripping of the chest, limpness of the legs, or tightness of the eyes. Grief can feel like the heart is literally breaking. Healing might be felt as ease in performing difficult tasks. The phenomenological subjective experience of emotion is difficult to communicate without attention to sensory-based vitality dynamics (D. N. Stern 2010). Awareness of the vitality currents that stream within the right hemisphere of the brain are revealed through images in dreams and inform the emotions, images, purpose, and meaning of our lived experiences. As we consciously engage, participate, and communicate the vitality of our dreams as they exist in our bodies, we begin to access the ancient wisdom of our body and mind.

As we differentiate the phenomenological elements of the dream— sensations, movement, emotions, and images, we can uncover the essential dynamics that have the most healing power and those that are connected to distortions. Focus on finding and exploring the safe, protective, transformative, healthy, alive aspects before exploring the disembodied and dissociated elements of the self that have been hidden with trauma, the lost parts of the soul. In order to effectively process the images in a dream, the intersubjective field must eventually hold and coregulate the intense dissociated affect. It's important to remember that it's not technique that helps people open to their hidden inner world, but rather the quality of safety and connection between helping professionals and clients, the nonverbal and verbal communication that encourages the flow of subjective experience into shared knowledge.

Once the phenomenological elements of images in a dream have been differentiated through somatic inquiry, helping professionals can identify the inner conflicts of the dream that emerge as polarities. These opposites are simply the extreme edges of the same experience; linkage can be restored through artful oscillation of these polarities, opening up a higher level of complexity, sometimes called the "third space." Talking about or expressing the particular sensations of an image stimulates a shift in the perceptions of that image; sensations naturally move along in time. Acknowledging shifting sensations of an image frees the sensations from the fixed perception of trauma so they can become fluid, reflecting the lost part of the soul coming into its own innate mobilization. Somatic inquiry into sensations of images gives a voice and animation to creative life that has not been accepted in experiences of relational trauma.

Following a somatic inquiry into the dream or imaginal perception, it is important to continue to hold the sensations and images of the dream and to embody them in different ways. For example, a dream could include the sensations of the earth being lifted up or the viscera opening and new life emerging while being held in relationship. Allowing the meaning to form into full consciousness through reflection fosters growth and development.

Throughout the process, helping professionals must remain curious, embodied, and fully present to differentiate client's neural states as they process images and sensations, to notice the small shifts that occur in subtle interventions and guide the healing images into embodiment. As healing images arise in dreams and lived experience, the traumatized body will defend against this reality with dissociated survival strategies. We gradually surrender in relationship to the healing images with humility, curiosity, and interest in the context of the intersubjective relationship. The healing images offer a new identity that can be frightening, one that arises from the lost soul within but is unfamiliar to the known sense of self. We need to gradually come into relationship with this unknown, lost part of the self, allowing the images to simmer on the heat of our complex emotions.

When exploring dreams and imaginal perceptions, the speaking language of helping professionals should hold respect for the unknown and unformulated bodily-based experience of the other and the self, along with a conviction that something new is arising. A somatic inquiry into dreams or imaginal perceptions should be both invitational and observant. The following are examples of what helping professionals might say to their clients to explore their experiences:

- "I am aware that something has shifted in the past few minutes. I am interested in what you have noticed?"
- "I'm sensing some inner movement, I'm curious about what you are sensing?"
- "When you describe the heaviness in your heart, I wonder if you can feel me with you?"
- "When you don't feel anything in your body, I wonder if any thoughts or images arise?"
- "When you remember that aspect of your childhood, I wonder what you feel in this moment?"

An Inquiry into an Imaginal Perception—Case 10.2: Keith

The following is an example of an inquiry into an imaginal perception with Keith, a client who was overwhelmed by addiction to alcohol and pornography. It demonstrates how embodiment of the imaginal, within the context of a loving intersubjective relationship, can provide a link to the vitality of healing and growth from within.

Since childhood, Keith had had a reoccurring dream about a tornado, similar to those he survived while growing up in the Midwest. Each time in the dream, a feminine figure would emerge in the midst of his terror and helplessness to hold his hand and bring him into the center of the tornado, a place of connection, quiet, order, light, and transcendence. Yet these moments of safety would quickly dissolve when the protecting "lady" disappeared, sending Keith back into the roar of the storm, the uncontrollable winds, and the drenching rains. One day, when he told me that he had just had the dream again, I asked Keith if we could take some time to process the dream together. Over the two years we had been meeting, we had developed the capacity to coregulate, and Keith was well able to self-regulate intense sensory experience.

Sharon: I'm wondering, Keith, if you could describe the dream you had as if you are in the midst of it and I am with you.

My suggestion to join him was an embodied imaginal intervention to link our relationship with his isolated and dissociated images.

Keith: OK, I kind of like the idea of having you there. We are hiding in the basement and the tornado is roaring so loud we can't hear each other.

Shivering from the cold of the basement and recoiling from the overwhelming sound of the storm, I realize that auditory and visual contact during this imaginal perception are going to be difficult, so I want to explore with Keith how else we might stay connected.

Sharon: I'd like to stay in contact since we can't hear each other. Do you have any ideas of how you might want to do that?
Keith: Why don't you put your foot near mine like you did before, so I can know you are here?
Sharon: OK . . . can you feel my foot near yours?

In an earlier session, I had asked Keith if I could make contact by placing my foot near his during an intense moment of terror. The contact, foot to foot, helped me to feel the ground and I settled a little more.

Keith: Yep, it helps me feel the ground when the fear gets really strong.

Now we both had an affective embodied experience to coregulate the fear.

Sharon: What would it be like to just notice the ground together, feel the sense of gravity from the earth and the sense we are together?

Here we felt the support of gravity while embodying our ability to stay in relationship. I watched carefully as Keith's face shifted from fixed-action patterns of grimacing and bracing to a softer expression. The muscles of his face organized into a subtle smile. I felt an inner reorganization in my own chest, gut, and face, a dropping of the defenses to the storm and a soft, warm, vibrating energy between us. In my imagination our relationship became the creative order at the center of the storm. Together we embodied this energizing space, while bracketing the chaos of the weather.

Keith: (*Opening his eyes and looking at me with curiosity*) Well it feels like the storm is over, it helped to have you there. I wonder why "the lady" did not show up this time?

Resisting the temptation to interpret, I initiated a somatic inquiry.

Sharon: Keith, I'm really curious about that also. Do you have any ideas of what might be happening?
Keith: Maybe I didn't need her when I had a real person with me.
Sharon: Wow! . . . I'm wondering what it would be like to imagine Janet with you in the dream.

Because Keith's pattern of avoidant attachment had affected his relationship with his wife, Janet, I hoped the sense of connection and coregulation we had developed could expand to include her. I had seen them together and had a sense that she would welcome his disclosure.

Keith: Probably better than you . . . she could hold me. I never told her about these dreams. Maybe I'll tell her and if the dream comes, she could hold me.

Here, Keith allowed hope to enter his imaginal perception, shifting the fixity of isolation. Recalling how Beebe and Lachmann (2014) emphasized the significance of feeling felt, I wanted to shift into embodiment once I had followed up with the suggestion about his wife.

Sharon: I'd be interested to know how it goes with Janet. It feels like I really got how awful things have felt for you. The basement was really cold and the sound was terrifying, but when we connected with each other and the ground, I felt safe.
Keith: I'm glad you are ok—I was kind of worried about you in there, like you might really get scared and not want to work with me.

Keith had also been concerned that his terrors would be too much for his wife to endure.

Sharon: It did feel a little scary at first, but most of all, it was really good to be with you.
Keith: OK. I wonder . . . if Janet and I get closer, the lady might never come back.

Sharon: Yes, that might happen. I'm curious to know what it would feel like to imagine Janet with you during a storm.

Keith: *(After a few moments of silence)* It feels safe and real. Janet is alive and warm, I can touch her.

The feminine spiritual figure in Keith's dream had offered safety in the midst of his implicit memories, but could not enter into his ordinary life. To bring safety back into the world of embodied relationships, first I, then Janet became Keith's companion, an embodied other who could feel the terror and helplessness with him, while helping him regulate his emotions with confidence and strength. Companioning Keith through the storm enabled him to perceive and imagine things a little differently in his ordinary life. An imaginal moment of coregulation with a partner created an opening that helped stabilize and regulate his bodily-based reactions to deeply buried overwhelming experiences. This inner experience helped Keith awaken his longing and hope to reach out to his wife, a small step in breaking the neural state of an avoidant attachment.

Stimulating Imaginal Perceptions

Since we enter into the embodied imagination through the doors and windows of sensory-motor perception, activities like mindful walking, meditation, reading poetry, listening to music, creating art, singing, chanting, and observing the natural world can stimulate embodied imaginal perceptions. Helping professionals may find it useful to initiate an inquiry that connects one of these activities with the spontaneous emergence of images, for example: "When you were walking in the forest (or insert any right-hemispheric activity), I'm curious to know if any images appeared?" Natural, emerging images that are stimulated spontaneously seem to offer a more direct route toward restoring innate right-hemispheric processing than intentionally created images. Sometimes a little more prompting is needed, such as, "When you recall (any specific experience), I'm wondering if you see any pictures in your mind, or hear any sounds or words?" This initial inquiry into the connectivity of lived experience can stimulate the disrupted innate processing system. However, people who have experienced severe relational-developmental trauma need multiple embodied imaginal perceptions in an intersubjective relationship to link lived experience with internal representations.

Although there are many activities that can stimulate the formation of imaginal perceptions, art making is one of the most effective. When the words in an intersubjective dialogue seem to be insufficient to describe the intensity of emotions, I encourage people to express their immediate experience with oil crayon marks on paper. Linda Chapman (2014) suggests that people who have experienced trauma can be encouraged to simply scribble to connect inner feelings with representations or image.

As the somatic inquiry continues, the corresponding marks of vivid color on the paper start to form new arrangements, continuity, and thematic images, bringing the "unformulated" (D. B. Stern, 2010) material into a new formation. An oil crayon journal of marks made during the therapeutic encounter can track the emergence of new ways of perceiving oneself. In the context of somatic empathy, a somatic inquiry can be directed toward the expression and communication of semi-conscious nonverbal images, sensations, emotions, and movement. For example, you might say, "When you notice that feeling of panic that comes when you are about to speak, I'm wondering if you could just scribble some colors on the paper that can help me get a sense of what it is like for you?" As I make this inquiry, I am physically close and serve as an enthusiastic art assistant, receptive to representations that may emerge as I hold the box of oil crayons.

Next I might continue by saying, "And, as you make these marks on the paper, I am wondering if another color will help express these complex feelings." Neural states and intense emotions all emerge in color, lines, shapes, contours, figures, and landscapes. Numerous sketches may be generated in a short period of time. Following a time of settling, I invite a somatic reflection on the affective experience. The sketches can be arranged on the floor, explored from different perspectives, and reorganized to reflect their relationship with each other. A dialogical inquiry can bring the images into more coherence by attending to what both of you notice and find intriguing. Take care not to define the exact meaning of any image or representation—simply welcome the return of the integrative processing. I often encourage an oscillation of attention between the images that hold fixity and those that hold vitality and fluidity, dialoging about the felt sense in the moment, the fluid images and any curiosity, wonder, or insights that may emerge.

A practice of reading poetry and prose and listening to music from one's own culture or another cultural heritage can also provide sensory-based imaginal healing, possibly of historical trauma. Poets and musicians who express a contemporary relationship to nature can offer sensory-based imaginal perceptions for transformation of implicit memories. The creation myths of aboriginal cultures and ancient scriptures of literature, music, film, dance, and other forms of art offer unfamiliar imaginal perceptions that can be embodied within our own lives, symbolically transforming implicit memories. Just as we choose our food carefully for physical health, choosing images and the sensations they stimulate is essential to mental health. See page 211 of the appendix for Exercise 10:1: Strengthening Transformation through Imaginal Perceptions.

Images and dreams take us into the unknown aspects of life; when acknowledged they can take us into a frightening wilderness where we witness the "not me" (Bromberg 2011) edges of ourselves and uncover our limited and habitual ways of knowing. It's important to remember that images may resist an easy interpretation and insist on their own identity despite our best attempts to find a known category or meaning. As we live in relationship to these unknown aspects of ourselves, we forge our developing identity with the guidance the images, sensations, and emotions provide. Oscillating attention between the images of divine vitality and images of horror and terror transform the creative energy of our inner world into higher levels of complex consciousness, where polarities offer depth and distinction rather than conflict and confusion.

References

Beebe, B., and F. Lachmann. 2014. *The Origins of Attachment: Infant Research and Adult Treatment.* New York: Routledge.

Bosnak, R. 2007. *Embodiment: Creative Imagination in Medicine, Art and Travel.* London: Routledge.

Bromberg, P. M. 2011. *The Shadow of the Tsunami: and the Growth of the Relational Mind.* New York: Routledge.

Chapman, L. 2014. *Neurobiologically Informed Trauma Therapy with Children and Adolescents: Understanding Mechanisms of Change.* New York: Norton.

Hecht, D. 2014. "Cerebral Lateralization of Pro- and Anti-social Tendencies." *Experimental Neurobiology* 23: 1–27.

Kalsched, D. 2013. *Trauma and the Soul: A Psycho-spiritual Approach to Human Development and Its Interruption.* London: Routledge.

Main, M. 2010. "Cross-cultural Studies of Attachment Organization: Recent Studies, Changing Methodologies, and the Concept of Conditional Strategies." *Human Development* 33(1): 48–61.

Panksepp, J., and L. Biven. 2011. *The Archaeology of Mind: Neuroevolutionary Origins of Human Emotion.* New York: Norton.

Parabola. 2014. "What Is a Parabola?" *Parabola*: 6

Porges, S. W. 2011. *The Polyvagal Theory: Neurophysiological Foundations of Emotions, Attachment, Communication, and Self-Regulation.* New York: Norton.

Sardello, R. 2008. *Love and the Soul: Creating a New Future for Earth.* Berkeley: North Atlantic Books.

Scheler, M. 1954. *On the Nature of Sympathy.* Translated by P. Heath. London: Routledge.

Stern, D. B. 2010. *Partners in Thought: Working with Unformulated Experience, Dissociation, and Enactment.* New York: Routledge.

Stern, D. N. 2010. *Forms of Vitality: Exploring Dynamic Experiences in Psychology, the Arts, Psychotherapy, and Development.* Oxford: Oxford University Press.

Stromsted, T., and D. Seiff. 2015. "Dances of Psyche and Soma: Re-Inhabiting the Body in the Wake of Emotional Trauma." In *Understanding and Healing Emotional Trauma: Conversations with Pioneers, Clinicians and Researchers,* edited by D. F. Seiff. London: Routledge.

11 Somatic Reflection

"These young people yearn for one thing, and one thing only—down under and behind every shout and cry of their lives they yearn to love. And without knowing it, they need, as do all of us, also without knowing it, to learn to be able to love."
(Needleman 2014–2015, 102)

Integrating Lived Experience into Meaning: Learning to Love

Somatic reflection is an embodied way of thinking about lived experience that is a "letting go of habits of mindlessness, as an unlearning rather than a learning" (Varela, Thompson, and Rosch 1991, 29). Varela, Thompson, and Rosch (1991) assure us that the habits of mindlessness can change, the mind and body can be connected and coordinated, and right-hemispheric processing can be brought into a coherent, meaningful expression of the self. This is a significant change in the tradition of reflection, moving from an abstract disembodied discourse that lacks a self to an embodied, open-ended unifying process. Somatic reflection disrupts habitual perceptions and ways of thinking and opens cognitive processes to the direct experience of the subjective self, providing exciting new answers to tired old questions. How does somatic reflection enhance intersubjective processing in a client-professional relationship?

On a subcortical level, somatic practices ground our feelings, down-regulate hyperarousal of the amygdala, up-regulate the depression of hypoarousal, differentiate traumatic bodily-based defenses from vitality, and process primitive emotions to stimulate changes in the peripheral nervous system. Subcortical systems that are in chaos can be reorganized with precise relational somatic interventions involving subtle sensory and motor experience. This lower right brain stem and limbic system processing restores regulation, converting chronic fear states into experiences of social engagement. In the context of a trusting intersubjective relationship, somatic reflection on this subcortical reorganization reveals the conflicted, hidden, and often shame-filled aspects of the inner world for mutual acceptance, embodiment, and incorporation. Following this conversion, the phenomenological methods of somatic reflection connect higher right-hemispheric images and archetypes with the regulated lower right hemisphere, bringing surprising clarity, aliveness, and meaning to our lives.

Converting the Chaos: Prereflective Processing

Somatic reflection is characterized by mutual phenomenological-based interactions that first differentiate and then integrate sensations and emotions in "pre-reflective" intersubjective relationships. In this often nonverbal dialogue, "unformulated" (Stern 2010) inner depths are experienced as visceral, emotionally laden "gut" knowledge (Tucker 2007) within the individual's level of optimal arousal. Often intense and overpowering, this visceral data brings to light the hidden force of trauma and can be gently felt in the optimal arousal zone as sensations or subtle inner movement in the healing process (Tucker 2007). These sensations or movements have "just enough" energy to lower hyperarousal of the amygdala and raise hypoarousal and mobilization to a level where reorganization can occur. Once regulated, the visceral data can be integrated with higher cortical symbolic representation, such as image and archetype.

The "pre-reflective" processing of chaotic sensations and emotions integrates these forms of knowing into an instinctive, intuitive visceral knowledge that is alive and moving toward love, the basic need of human life. This alchemical processing of direct experience reveals the treasure of authentic, often wordless visceral ways of knowing, an inner sense of self that is visible in posture, voice, and eye gaze. It is the *way* of knowing, not necessarily the knowledge itself, that brings vitality and congruence to lived experience and to the reflective processes of more complex consciousness.

Sharing reflections on the direct lived experience of the changing bodily-based systems expands unconscious inner neural-emotional states into more complex, higher order affective states. Converting the survival-based chaotic neural states to relational connectivity and then reflecting on this experience allows people who have experienced trauma to shift from self-limiting, dissociative, disembodied ways of being to more caring relational connections with expansive ways of seeing, hearing, feeling, and making sense out of lived experience. Somatic reflection benefits practitioners, too, by enriching one's understanding of another, enhancing body-based empathic ways of knowing.

A body-centered dialogue, somatic reflection can be experienced in a number of forms: nonverbally, verbally, and through written expression or art. (See Exercise 11.1: Reflection on Images, Metaphors, and Archetypes that Emerge in Memories and Dreams on page 212 of the appendix for a suggestion on engaging in somatic reflection through art.) The creative expression of a somatic reflection leads to developmental growth: unformulated inner truth arises in expressive forms and the vast human reservoir of unresolved, generational trauma can be articulated and integrated in a communal way,

through ceremony, drama, music, literature, and media. For example, Ram-
giri Braun (2014–2015) describes his somatic reflective process several years
ago at the German Nazi concentration camp Auschwitz. He joined a culturally diverse group who came together to bear witness and to reflect together
on the lived experience of sitting in the spaces that contained human beings
at Auschwitz.

While sitting in the children's and women's camp, Braun felt a violent,
tearing, immense weight in his chest, and ancient spiritual archetypal
images of destruction arose. As an embodied witness, Braun endured the
powerless horror and isolation in his body until images of Kali arose that
opened him to the shared human reality of his current experience. In a pre-
reflection, Braun shared his experience with his meditation group and also
listened to their pre-reflections. Inspired by this community-based intuitive intersubjective field, he concludes that we all wish to know reality as it
is and with this integrity and readiness for truth, we open to transformation. Continuing to deepen his personal reflective inquiry, Braun wonders
if meaning can come out of suffering of this magnitude.

His reflection then takes a form of prophetic contemplation; the meaning of his experience has expanded from current time to the history of
humanity as he imagines the millions of people who have suffered from
senseless destruction, and a new consciousness arises within him, one that
"has the power to end all war inside and among us." His arousal of awareness was spontaneous, embodied, visceral, and interpersonal: Braun was
flooded with sensations of warmth and love and the visceral knowledge
that awareness of this love in his and all human hearts can transform consciousness from states of darkness and illusion to freedom, love, and peace.
His reflection deeply affected his sense of compassion for the personal and
communal Self as he realizes that suffering comes from being disembodied
and separated from ourselves, an estrangement that leads to confusion and
can be shifted by systematically opening "our minds, eyes, and hearts" (47).

Similar to Braun's reflective process that began as he followed his visceral
awareness into archetypal images, dialogue, and then more complex reflections on meaning, somatic reflection follows a series of phenomenological
phases. Each phase integrates an intuitive body-centered way of knowing
with more complex phenomena. This reflective process flows out of the
reconnection of body and mind, as subjective and intersubjective phenomena merge into shared consciousness, integrating discrete bits of perception,
emotion, images, and synthesizing knowledge and awareness through the
use of spontaneous language. See Exercise 11.2: Inviting Images to Speak
the Embodied Truth to witness how embodied experience becomes spontaneous language in a somatic reflection. See page 212 of the appendix.

Somatic reflection requires a shared acknowledgement of small changes
in perception, regulation of disturbing affect, and transformation of the
stream of affective data from chaos into meaningful, embodied, and incorporated knowledge. It is *incorporated* knowledge, recognition of the *visceral*

truth of *that which is* that unifies the sense of self. This integration brings clarity to the emerging sense of self in relationship—who a person is in the moment and over time. Braun's sense of self at the conclusion of his reflective process had shifted from a horrified individual meditator in a diverse group to a shared human heart of love, beauty, and goodness. Let's explore what we mean by a sense of self.

Sense of Self and Flow States

The sensations, feelings, images, and patterns of thought that create a personal subjective inner world have been unconsciously and at times, consciously, formed throughout life and currently exist as a sense of self in the moment (Damasio 2010). Our earliest moments of consciousness as a self-in-relation awaken us to the sense of our individuality and personhood. The self is never created alone; it is formed in the context of interpersonal relationships and community. Our consciousness in the moment reflects the confusion and integration of all we have lived. Our emergent philosophy of life is formed in bits and snatches from our perceptions, the processing of our lived experience, and the meaning we glean from our lived experiences. The culture of our ancestors, our families, and current relationships continues to influence how we process our own lived experience and contributes to the flow of meaning and our changing sense of self. As a lifespan, often unconscious, developmental process (Peavey 1997), meaning making is naturally constructed in the internal subjective world as we feel our bodies and imagine the experience of others (Margulies 1989). Our individual relational, spiritual, and religious experiences; the written and unwritten laws of society, and our personal relationships with the natural world all affect the fluid construction of meaning making. Somatic reflection brings this unconscious natural process into explicit expression with a body-centered awareness that discerns the truth of *what is* from our personal and communal illusions, strengthening the self in relation to the truth and wisdom of inner knowing and the "objectivity" of the outer world.

Somatic practices reveal the differences between the illusions of our minds, as we discussed in the prior chapter on imagination, and the responsive and immediate truth in our bodies. The meaning of our inner subjective lived experience is not just mental; it is based in our bodies. Objectivity can be thought of as the meaning shared by a specific culture about particular events, behaviors, and emotions. A brief glimpse of different ages of humanity and flourishing cultures affirms that objectivity is based on agreed upon norms and values, many of which cause confusion to the integrity of subjective knowledge. Individuals, particularly those living in an intercultural world, engage in an unconscious dialectical process where inner subjectivity is considered in relationship to the current objectivity or shared illusions in an effort to adapt to the current reality, yet know reality as it exists for them in a visceral subjective way.

Often, in a dangerous world, one's inner subjective truth is ignored for survival and the self becomes disembodied, dissociated from lived experience, confused, conflicted, and faced with difficult choices: do I adapt to the current disembodied and distorted perspectives of the dominant culture or find another way of knowing that is grounded in a visceral, alive process of meaning making? Writers reflecting on World War II, such as Merleau-Ponty, Elie Wiesel, Viktor Frankl, and Morris Berman have felt the urgency of this dilemma. Their thinking supports the emergence of developmental neuroscience and interpersonal neurobiology, pointing the way toward the resolution of this dialectic. Right-hemispheric processing of the "qualia" of the body—the fast moving sensory experience with primitive emotions, spontaneous images, and the felt sense of love and connection between people—constructs a way of knowing that is radically distinct from abstract logic and reason of the left hemisphere, yet provides a firm foundation for living in a multicultural, fast changing world. The question is not "right" or "left" hemispheres of the brain (McGilchrist 2009), but when to engage each side of the brain, and how to enhance their respective ways of knowing.

A similar dialectic occurs between two individuals in an attuned, resonant relationship. Just as in the infant-mother dyad, the subjectivity of both is highly valued and essential to optimal development. The process of dialectically attending to one's own subjectivity while valuing the subjectivity of another creates a new self-state of intersubjectivity that is shared by both, an empathic bond and sense of "we." Once a relationship has found the rhythmical, oscillating balance of mutual subjectivity, interpersonal dynamics begin to "flow." When engaged in relational flow states, a sense of unity and connectivity emerges; we lose a linear sense of time and feel that we are a part of the activity of creation. There is an inspired vitality to shared states of flow that intuitively accesses prior knowledge, imagination, connection, and synchronistic thinking. When engaged in the neural state of social engagement (Porges 2011) and aided by the curiosity of the shared "seeking system" (Panksepp and Biven 2011), the neurons of social engagement are prompted to fire and rewire at top speed with myelination while being supported by streams of oxytocin and dopamine. Flow states are times of intense learning, changing, and codeveloping of essential meaning of the intersubjective lived experience for both individuals. This sense of flow can emerge in groups of people who value mutuality, are interested in exploring emerging phenomena, and find delight in the discovery process of dialogical exchanges, like somatic reflection.

Just as there are flow states between people, these states exist within us as well. When we are embodied over time, vitalized by the interconnected presence of others, and have regulated the subcortical chaos of our own trauma, our lived experience is swiftly processed; an achievement Schore (2014) calls self-regulation. With optimal right-hemispheric processing, we are able to discern our subjective truth in the moment, empathically connect with the subjectivity of others, and experience a "gut know-ing" that is mapped in the sensory motor cortex of the brain, a kind of inner gyroscope that serves as a guide for ongoing development of the self-in-relation. The flow of right-hemispheric inner dialectical process-ing generates an intuitive state of well-being and creative adaptation to the environment, a "state of grace." The fundamental split of trauma— between the elements of right-hemispheric processing, the body, and the mind—is apparent in our inner unconscious suffering and often appears in dreams as incongruent, unfamiliar, and frightening figures and experi-ences and an ordinary everyday sense of anxiety.

Once suffering, including sensory anguish and stunted primitive emo-tions, are brought into consciousness in the containment of an intersubjec-tive field, the particular sensations that have formed the primitive survival emotions can be converted, metabolized, and transformed into images, and then reflected upon for meaning. When we acknowledge our suffer-ing in relationship, connection occurs through love and compassion and meaning emerges. We can somehow manage the pain and discomfort from a different, more expanded consciousness. For example Anne Marie, a young woman suffering for many years from the physical, emotional, and mental anguish of post-encephalitic syndrome, found that she was able to companion and thus ease the suffering of a beloved relative dying from cancer. Following the death of her aunt, she reflected upon the opportu-nity to share states of deep distress and help to relieve another's suffering. She concluded that her lifetime of suffering now had meaning for her. This is not an easy reframe, but a deep immersion in the horror and terror from trauma and the strength of the intersubjective field to transform inner separation into love and meaning.

Inner separation and alienation often begins with shame—a feeling that must be acknowledged and converted into connection and humility in relationship in order to heal trauma. Resisting states of unresolved shame results in addictions, grandiosity, and perfectionism. As a neural state, shame is at the core of immobility with fear. A complex state that includes the loss of innate vitality, shame is permeated with helplessness, hopeless-ness, and powerlessness. Shame gets its painful power from the loss of vitality, alienation of self and others, and a thwarting of a fundamental human need for love and connection. Laurens van der Post (1960) speaks of the silent power of shame people use to "turn their back" on those that deviate from the dominant culture's social norms, often resulting in the immediate death of those that have been thrown out of their communi-ties. Addictions are often fueled by shame; when triggered by even very subtle messages that one has failed, the hidden pain becomes overwhelm-ing and the addiction blooms. Somatic reflective processes, in the context of an intersubjective relationship, can gradually transform the alienation of shame into a profound sense of belonging in relationship, humility in terms of one's own humanity, and fluid interconnection with all. In a subtle, gentle way, somatic reflection can gradually mobilize the sensations of shame, holding them in a sacred crucible of relationship, and support the developmental thrust for one's own sense of inner embodied autonomy balanced with the human need for intimate relational connection.

Engaging the Embodied Reflective Witness

At the heart of somatic reflection is the activity of an embodied reflective witness. The embodied reflective witness actively participates in the present moment to create a fluid, yet stable sense of self. By consciously connecting the emerging neural state in the moment with an embodied reflection-in-action, lived experience is transformed into more expansive ways of knowing. Reflection-in-action (Schön 1990) "reshapes what we are working on while we are working on it," a transformation clearly demonstrated by Braun and his embodied witness at Auschwitz. By remaining in the present moment, the neurons connected to an experience are actively firing and rewiring as the reshaping continues. For a person suffering from an early trauma, the practice of being an embodied reflective witness may have never developed and will take time to be generated in the intersubjective field. The consciousness of an embodied reflective witness intuitively reflects-in-action on vast amounts of data, knowledge, values, and desires, remaining open to see, hear, and feel from a variety of perspectives. The reflective witness brings new sensory data through the peripheral nervous system, to the brain, then back to the body with new action.

When the usually unheard communication of the body is included in somatic reflection, innate bodily-centered wisdom for healing becomes available. With access to this inner intelligence, people begin to trust themselves and surrender into the guidance of sensory cues in a healing process. In any relationship, feelings of trust and safety determine the degree of healing and learning that occurs. In relationships marked by deep trust, the darkest side of another and the confused perceptions and illusions that have taken root within them, are felt and witnessed with compassion. When we feel acceptance and trust from another, our defenses may be activated. The defenses that emerge in the intersubjective field reveal patterns of fear from the past and unconsciously trigger breaches in the relationship, particularly enactments. The emotionally based defenses rise out of dissociated memories and when detected are then available for reconsolidation. Shame can be transformed into connected humility; rage into organized, purposeful action; anger into mobilization for justice; regret and guilt into empathy and compassion for the self; and sadness into a commitment to love despite inevitable losses. In a state of acceptance and love, the embodied, helping professional becomes a "totemic witness" (Stanley 1994). A totemic witness holds the suffering and vitality of generational and current history and takes responsibility for the creation and maintenance of a sacred space for living, loving, and healing. By serving as a totemic witness, a helping professional supports the other to gradually reorganize the darkest elements of the inner world and access symbolic support to integrate and embody the truth of lived experience with safety and compassion (Stanley 1994). Before moving to explore the steps of a somatic reflection with a client in the following section, you can practice being your own totemic witness in Exercise 11.3: Written Somatic Reflection on Memories. See page 213 of the appendix.

Steps of a Somatic Reflection

A somatic reflection can initiate a therapeutic encounter, be embedded within an encounter, conclude the processing of lived experience, or mark the closure of a therapeutic relationship. Somatic reflection begins with somatic awareness—an embodied higher cortical process, a totemic witness, that invites the integration of previously disconnected elements of lived experience into cohesion and connectivity. It is important for helping professionals to continually and intuitively reflect-in-action by recalling diverse moments of intersubjective connection, disconnection, and information regarding neural states, emotions, images, and thoughts, then integrate this material with right-hemispheric speed and acuity. The shared experience of somatic reflection informs the ongoing inquiry and interventions and gradually becomes more explicit in the therapeutic conversation. Once there has been some integration of subcortical elements, such as sensations with emotions, or movements with images, a somatic reflection has begun. At first, the moments of reflection and integration are short and to the point; however, as connectivity with higher cortical processes is formed, they become more frequent and expansive. The following example demonstrates the use of somatic reflection at the closure of a therapeutic session with a client.

Ryan was a thirty-two-year-old husband, father, and "successful" sales associate of an upstart multinational corporation. Ryan initially came to therapy at the insistence of his wife, Gina, when she gave him an ultimatum regarding his drinking and disconnection from her. At the beginning of our seventh ninety-minute session together, Ryan talked about his stressful week of travel, sales, and exposure to alcohol; all of which exacerbated his feelings of overwhelm and increased his tendency to dissociate. As I listened, I recognized the need for both of us to lower the fast rising sensations of hyperarousal before we could feel connected with each other. At my invitation, we took a few moments to ground, regulate, and reflect together. Recalling a moment earlier in the session when his eyes lit up, a moment of "heart," I invited Ryan to reflect-in-action on the moment his four-year-old daughter ran to greet him when he came home. We differentiated that moment into diverse phenomena and reflected-in-action on the accompanying sensory experience: the look on her face before she saw him, the moment of recognition when he caught her eye, and the moving image of her long legs and hair flying as she ran to greet him, bringing our relationship into the optimal arousal zone. Near the end of the first hour, we began to oscillate the moments of high stress from the week with his feelings about his daughter and her heartfelt embrace. When he began to smile, relax, and open his eyes, I recognized his growing ability to regulate intense subcortical arousal, and initiated a more complex somatic reflection on the shared lived experience of our session together. The path of a somatic reflection on shared lived experience dialogically reviews the bits of related phenomena that intuitively arise in the intersubjective field for integration. Embedded in the following phenomenological somatic reflective process, is a stylized reflection process with Ryan, one that follows a sequence and includes approximately eight phases.

1. Recall States of Mind before the Experience

Open a dialogue to recall and communicate the expectancies and felt sense of each before reflecting on shared lived experience.

Sharon: I'm wondering, Ryan, what was happening for you today before we met? What did you imagine might happen in our session today?

Ryan: I was feeling like I had failed again. I barely remember the last night of my sales trip. I had four drinks and was out of it . . . again. I guess I was so ashamed of myself and worried that I won't ever change and that you and my wife will give up on me.

Sharon: (*First responding with nonverbal eye gaze of acceptance, soft voice, and a gesture of connection*) Ryan, I am so grateful that you came today and have the courage to continue your work.

2. Recall the Vivid Moments of a Shared Lived Experience and Embody Those that Offer Vitality

Sharon: I think some things happened between us today that are part of the change you are working for. I'm wondering if we could go back and recall what we accomplished together.

These questions are designed to identify the aspects of the session that may have the most impact for changing the fixed-action patterns of trauma.

Sharon: When you think back to the time we came together today and up to this moment, what has been most vivid for you? Can you describe your experience of that moment?

Ryan: I love the image of Isobel running toward me. I see her hair flying and her long legs moving and her eyes shining, all just to see me.

Speaking in the present tense, Ryan indicates he is in a reflection-in-action; his neurons are firing and rewiring. Visible emotion is moving within his guts, action that is reflected in his face.

Sharon: When you recall that moving image, what do you notice in your body right now?

Ryan: It's a kind of rising up. The cramp in my belly loosened (*the shame*) and a kind of warm feeling is coming up into my face and eyes (*vitality*).

We allowed time for the completion of this emotion between us. I witnessed the small subtle shifts of ventral vagal connectivity in his face. Some of his shame had dissipated as it came into the intersubjective field, an up-regulation of the neural state of immobility with fear. Now there was more animation between us.

Because right-hemispheric experiences can be elusive, I keep track of the session in writing. For example, I note shifts in neural states as we talk about a topic, the dynamics of a somatic intervention, the exact poignant words spoken that seem to articulate a change moment. I also ask clients if they are interested in what I notice as vivid experiences. If they are interested, and most often people are very curious to know my experience when I have truly listened and responded to them, I recall the annotations that seem important, including the effect on me.

Sharon: Ryan, when you described Isobel running toward you, I felt tears and my chest expanded. When you acknowledged how overwhelmed you were in Chicago, I felt I wanted to reach out with my heart to hold you.

Self-disclosure in terms of the effect the interactions have had on you as the helping professional is an essential aspect of a two-person therapeutic relationship (Quillman 2012) and normalizes the transformation of shame into relationship.

3. Recall Arousal and Emotions in the Encounter

A reflection on the lived experience identifies the dissociated affect and states of vitality that are present in the inner world. Depending on a person's ability to regulate intense emotions and stay within his or her own optimal arousal in the moment, I begin an up-regulation from hypoarousal with the emotions that held vitality and aliveness, usually the more pleasant emotions.

Sharon: Ryan, when you recall the feelings you had today as we worked, I am wondering what moments you felt most alive and hopeful?

If someone has a difficult time recalling any such moments, I may offer my recall.

Sharon: Ryan, when you were describing your plan for the garden, the way you will plant the flower seeds with Isobel, I noticed a new light came into your eyes. I'm wondering what that moment felt like for you?

At other times, when I am confident that we will be able to regulate and return to a person's optimal arousal, I may begin the reflection with the more uncomfortable emotions, as I did with Ryan.

Sharon: Ryan, I'm wondering what feelings were most difficult for you during this time together?
Ryan: I know that when I feel that black pit in my belly, I give up. That's when I get overwhelmed.

I sensed he was referring to his felt sense of shame and beginning to drop down into a low arousal state. My response was contingent on his, followed the phenomena of his experience yet guided us into a ventral vagal states of social engagement.

Sharon: When you recall those feelings, I am wondering what they are like in this present moment as you are with me?
Ryan: I'm getting that warm feeling coming up into my chest and face and feel lighter all over.

This inquiry differentiates the past alienation of shame from the present connection in relationship—a moment of coregulation.

Sharon: I am curious to know what helped you to negotiate those feelings in our time today?
Ryan: It felt like that lump in my belly finally loosened when I saw the love Isobel had for me.

Following the expression of these complex emotions, I attend to aliveness and vitality in a more expansive point of view.

Sharon: I'm wondering what sensations, feelings, and emotions were most pleasant for you in our time together today? When you recall those experiences, what do you notice now?

In the reflection phase of a therapeutic encounter, the green shoots of healing, growth, and development begin to emerge out of the soil of the intersubjective field. It is important to identify, protect, and support the growth as it emerges, to become the totemic witness. Here are a series of phenomenologically-based questions you might ask.

- I am wondering what might have felt different to you in our time together today?
- What was surprising for you in our work today?
- What seemed to be fresh and alive for you today?
- When you sense this change, what do you notice now in your body?

4. Identifying the Emerging "New"

The implicit memories that have been in dialogue begin to form and reform into new patterns of perception, arousal, emotion, and meaning. It is important to articulate the edges of the new perspective; it literally gives clients an anchor and a chance for life. This is the midwifery of therapeutic encounters—holding the space, encouraging the deliverance of the new life within. Finding fresh words for the changing phenomena of internal states can be challenging, and the process of verbalization needs to move slowly and reflectively. This is the emergence of the "speaking language" (Merleau-Ponty 2002), the knowledge contained in the body. A somatic inquiry can help that inner voice be articulated, heard, and witnessed.

Sharon: Ryan, when you recall that feeling in your belly and how it shifted from a black pit to warmth rising up, I am wondering what is happening for you now?

Ryan: I am still feeling that warm feeling in my chest and throat.

An open-ended reflective question, a reflection-in-action about the past while in the present moment allows the continuity of emerging phenomena to guide the healing. Whatever the response, the helping professional can follow as the phenomena unfolds. For example, you might ask, "When you felt that tightness in your belly, what did you notice next?" In this inquiry with Ryan, I am focused on restoring the flow of continuity of processing lived experience rather than the dissociation that comes with shame.

Sharon: When that energy moved up through your chest into your throat, I wonder if you have any words in this moment to describe it.

Ryan: (*After a few moments of silence*) It's hard to find the right words . . . It's like a rising up of who I am so I can be seen.

Be sure to take your time and see what phenomena come up. In this body-centered inquiry, we are verbally supporting the flow of the inner world with the direct speaking language of the body. When helping professionals stay attuned to the same areas in their own bodies, the intersubjective field becomes the crucible for opening a new, interconnected experience that can become part of our language together. We can inquire about new images that access the dissociated, intense affect.

Sharon: In our time together, I am wondering if you noticed any images that feel vivid.

Ryan: I had the image of my boss sending over the drinks, he drinks a lot and likes company at the bars, so I go along with him and drink even when I don't want to.

For Ryan, that image brought up thoughts of shame. I was interested to sense the current somatic experience of the shame.

Sharon: When you remember that image, what happens in your belly in this moment?

Ryan: It opens and clears and I just had the image of Isobel running toward me, hugging me while I ask for a ginger ale in the bar. My boss smiles. He is glad I am taking care of myself and staying with him at the same time. He can see me now.

The images can emerge as insights or constructions of thought.

Sharon: When you recall our experience together today, I am wondering if you have a feeling of how it has affected your sense of self?

Ryan: It feels like I have more strength to say what I need even if it is disappointing someone.

The emergence of connections can come in any form in right-hemispheric processing. It's important to note that what feels noteworthy for you as a helping professional may not be significant for the other, yet it is valuable to speak about what you noticed.

Sharon: When you talked about seeing your wife at the train station, I noticed a sparkle and radiance in your eyes and face. I am wondering what it felt like for you?

Ryan: Yeah, things are getting a little easier between us. I'm not as shut down as I was with her. Just now, I felt glad to see her.

5. Association of the New Material with Prior Knowledge

New emerging ways of perception and knowing need integration with prior knowledge. This inquiry is looking for the continuity of knowing, links that make the new change acceptable. We are seeking to strengthen the continuity of self. In this way the new change can be experienced as natural, normal development.

Sharon: Ryan, I really appreciate your sense of enthusiasm and connection with your family and I wonder if this is a familiar feeling in other relationships in your life?

Ryan: Yep, that's why I love sales, getting to know a client and figuring out just what he needs to get the job done. I really like that kind of connection.

6. Valuing the New

When we are conscious of the value of a new aspect of the self, we are able to discern the meaning that was previously hidden from awareness. The value of our lived experience when reflected upon becomes the emerging meaning of our lives.

Sharon: Ryan, when you recall how Gina and Isobel have been there for you, I'm wondering the value of their presence in your life for you?

Ryan: When I remember seeing them at the train, I feel that warm sense in my chest and face and I know they are the most important part of my life.

7. What Do You Imagine Might Change with This New Knowledge?

In this phase, we are preparing for the ordinary ways that the change will continue. This inquiry can open up the obstacles and challenges that will emerge due to the change and is useful to attend to the awareness of what might lie ahead. Awareness of the challenges can provide an opportunity to prepare to meet those emerging changes.

Sharon: Ryan, when you consider how this new sense of connection with others will affect your life, I am wondering what you imagine could happen?

Ryan: I know that I can go back to remember Isobel and Gina waiting for me at the train station and the hope rises up again. I think when I feel this hope I don't feel stuck anymore.

8. The Effect of the Shared Lived Experience on a Sense of Self

Sharon: Ryan, when we ponder what we did here today, I am wondering how it affects your sense of yourself and who you are with other people.

Ryan: It was really weird how that black lump moved up from my belly and opened up my chest. *(After some quiet time)* This is who I really am.

This somatic reflection with Ryan provided a contrast between his innate urge to receive the love from his daughter and wife and the inner over-whelming "black lump" of shame that created an autonomic distance in his relationships. With the accumulation of a ventral vagal state of social engagement with Isobel, Gina, myself, and his sales clients, the immobil-ity with fear held in his viscera—the source of his shame—released and simply became energy in his body that opened his chest and consciousness, a bodily based reorganization that restored connectivity and cohesion. Somatic reflection allowed the remnants of his fear, shame, and immobil-ity to be uncoupled.

Somatic Reflection in a Group

There is much to be gained from participating in somatic reflection in a group setting. Used in educational modules for Somatic Transformation, the Phenomenological Encounter Process is a structured reflective process that helps participants shift perspectives about themselves and others and enhances empathic abilities (Stanley 1994). The goal of the Phenomeno-logical Encounter Processes is to develop an embodied awareness of neu-rological states and hidden emotions before engaging in reflective thoughts regarding self and other. These encounters help people identify barriers to somatic empathy and reveal bodily-based knowledge of the relationship.

In coreflective dynamics, people learn to trust in their own inner ways of knowing, building a stronger foundation for choice, commitment, and accountability. Participants in the Phenomenological Encounter Process have found that self-awareness was less threatening than confrontation from others in a consulting group, and they felt more compassion for the self and the obstacles faced by others. Reflection opens people to a more hopeful perspective, yet, paradoxically, people who follow practices of somatic reflection recognize the power they have to hurt and cause suffer-ing and consciously develop caring practices.

Reflection-in-action through the Phenomenological Encounter Process is a vehicle for practitioners to articulate their subjective inner world and distinguish it from the subjective inner world of another, a discernment that allows them to become more effective at maintaining boundaries and closeness. It also gives them an immediate, empathic connection by imagining the same lived experience from another's embodied state. June Singer (1990) speaks about an invisible world that comes into awareness when we experience our lives and voice our concerns in the present tense with an active voice that will "bring about an evolution in those concerns" (121). Participants in the Somatic Transformation educational process are encouraged to write a reflection-in-action on daily encounters with people in their life, in the present tense with an active voice as suggested by Singer. See Exercise 11.4: The Phenomenological Encounter Process on page 213 of the appendix.

References

Braun, R. 2014–2015. "Resurrection." *Parabola* 39(4): 42–47.

Damasio, A. 2010. *Self Comes to Mind: Constructing the Conscious Brain.* New York: Pantheon.

Margulies, A. 1989. *The Empathic Imagination.* New York: Norton.

McGilchrist, I. 2009. *The Master and His Emissary: The Divided Brain and the Making of the Western World.* London: Yale.

Merleau-Ponty, M. 2002. *Phenomenology of Perception.* Translated by D. Landes. New York: Routledge.

Needleman, J. 2014–2015. "Why Can't We Be Good?" *Parabola* 39(4): 96–109.

Panksepp, J., and L. Biven. 2011. *The Archaeology of Mind: Neuroevolutionary Origins of Human Emotion.* New York: Norton.

Peavy, R. V. 1997. *SocioDynamic Counselling: A Constructivist Perspective.* Victoria: Trafford.

Porges, S. W. 2011. *The Polyvagal Theory: Neurophysiological Foundations of Emotions, Attachment, Communication, and Self-Regulation.* New York: Norton.

Quillman, T. 2012. "Treating Trauma through Three Interconnected Lenses: Body, Personality and Intersubjective Field." *Clinical Social Work Journal* 41: 356–365.

Schore, A. N. 2014. "The Right Brain Is Dominant in Psychotherapy." *Psychotherapy* 51(3): 388–397.

Schön, D. 1990. *Educating the Reflective Practitioner.* Oxford: Jossey-Bass.

Singer, J. 1990. *Seeing through the Visible World: Jung, Gnosis, and Chaos.* New York: Harper Row.

Stanley, S. A. 1994. "The Process and Development of Empathy in Educators: A Phenomenological Inquiry." PhD diss., University of Victoria.

Stern, D. B. 2010. *Partners in Thought: Working with Unformulated Experience, Dissociation, and Enactment.* New York: Routledge.

Tucker, D. M. 2007. *Mind from Body: Experience from Neural Structure.* New York: Oxford University Press.

Van der Post, L. 1960. *The Lost World of the Kalahari.* London: Hogarth Press.

Varela, F., E. T. Thompson, and E. Rosch. 1991. *The Embodied Mind: Cognitive Science and Human Experience.* Cambridge: MIT Press.

12 The Old/New Paradigm for Healing Trauma

"Sometimes we are misled by the promises of gurus and systems outside our-selves . . . This is the great falsity of all colonization, be it territorial or spiritual. It robs the native land, or native soul, of the sense of its own indigenous treasures and resources."

(O'Donohue 2010, 19)

The Old/New Paradigms: Essential Elements for Healing Trauma

Emerging research of the new paradigm—the neuroscience of relational human development—teaches us that the inner world of people suffering from trauma is based on a rigid, dysregulated nervous system that pro-duces dissociated and conflicted emotional states, with feelings of emp-tiness, despair, rage, anger, and anguish. These chronic states of trauma result in difficulties sustaining nurturing relationships and profound loss of meaning in life. Trauma dynamics not only disrupt attachment rela-tionships between children and their caregivers but affect future genera-tions through war, oppression, genocide, slavery, and poverty. The effects of trauma include physical and emotional illness, disabilities, relational betrayal, and the formation of social structures based on power dynamics rather than interpersonal connectivity. While it is true that more must be done on a global level in our educational and healthcare systems to address trauma, ultimately healing begins within the inner world of each person, in the connectivity of nurturing relationships, and the conscious develop-ment of small groups of people dedicated to meeting and alleviating the massive damage caused by trauma.

In many ways, the "new paradigm" is simply the reemergence of an old paradigm, a phenomenon supported by research regarding neural development over the span of human evolution (Porges 2011). Current research in neurobiology offers vast data related to relational healing from trauma (Schore 2012) that is highly congruent with the principles of healing contained in the ancestral legacies of human beings (Narvaez et al. 2014). While hyperarousal and aggression—the responses to fear and terror—can unite a population to eradicate an adversary, an alternative path based on authentic social engagement, rather than survival of the most powerful, has actually been the dominant way of knowing and interacting for thousands of years. Narvaez et al. (2014) offers an abundance of research into highly successful human ways of knowing and shared subjective ways of relating, ancestral legacies established over the course of evolution that lead to a larger and more inclusive view of what it means to be human than a narrow window of survival offered through aggression and control. The research of Allan Schore (2012), Stephen Porges (2011), Ian McGilchrist (2010), and others is in tune with this ancestral view of our human legacy of love. Their work recognizes the primacy of right-hemispheric ways of knowing and the possibilities for healing our shared historical and individual trauma through relational body-centered practices.

My own informal phenomenological research over seventeen years of teaching somatic practices, combined with the academic study of neurobiology, ancient wisdom, and Indigenous cultures, reveals three essential elements for healing trauma: *enhancing perception through the senses; knowing through direct experience; and relating to humans and nonhumans with a sense of mutuality, humility, and interconnection.* Relational body-centered practices based on these three elements of the old/new paradigm offer innovative ways to shift the inner survival-based nervous system from the chronic arousal of fear, terror, and horror to patterns of resilient, optimal states of regulation, where even the most horrific traumatic events can be incorporated in relationships of love, trust, and affection. This change is initiated through authentic, intimate, heart-to-heart, body-to body, right-brain-to right-brain encounters. Such a transformation may sound simple but is actually complex and challenging if it is to endure and be transmittable.

"Top Down" Versus "Bottom Up"

Generations of helping professionals who work with traumatized people have been trained in a variety of philosophical, religious, scientific, and psychological theories based on "top-down" approaches that were developed by enlightened leaders, abstract scholarship, and charismatic gurus. Practitioners were expected to faithfully adhere to a specific approach or invent their own "eclectic" practice by combining congruent approaches. Top-down theoretical approaches organize what and how people see, hear, and feel in terms of logical, abstract principles or a diagnosis of a particular pathology. The tendency to submit to the control of authorities for habits of perceiving, knowing, and relating can be accelerated in times of communal danger and threat, resulting in the loss of diverse individual perceptions and the increase of conformity in knowledge and behavior. For example, in a war or disaster, survival may appear to be dependent on obedience to a strong leader rather than consensus of a group. In educational groups and trauma therapy, I have continually witnessed how people who are dominated by trauma will submit and comply with the techniques and interpretations of people who wear a mantle of authority, dissociating from their own internal "gut-based" knowing or reacting to authoritative top-down protocols with anger and aggression.

A number of hunter-gathering, nomadic, wisdom, and Indigenous cultures described by historians and anthropologists, such as Berman (1989), Diamond (2012), Atleo (2004, 2010), Ray (2008), and Narvaez and Schore (2014), have a "bottom-up" approach that values subjective experience based on keen perception of individuals, the development of knowledge through the communal processing of shared lived experience and egalitarian social structures that value fluid, diverse perspectives, rather than obedience and conformity.

The new paradigm in developmental neuroscience points to the "old" way: a bottom-up approach that recognizes the capacity of human beings to accurately perceive and wisely respond to their bodily-based subjective lived experience while compassionately taking into consideration the bodily-based subjective lived experience of others (Schore 2012). The philosopher Merleau-Ponty (1962) reminds us that our own subjective lived experience is most fundamentally perceived through the body. Developmental neuroscience recognizes that the primary modes infants use to communicate their subjective experience is through the eyes, ears, and feelings of gesture and touch. This sensuous, direct connection with others from birth throughout the life span of interconnected attached relationships contributes to the accuracy of current perceptions and the value of knowledge gleaned from subjective lived experience. Let's take a moment to explore these elements in a more specific way.

Perceiving

A psychological definition of perception is a "single unified awareness derived from sensory processes while a stimulus is present" (*Webster's Unabridged Dictionary* 2001). Our external sensory experience focuses primarily on vision, hearing, and touch. However, our internal states of digestion, respiration, and circulation are monitored by the process of *interoception*. Interoceptors are located on the heart, stomach, liver, and other organs that provide us with information regarding the well-being of the viscera, the health of specific organs (Porges 2011). The ability to sense internal states in order to recognize symptoms of neural dysregulation and create shifts in chronic states of arousal is at the core of somatic practices.

Somatic practices beginning with mindful embodiment allow us to take personal responsibility for our own health and well-being, engage in skillful action to attend to dysregulated patterns of arousal, and do the same for others. Engaging in interoception—observing gut-level visceral activity through somatic sensory-based awareness—is a little known practice in Western culture, yet it is a highly refined and valued ability in hunter-gatherer, Indigenous cultures, and other wisdom traditions such as Tibetan Buddhism (Ray 2008). Porges maintains that the "ability to sense and regulate internal physiological states is at the base of competencies in higher order behavioral, psychological, and social processes" (2011, 82). The "nervous system provides the management skills necessary to regulate internal physiological systems" (2011, 85). The practice of paying attention to bodily-based visceral states provides essential afferent feedback to the nervous system and the necessary information to the vagal nervous system to maintain social engagement.

The term *neuroception* (Porges 2011) describes how the stimulation of fear, terror, and horror create sensory processes that result in a "single unified awareness," a consciousness that radically changes our unconscious ways of knowing and relating and results in states of mobilization that interfere with the detection of social cues. For example, when in a state of mobilization by fear, such as withdrawal or aggression, it is very difficult to perceive and respond with social connection. Immobilization of the dorsal vagal has coupled with sympathetic mobilization, significantly dulling accurate perception of current experience. The wounds of trauma generate distortions in the perceptual processes of the brain stem, particularly interoception, and affect how we see, hear, taste, and feel in any given moment. Unconscious implicit memories can arise through our perceptual system to convince us that danger or life threat is immediate and we must fight, flee, or freeze to survive even in environments of safety and security.

Practices of embodiment, somatic awareness, and empathy can help people discern between the lived experience of haunting traumatic memories and the accurate, fresh, immediate experience of seeing, hearing, tasting, and feeling current reality. It is only when we can stay fully embodied, somatically aware, and emotionally present to ourselves and others in moments of uncomfortable, distressing, and even excruciating sensory experience that past memories can be uncoupled from the present subjective experience. It is inhumane to expect a traumatized person to attend to the sensual and imaginal torment of embedded trauma without the support of others. When the suffering is met, shared, perceived, and known by compassionate others, a person can release the fixed-action patterns of hyperarousal that include reflexive gripping in the body and reactive aggression as well as the fixed-action patterns of hypoarousal that trigger unconscious disembodiment, dissociation, and disconnection. The tiny muscles and tissues governed by neuroceptions, and accessible to change through interoception, are highly sensitive to the compassion and caring of another, releasing the ghosts of the traumatic past that reside in the body. Once these "ghosts" have completed their lament; they have been seen, heard, and felt by another; mourned; and finally freed, a traumatized person can begin to move on. The diverse, sacred ceremonies of hunter-gatherer and Indigenous people and embodied meditative practices of wisdom cultures (Ray 2008) are the primary ways human beings have restored health to traumatized people throughout history.

Knowing through Direct Experience

Both the old and new paradigms value knowledge that is mediated through direct bodily-based experience and the right hemisphere of the brain. Knowledge may be organized in the left hemisphere in logical systems, sequence, and abstraction—forms of knowing that are available for intuitive access—but remains fluid and responsive to momentary changes in the environment, a task that is beautifully accomplished by the right hemisphere of the brain (McGilchrist 2009). Direct ways of knowing begin with bodily-based perceptions that stimulate specific neural states, or neuroceptions, that can bypass logic and rational processes. Knowing begins with accurate external perceptions of vision, hearing, and touch and the interoceptions that move us toward or away from social encounters with others. This urge to move toward or away from something or someone, becomes an emotional knowing that leads to more specific modes of comprehension through imagination, a way of knowing which can contain and communicate the intensity of emotion in highly significant ways. Reflection on shared sensory experience, emotions, and images facilitates integration of these different forms of knowledge into clarity and meaning that can then be easily translated to the left hemisphere.

We can practice ways of discovery and knowing that go beyond generalities, categories, and systems with somatic methods of phenomenology, such as somatic-based inquiry of one's internal states and those of another. Somatic inquiry comes from a place of wonder, curiosity, and creativity and is radically different from a top-down analytical, projective, or diagnostic interpretation. Somatic inquiry requires respect and reverence for the unique subjective experience of the other and a recognition that the most painful memories of trauma have been deeply hidden within the inner world. The "unknown" inner core of trauma must be approached slowly, carefully, and with reverence; go too fast and it will explode into violence and aggression; too slow and this core remains dormant, unconscious, and in control of the inner world.

Skilled phenomenological methodology guides an alive, intuitive, interactive exploration of trauma as it emerges in the intersubjective field. Clinicians learn to discern and track barely perceptual cues that indicate both healing and trauma as the intersubjective field grows in safety, intimacy, and recognition of a mysterious beauty that is present despite the trauma. A somatic inquiry is first interested in the immediate perceptual experience of the other, not in the stories of how the current state came to be. The stories are important, but they do not change until the underlying neuroceptions shift from fear and terror to safety and love. While conducting a somatic inquiry, practitioners are continually engaged in mindful attention to the subtle cues that indicate safety, danger, or life threat.

The shift from a dominant explicit way of knowing to more implicit modes involves letting go of a fixed sense of self and the world. Terry Marks-Tarlow speaks of intuition as trusting the body's responses for guidance in the moment and clinical intuition as the right-brain mode of perceiving "immediate sensory, emotional and imaginal data" in helping relationships (2012, 3). Intuition, based on "flashes, hunches and gut feels," is a holistic way of knowing that can be refined, amplified and evaluated for accuracy with somatic inquiry. For example, I may inquire with a client, "Joan, when you were describing the movement of the jellyfish with your gesture, I was imagining that movement was what you were feeling in your chest in that moment. I wonder what you recall?" If I am accurate, Joan will feel felt by me; if I am inaccurate she has an opportunity to correct me and shift my assumption. Intuitions are implicit communications that can be noticed in dream states, meditations, and ordinary interactions and contribute to the depth of a reflection on lived experience.

Relating in Mutual, Interactive Ways

Relationships come to life when power is shared and the subjective reality of each is honored. In the new paradigm of relational healing (Bromberg 2011), a two-person psychology describes the primacy of subjective experience and connectivity in embodied, intimate encounters. These spontaneous "moments of meeting" (The Boston Change Process Study Group, 2010) engage authentic emotional responses of each resulting in the aliveness of intersubjective connection. It is this intersubjective connection that stimulates inner sources of vitality that can touch into and melt the icy deadness of traumatic neural states.

Subjective-intersubjective ways of knowing the self and the other are open to ongoing change, revision, and surprise through perceptions and implicit ways of knowing that are in contrast to therapeutic certainty through physical, psychological, and spiritual top-down theories and protocols. Held in the safety of a contained intersubjective relationship, the buried and dissociated emotions from historical and personal trauma are implicitly recalled in the form of barely perceived sensations, movements, emotions, images, and archetypes. These unresolved implicit memories arise as current neurological states of hyperarousal and hypoarousal that require attunement and resonance by another in order to restore vagal homeostasis and reorganization into higher cortical states of being. If not regulated in the context of a trusted intersubjective field, the patterns of dysregulated neurological states continue in behaviors of violence with active or passive aggression, dissociated states of helpless immobility, and chronic inner emotions of rage, anger, despair, and shame that present to clinicians as anxiety, tension, powerlessness, and stress.

Attention to a wide variety of emotions in the safety of the intersubjective field allows implicit memories to resolve in the context of the current relationship. This resolution is possible when helping professionals are able to recognize and regulate the neural state of an emotion, then the healing value of a particular emotion, next guiding each affective experience into meaning and wisdom rather than judging uncomfortable and painful emotions as disruptive and negative. Emotions are very human ways of knowing the inner and outer environment and represent the transformation of ways of knowing, beginning with perceptions, to the natural conclusion of meaningful information regarding safety, justice, respect, love, and equity. For example, perceptions of danger and life threat lead to emotions of fear and terror that motivate us to act in ways to ensure safety. Anger motivates us toward justice, disgust protects us from toxicity, while sadness acknowledges loss and, when shared, reunites us to others. Joy elevates us into sustaining bonds of connectivity.

The Value of the Old/New Paradigm

The old/new paradigm applies to the healing, growth, and development of human beings who carry a legacy of generational trauma, are vulnerable to adverse events, and have been deprived of a secure attachment. Throughout this book, the practices of embodiment, somatic awareness, empathy, inquiry, congruent intervention, and reflection offer tangible, practical ways to amplify perceptions of current reality, know through direct experience, and change through embodied affective interpersonal relationships.

With somatic awareness of emotions we can guide our internal unknown experience into knowing through images and reflection. Somatic empathy allows us to receive the felt sense of the unique perceptions and knowledge of the other in their own terms, rather than project our own experience and interpretation upon them. Embodiment, somatic awareness, and somatic empathy are all internal subjective practices of the mind and body, ways of acting that begin first in the intrapersonal world of the practitioner and then enable that helping professional to truly know and accompany others in their shifting, yet healing, moment-to-moment experiences of loss, anguish, sorrow, pain, yearning, and joy.

Somatic inquiry allows helping professionals to shift from treating the pathology of the other, a top-down approach, to mutually exploring hidden realms of pain and sorrow with compassion and empathy. Practices of somatic inquiry opt for openness and wonder instead of analysis, unknowing rather than certainty, and curiosity about the internal world of the other instead of projection, diagnosis, interpretation, and management. The practice of somatic inquiry requires a respect for the innate subjective wisdom of the other, a realization that the most important aspects of the other are unknown and rich in mystery, wholeness, and beauty. A somatic inquiry is first interested in the perceptual experience of the other, not the opinions of how the perception came to be. When regulated into safety and connection with the other, a somatic inquiry continues to attend to and synthesize the unresolved elements of trauma that emerge as right-hemisphere phenomena: sensation, movement, emotion, image, and archetype.

Somatic reflection synthesizes information from a somatic inquiry into a body of lived experience that can be assimilated by the left hemisphere and known as one's subjective truth, providing a logical, sequential connection with a person's abstract way of knowing, a glimpse of truth-in-the-moment that remains open to new lived experiences and new logical syllogisms. Each somatic practice in this book supports a right-hemispheric to right-hemispheric way of knowing, one that is grounded in the ecology of "right relations."

Navigating the Inner Realms of Trauma

The relational focus of emerging neuroscience is a call to action for a radical shift from the "rugged individualism" of the dominant Western social environment to explore the wisdom of cultures where people live in congruity with their own subjectivity and integrity, yet actively participate in an interconnected, socially engaged community, a balance that our Indigenous ancestors achieved over thousands of years (Davis 2009). For example, Wade Davis describes the complex social organization of the Indigenous people of the Trobriand Islands. This community belonged to a complex trading circle in the Pacific, known as the "Kula ring" that was based on "balanced reciprocity," where intricate navigational skills required social organization. Exchanges between people of different islands were complex and spiritually significant. Davis describes the right-hemispheric orientation of these people that was reflected in their method of navigation. "The genius of Polynesian navigation lies not in the particular but in the whole, the manner in which all these points of information come together in the mind of the wayfinder, who must process an endless flow of data, intuitions, and insights derived from the observations and the dynamic rhythms and interactions of the wind, waves, clouds, stars, sun, moon, the flight of the birds, a bed of kelp, the glow of phosphorescence on a shallow reef—in short, the constantly changing world of the weather and of the sea" (2009, 60).

The process of the Polynesian wayfinder is similar to that of the somatic practitioner seeking to heal trauma. Information from developmental neuroscience and theories such as affective regulation therapy (Schore 2012) are challenging helping professionals to develop intuitive (Marks-Tarlow 2012), complex, integrative skills to navigate murky inner subjective worlds that have been disrupted by trauma. Affective, somatic education in the context of authentic intersubjective relationships can pave the way for more empathic, sustainable, interactive, bodily-based practices than techniques and strategies learned in a disconnected educational environment. Our perception expands when we feel engaged, connected, and supported by others, a contrast to the moments when we feel alone in groups and must rely on our personal resilience. Social engagement and the ongoing development of embodiment, empathy, and intuition leads to healthy relationships, groups, and communities in which to raise our children and grandchildren. How do we create this change we wish to see?

Perhaps a first step for helping professionals is to develop trusting relationships within an embodied professional community. While the facts and data pertaining to developmental neuroscience and effective practices can be gleaned through traditional, impersonal learning experiences such as books, lectures, online courses, large training groups, and conferences, the intangible clinical expertise needed for relational embodied practice requires a heartfelt sense of personal safety and wholeness through connection with others.

Shared affective experiences can help professionals become aware of unconscious defenses, revealing and softening power-oriented relational strategies and providing opportunities to grow beyond unconscious self-survival dynamics into transparent, kind, and loving ways of being. In well-designed and facilitated small learning groups, the shared sense of "feeling felt," known, and cared for releases a person from the burden of lonely defensive survival and slowly opens the group to loving practices of social engagement. Change occurs while immersed in the context and dynamics of social engagement, relationships that actually touch into and alter our more sensitive places. Reflecting on the *idea* of belonging and interconnection can prepare the way for change; however, it is the actual lived experience of embodied, empathetic, and intuitive ways of healing in relational communities that energizes our neural-emotional social growth and development.

Relationally oriented, embodied learning communities can grow into ongoing consultation groups, forming small tribes of people who explore ways to reduce unnecessary suffering. Professional education with relational bodily-based practices is holistic and requires the tender lived experiences of "balanced reciprocity," similar to those needed by traumatized people—connected, congruent, and contingent affective dynamics that strengthen clinical expertise. It is essential that these experiences happen on a professional level in the context of authentic relationship—with people who are willing to open their hearts and souls to one another.

While it is extremely important for helping professionals to develop relational learning communities to further develop their clinical expertise in somatic practices and work through their own unresolved traumatic experiences, more must be done on a global level to help communities not only heal from trauma, but eradicate the conditions that allow it to happen in the first place. Prevention of trauma includes the need for individuals to take responsibility for the integrity of their own inner world, express their subjective bodily-based experience with transparency and honesty, and prepare for inevitable adversity with disciplines that strengthen mental, physical, and, particularly, interpersonal health. In a postcolonial era, we have much to learn from Indigenous communities who are working toward healing and preventing trauma by reclaiming their own ancient creation myths, traditional expressive language, embodied relational practices, and rituals and ceremonies.

Elissa Washuta (2014), a Native American woman and professor at the University of Washington, describes her intense physical and mental struggle to attain health and overcome her own historical trauma in her autobiography with an unusual vulnerability, vivid sensory-based imagery and emotional honesty. She writes of the somatic sensory perceptions of her suffering, the effect of pharmaceutical medical interventions, and her growing trust in a transformative bodily-based healing process. "My brain steams inside my skull, overheated as I consider driving my car into the Sound, surfacing, and binding my busted legs into a mermaid's tail. . . . I want to turn half-creature and breathe through gills, replace my human brain with something that needs to only know smell and light and balance, an understanding without nuance and shade. I tell my GPS [her inner guidance system], 'Fucking tell me where to go and I will.' Ten seconds later, she tells me" (189). This is the final sentence in her book.

Washuta's wisdom lies in her choice to release the domination of Western culture's definitions and practices of mental health that she has internalized over her own body in favor of Indigenous way of knowing through her perceptions—breathing, smelling, seeing light, and feeling a balance. She then enters into the process of healing by trusting her own intuitive, bodily-based way of knowing, relying on the emergence of ancient wisdom she does not need to share with us. Washuta implicitly reminds us that right-hemispheric ways of knowing how to mitigate trauma have existed throughout human history and further research and support of Indigenous efforts to restore and renew ancient ways of knowing will benefit all, particularly Western-oriented researchers and practitioners interested in developing creative, natural processes for preventing and healing trauma that are congruent for a multicultural world.

The field of interpersonal neurobiology is creating a shared intercultural meeting place of emerging research through neuroscience, philosophy, and bodily-based practices that explore the wide diversity of lived experience as it exists ecologically in human beings around the globe. The therapeutic model and educational processes of Somatic Transformation continue to be a fluid, dynamic synthesis of emerging neuroscience, ancient culture and wisdom, and phenomenological ways of knowing that can be used to heal personal and generational trauma. As Simone Weil (1952) points out, unacknowledged suffering leads to violence, while acknowledged suffering ends the cycle of violence. It is only through relationship that the unresolved suffering can be transformed into love and connection.

References

Atleo, E. R. 2004. *Tsawalk: A Nuu-chah-nulth Worldview*. Vancouver: University of British Columbia Press.

Atleo, E. R. 2010. *Principles of Tsawalk: An Indigenous Approach to Global Crisis*. Vancouver: University of British Columbia Press.

Berman, M. 1989. *Coming to Our Senses*. New York: Simon and Schuster.

The Boston Change Process Study Group. 2010. *Change in Psychotherapy: A Unifying Paradigm*. New York: Norton.

Bromberg, P. M. 2011. *The Shadow of the Tsunami: and the Growth of the Relational Mind*. New York: Routledge.

Davis, W. 2009. *The Wayfinders*. Toronto: House of Anansi Press.

Diamond, J. 2012. *The World Until Yesterday: What We can Learn from Traditional Societies?* New York: Viking Press.

Marks-Tarlow, T. 2012. *Clinical Intuition in Psychotherapy: The Neurobiology of Embodied Response*. New York: Norton.

McGilchrist, I. 2009. *The Master and His Emissary: The Divided Brain and the Making of the Western World*. London: Yale.

McGilchrist, I. 2010. "Reciprocal Organization of the Cerebral Hemispheres." *Dialogues in Clinical Neuroscience,* 12(4): 317–334.

Merleau-Ponty, M. 1962. *Phenomenology of Perception*. Translated by D. Landes. New York: Routledge.

Narvaez, D. and J. Panksepp. 2012. *Evolution, Early Experience and Human Development: From Research to Practice and Policy*. New York: Oxford University Press.

Narvaez, D. and A. Schore. 2014. *Neurobiology and the Development of Human Morality: Evolution, Culture, and Wisdom*. New York: Norton.

Narvaez, D., K. Valentino, A. Fuentes, J. J. McKenna, and P. Gray, eds. 2014. *Ancestral Landscapes in Human Evolution: Culture, Childrearing and Social Well-Being*. New York: Oxford University Press.

O'Donohue, J. 2010. *Four Elements: Reflections on Nature*. Dublin: Transworld Ireland.

Porges, S. W. 2011. *The Polyvagal Theory: Neurophysiological Foundations of Emotions Attachment, Communication, and Self-Regulation*. New York: Norton.

Ray, R. 2008. *Touching Enlightenment: Finding Realization in the Body*. Boulder: Sounds True.

Schore, A. N. 2012. *The Science of the Art of Psychotherapy*. New York: Norton.

Washuta, E. 2014. *My Body Is a Book of Rules*. Pasadena: Red Hen Press.

Webster's Encyclopedic Unabridged Dictionary of the English Language. 2001. New York: Gramercy.

Weil, S. 1952. *Gravity and Grace*. Translated by E. Crawford and M. von der Ruhr. London: Routledge & Kegan Paul.

Appendix: The Practice of Somatics

Somatic practices are developed over time and best incorporated in relationships. When cultivating somatic ways of knowing, it is helpful to remember this form of learning is first explicit, then, as it is embodied, it becomes implicit and intuitive.

Exercise 1.1: Embodiment—Sensory-Motor Awareness and Regulation

The nervous system communicates with the brain through sensation. Interaction with your current sensory experience allows you to regulate your neural-emotional state. As you select the focus of your somatic awareness and shift from a particular sensation to another allow any instinctive micromovements your body wants to make. This exercise can be done in stages as people develop ease with embodiment.

Stage One: Opening to Embodiment

1. Establish a sense of connection with a partner through eye gaze, proximity, and attunement. As the first witness in the partnership, invite the other into the following observations.
2. Take a moment to notice any sensations or subtle movements in your bodies. Allow your attention to explore your feet, legs, arms, and hands.
3. Engage in small, slow, gentle, contraction-expansions, for example lifting the heels and then releasing them or opening and closing the hands, to locate your body in present time and space. Observe tension or ease in each area with interest and curiosity. Walk around the room slowly and describe the sensations you feel in each moment. Dialogue about your experience with your partner.

Stage Two: Animating the Ventral Vagal Nerves

4. Now allow your attention to focus on your face, jaw, forehead, and chest. Again, observe and bring micromovements of expansion and

contraction, such as raising and lowering the eyebrows, allowing the jaw to drop with gravity and slowly return, and moving your head in different directions. Notice any sensations of ease or tension and come to rest. Dialogue with your partner.

Stage Three: Accessing States of Vitality

5. Take a minute or so to recall and savor moments of pleasure or vitality you have experienced over the past few days and describe them to your partner.
6. Now scan your body, arms, legs, and hands, then face, jaw, neck, and shoulders. Dialogue with your partner: Has the felt sense in your body changed in any way as you remember those moments?

Exercise 4.1: Embodiment—Grounding and Restoring Rhythm

This exercise stimulates proprioception, your bodily-based way of knowing where you are in time and space. Used mindfully, somatic perception can diminish the power of past memories of trauma to overwhelm the present moment.

1. Engage with a partner as you restore a sense of innate rhythm, a usually unconscious inner dynamic that is thwarted with trauma.
2. As you imagine the earth beneath you and settle into gravity, bring a little movement into your ankles, one at a time. Lift the heel of one foot then slowly release it. Explore just the right rhythm for you as you lift and release each foot. Take some time to enjoy the movement, like a dance.
3. Now alternate the movement of lifting your toes and lifting your heels in a rhythm and sequence that feels playful and pleasurable.
4. Take a few moments to sense any vibration, pulsations, or peristalsis in your body. Notice any warmth, coolness, looseness, or tightness. Notice with interest and curiosity.
5. Play with very slow movements around areas of tension, discomfort, or pleasure.
6. Dialogue your experience with your partner.
7. If your eyes have been closed, take time to let a little light in. If your eyes are open, orient to what you see in this moment by slowly moving your head and eyes.
8. With open eyes, keep your gaze soft as you bring attention to the environment. Slowly organize your eyes, ears, head, neck, and shoulders into one slow, fluid movement as you explore the room and let your soft gaze take in that which is pleasurable in the environment, such as color, light, lines, and ground.

9. Continue to move your eyes, ears, neck, and shoulders in very slow, fluid movement to the right and then to the left as you orient to the present moment environment and track the changes in your inner sensations.
10. Then take a few moments to close your eyes, let the stimulation settle and reconnect with your partner to dialogue about your experience. What are you learning about your body and inner ways of knowing?

Exercise 4.2: Fostering Mutual Embodiment

1. With your partner, take a few moments to sit in each other's presence, wordlessly noticing, attuning, resonating, and respecting the boundaries of each.
2. Observe your comfort or discomfort with eye gaze and posture, making small movements to increase your comfort.
3. With a sense of interest and curiosity in your own inner sensory experience and that of the other, begin to identify perceptions in the moment. For example, the first person may begin by saying, "Now I see . . ." and describe what you are seeing in the moment. Your partner should silently attune to what you are seeing.
4. Next, say, "Now I hear . . ." and describe what you are hearing in the moment. Again, your partner attunes silently.
5. Finally, say, "In this moment, I am feeling . . ." while your partner silently attunes to that feeling.
6. Alternate roles so your partner identifies present moment sensory perceptions while you silently attune. Repeat this exercise three times.
7. Reflect on the experience with your partner. What was it like to shift modes of perception? How did it affect your body? What was it like to feel your own experience while you attuned to the experience of the other? What was the value of your exploration?

Exercise 4.3: Weaving a Cocoon for Protection

To restore embodiment when we are alone or with another, it is essential to feel safe, protected, and connected. Weaving a Cocoon is a somatic imaginal process that creates a sense of containment and protection.

1. Begin by lying down, sitting, or standing in a comfortable pose. Bring your awareness to six inches beneath your body.
2. Allow your mind to move down into the earth and locate a sense of gravity that can invite your body to release into it.
3. Now, bring your attention to the area six inches above your body, six inches in front of you, and then six inches behind. Each time, use attentional marking to weave a cocoon around you, an embodiment of your personal boundaries. Invite those boundaries to fill with the energy from your heart.

Exercise 4.4: Feeling Embodied Compassion

1. Identify with your imagination a person who has compassion for you and recall the sensations of receiving it. This person can be living, dead, or a spiritual guide. Alternatively, imagine the sensation of feeling compassion for yourself.
2. Scan your body as it rests in your cocoon and notice where you might be feeling some tension or discomfort in your arms, legs, shoulders, or face.
3. Slowly allow your hand to gently touch the area of discomfort with compassion.
4. Notice the sensation of the compassion and any warmth, safety, vibrations, or pulsations that come from the touch.
5. Allow yourself to engage in this meditation as long you like.

Exercise 4.5: Listening to the Voice of the Body

Our natural rhythm provides us an innate regulation that is disrupted in trauma. As we listen to and feel the body's messages, the natural regulation can be restored through the safety and connectivity of a trusted partner.

1. Following rhythmical music and perhaps dancing, listen to the sounds and subtle movements of your body; the vibrations, pulsations, and peristalsis.
2. As you pay attention to the vibrations, pulsations, and peristalsis, notice how various systems coordinate and bring you into regulation.
3. If the vibrations and pulsations are too strong, return to the preceding calming and centering exercises. Awareness combined with micromovement can also down-regulate the system.
4. If the vibrations and pulsations are too weak, as happens in hypoarousal, they need to be stimulated and up-regulated in relationship. The practice of right hemisphere communication with attuned eye gaze, resonant and contingent prosody and *feeling with* another within an intersubjective field stimulates hypoaroused states. In uncomfortable states of arousal, somatic awareness with stretching, a long, brisk walk, yoga, Tai Chi, Feldenkrais, meditation, dance, massage, and other body-centered practices stimulate vitality so that regulation can be restored.

Exercise 6.1: Accessing Vitality

People who have experienced trauma disembody to avoid uncomfortable and frightening internal sensations. Yet shutting down intense discomfort also closes the pathways of vitality that bring joy and pleasure. In order to replace dissociated fear and distress with a "vagal brake," we need to first catch people in brief moments of calm, pleasure, and joy. Joy and vitality come unexpectedly in a sustained, safe, and nurturing relationship.

1. Take a few moments to recall moments of delight and joy in your life. If there is no explicit memory of them, it is necessary to generate them in an embodied intersubjective field of a sustained therapeutic relationship so they can be noticed and amplified in the following exercise.
2. Talk about these experiences, one by one, with your partner. Notice what you feel in your body after you describe each experience. Notice if any experiences of distress or discomfort emerge. Notice how that feels in your body and consciously bracket, with the help of your partner, those sensations which are uncomfortable and then return to recall the moments of joy. If joy was interrupted by distress, oscillate your somatic awareness between the two polarities for a few moments and return to somatic awareness of the room and relationship.
3. Now your partner will describe his or her experiences of joy they have shared with you. Oscillate your attention between your own inner sensations and your perceptions about the other person's inner world. Be prepared to assist your partner in oscillation to stay in the optimal arousal zone.
4. Reflect together on the shared experience. Identify any unusual, intriguing aspects of your inner knowing. Notice what was helpful in differentiating sensory neural states.

Note: Differentiating neural states of joy and distress through oscillation allows coupled circuits to untangle. Oscillation of polarities is a dialectic that leads to transformational change and opens us to a more complex and multilens perspective, with the synthesis of loneliness with connection, joy with sorrow, and love with pain.

Exercise 6.2: Honing Nonverbal Somatic Awareness

Practice developing your capacity for somatic awareness in this partnered nonverbal exercise. You may make prosodic sounds of support, like *ohhh*, *umm*, or *hmmm*, if it feels natural. Take time to be wordless yet present.

1. Stand or sit across from your partner at a comfortable distance. Take a few moments to become quiet and simply notice what is happening in your body.
2. Then explore a shared rhythm of eye gaze and look on the periphery of your vision, a connection that is not intrusive for either of you. Allow your eyes to communicate your bodily-based feelings.
3. Your partner should attune, resonate, and feel with you—not interpret or fix.

4. As you scan your body, notice where there may be sensations of pleasure or ease. Bring your focus to these sensations and slowly enter into them more deeply with your consciousness, letting your somatic awareness follow any changes. Allow your face to reflect your experience—this can assist your partner in attuning and offering contingent, nonverbal interactions.
5. Watch your partner's face to receive nonverbal communications of presence, nurturing, and caring.
6. Next, notice any areas in your face, arms, legs, shoulders, or back that may have tension (these are areas where tension can be relieved with micromovements of voluntary muscles). Bring awareness to this area and sense into the tension. Observe how the tension responds to your awareness.
6. Sense into the contraction and tension and see if movement would create a little release or expansion. Experiment with micromovements of contraction and expansion.
7. Recall an area of pleasure; feel the sensations and let things settle as you engage fully with your partner. Take a few moments to describe your experience of somatic awareness before you switch roles.
8. Talk about your inner experience when you were the client and then when you were the observer. Shift and listen to your partner reflect on his or her experience.

Note: Establishing a shared rhythm of eye gaze helps to strengthen the ventral vagal neural state needed for social engagement in relationship. With this optimal state, sensations moving up the body to the brain can change in the moment, and the movements coming back down from the brain can be amplified to make changes in the "closed system" of the peripheral nervous system and autonomic nervous system.

Exercise 7.1: Practicing Bodily-Based Awareness, Attunement, Resonance, and Responsivity

This exercise incorporates somatic empathy in an attuned, resonant, and embodied connection with a partner.

1. Choose a safe place to practice, keeping in mind that a safe place for one person can feel dangerous to another. Discern your sensations that indicate safety, danger, or life threat and then listen to the discernment of your partner.
2. Experiment with somatic interventions to attain a sense of safety. Once you both feel safe, take a few moments to orient slowly to the space and the other person. Notice if it is easier to look to the right, or to the left, to sit close together, or further apart. Actively explore what feels safer and what diminishes a sense of safety. The goal here

is to learn to identify the sensations that indicate you are safe in this moment.

3. Notice internal sensations that arise on the periphery of your body. Notice feet, knees, legs, hands, arms, and shoulders and initiate micromovements that you hold in consciousness. Do you sense cold, warmth, vibration, pulsation, tension, flaccidity, or other sensations? Be curious and observe. Don't assess the internal viscera which can contain intense emotions—stay on the outside. What sensations indicate safety and what sensations indicate vigilance?

4. Now verbally communicate to your partner. Share something that is true about yourself—that you value—and what body sensations you notice. For example, you might share something like this: "I am dedicated to caring for abandoned animals." Briefly describe your truth and its value to you. Notice any sensations you feel as you speak and watch your partner's face as he or she listens. Notice how the other's reaction feels in you. Stay curious and bring wonder to your exploration.

5. Shift roles and as you listen to your partner, hold a dual awareness—where you are present to the other but also sense with curiosity and interest what is happening in your own body. Let go of thoughts and assumptions and return to sensations. Observe any changes, movements, tightening, or releasing. Be interested if you feel numbness or distance from your body. Suspend judgment and increase wonder, curiosity, and interest.

6. Notice where you might feel arousal of vitality or any discomfort or tension. Notice your face for the beginning of a smile or tightness in your jaw. Begin to notice your chest and throat for expansion or contraction.

7. Nonverbally attune and resonate to each other, sensing your own breath, rhythm, discomfort, and comfort. Begin by initiating some micromovements, such as nodding your head, rocking, or swaying. See if your movements synchronize. Notice the disconnections as well as the attunements.

8. Reflect together on this experience. Take a few moments to verbally describe to each other your self-awareness and awareness of the other. Allow the verbal dialogue to emerge with responsivity and reciprocity by building upon the observations of each. Note your difficulties and your accomplishments.

Exercise 7.2: Becoming a Participating Witness

In this exercise, the goal is to deepen somatic empathy by entering into a direct participation with another other from the safety and warmth of your own heart. When we witness through the heart, an organ of sensory perception, we are better able to self-regulate and regulate others.

This exercise can be done alone (follow steps 1–12) or in a small group (follow steps 1–16).

1. Take time to carefully witness what is happening in your body, eventually selecting attention to your face. To do this, drop down into a quiet state, surrender to the sensations in your body and particularly those of your face. Don't try to change your sensations. Notice what it is like to be a participating witness. You are here now while you witness any sensations and movements in your face.

2. As you take time to settle, notice where you experience tension in your face and where you notice an expansion. For more expansion, make micromovements in the muscles in your face. Notice the difference and oscillate your attention back and forth between the expansion in your face and a place of contraction.

3. After a few moments take some time to simply rest, and witness how your body can release into gravity. Consider how you can allow gravity to pull you closer to the earth.

4. As you release into gravity, play with an inner smile. A small smile within will stimulate a ventral vagal neural state.

5. Invite the inner smile to witness your eyes.

6. Your eyes might blink, spasm, and discharge tension in other ways. Continue the smile to your eyes from within, observing any changes.

7. Allow the smile of your eyes to move down to your heart. As you smile to the eyes of your heart, let your attention and eyes rest in your heart. Attention to the heart provides an open, secure place from which you can observe your body and the other without strain or vigilance.

8. If you would like support for uncomfortable sensations, place your hands on your face, gently cupping your eyes, or place your hands on your heart. With this touch, you can stimulate the ventral vagal circuit.

9. Explore micromovements of your jaw and eyebrows to release the tension and then rest. Observe how your body sensations move, shift, or are simply quiet in this moment.

10. When you feel ready, reorient to the room and reflect on the sensations of this meditation. You might notice how your neural state may have shifted.

11. Attend to very subtle cues in your body and reflect on your experience.

12. Consider how you were able to detect sensations and how selective attention to particular sensations enabled you to shift neural states. If in a group setting, continue with steps 13–16.

13. Take time in a small group for each person to describe his or her own experience of the participating witness meditation.

14. As each person speaks, listen with your body and mind. Notice how the eye gaze, voice, gestures, and presence of the person speaking affects your body in the moment.

15. Take some time to notice the sensations that arise when each person speaks and then discuss which sensations offer cues to the five different neural states: hyperarousal, hypoarousal, high arousal, low arousal, and optimal arousal.
16. Support each other in regulating arousal through grounding or vitality exercises.

Exercise 8.1: A Somatic Dialogical Inquiry

In this partnered exercise, you will practice a somatic dialogical inquiry through languaging, an important part of establishing congruency in human relationships. The spaces of energized silence between the words are equally potent—at times more so.

1. Take a few moments to gaze at your partner; notice what you see and wonder what you might not see, feel, or know about the other. Notice what happens in your body as you wonder about the other. You are developing the rhythm of an internal interactive oscillation as you move your awareness between yourself and the other.
2. Guided by your observations of your partner's face, eye gaze, tone of voice, and gestures as well as your own, begin languaging slowly (Step 3 offers specific suggestions for how to begin languaging), creating responses that are contingent on the nonverbal and verbal communication of the other. Contingent dialogue is phenomenological, unplanned yet intentional and intuitive, dependent on conditions in the moment. Each contribution follows the other. When in doubt, stay present and embodied, and listen for the guidance of your bodily-based wisdom. Notice the specific level of intimacy that you are able to sustain without raising defenses of withdrawal, aggression, or dissociation in yourself and your partner. A ventral vagal neural state is essential to developing the depth of intimacy needed to explore dissociated aspects of the self.
3. Begin languaging on the social level by taking responsibility for your curiosity. You might say something like "I am wondering what is happening for you in this moment," and then follow the emerging phenomena into the language of present moment sensation. In a verbal inquiry, the invitation to explore is open-ended, and characterized by wonder. With invitational words and tone of voice, the other person is free to describe the subjective experience in his or her own terms and at the level of intimacy that feels right in the moment.
4. Oscillate between speaking and listening with each other. A listener in a dialogical inquiry watches, hears, feels, and wonders about the other while gathering cues; suspending judgment, bias, and reaction. Both participants observe their own inner vibrations, pulsations, neural states, emotional feelings, and spontaneous images, allowing language

to emerge spontaneously from sensory-based perceptions. This flow of internal information and energy is combined with a conscious effort to be contingent with the current neural state, emotional tone, and imaginal language of the other. The goal here is not to sort out any areas of disagreement as is common in a discussion, but to find an intriguing, bodily-based place of safety with the other. During this phase of the connection, you might ask, "What can you imagine I could do to help you feel more comfortable in this moment?"

5. Next, watch for a felt shift from a general social level to an intersubjective level of intimacy. This shift feels like an energetic presence in your heart, a resonating sense in your gut, or a feeling of moving out toward the other; the other is no longer a stranger but an intriguing person in his or her own right.

6. Deepen your intention to attune and resonate with the other's experience as he or she describes it. Continue to explore the embodied, shared, subjective experience in the moment until this natural yearning to know the other emerges. This is the level where primitive emotions emerge and can find space and expression in the bodies and language of each. However, primitive emotions may *not* emerge in this encounter.

7. On the intersubjective level, monitor the felt sense, the emotions, and images that emerge, languaging them in ways that respect the connection, the new material, and your own responsivity, entering step by step into the depths of each other's lived experience. Queries on this level might take this form: "When you say that you have been angry with me, I'm wondering what you notice happening between us in this moment?" or "I feel touched when you talk about your sense of loneliness, I'm wondering if you can feel me with you in this moment?"

8. As trust and acceptance of each other's subjective reality sustains the intersubjective field, the dialogue may now enter into a deeper, more unconscious level, the inner core of dissociated neural states and primitive emotions. With the trust established in the intersubjective field, one person suspends the exploration of their own lived experience, to accompany and embody with the other the deeper intrasubjective realms of joy, ecstasy, terror, and horror. This is where the listener might unconsciously experience discomfort, inadequacy, or come face to face with the terror of unknown and unresolved trauma. When this happens, both people may disembody and dissociate, and enter into an enactment. If that happens, you may become confused and feel an urgency to fix it, all indicators that intrasubjective languaging is over in this moment. These breaches are part of intersubjective dialogue, and if they can be observed and acknowledged as enactments in the moment, repairs can be made and trust

can become stronger. It may take some time of reflection and consultation before listeners can return to the dialogue and acknowledge their responsibility in the breach and enactment. A somatic inquiry at this stage of the process might sound like this: "I'm feeling uncomfortable about my reaction to you last week. I remember saying to you that you had improved so much and when I saw your face, I realized that I was trying to fix you, not really hear you. I remember how you were describing the fear and terror of the suffering and I want you to know that I am aware that I missed the moment to be with you in your pain."

9. As participants trust the humility and truth behind the acknowledgment of relational breaches, the bridge between the two intrasubjective worlds is strengthened and a spontaneous synchrony becomes more accessible. Somatic inquiry at this level incorporates the imagination with bodily-based responses. An example of a somatic inquiry at this level might be: "I can sense the 'green pasture' in your image, and 'see the tail of your cherished dog, wagging wildly in recognition.' I'm wondering what you notice right now in your body." Following the bodily-based response with gaze, tone of voice, and gestures allows the bumps, breaches, and separations that happen in all human relationships to be rewoven.

10. A dialogical inquiry leads to the construction of meaning through somatic reflection. For example: "When you recall your experience of our session today, what moments feel important to you now?" and "How do you sense that in your body in this moment?"

**Exercise 9.1: Directed Eye Movements
for Integration of Opposites**

The goal of this eye movement exercise is to stimulate integration of polarities that have been fixed for some time. As phenomena are differentiated in a somatic inquiry, a conflict of opposites is often revealed.

1. Describe the following exercise to your partner with whom you have a stable intersubjective field.
2. When you are aware of a resistant inner conflict, differentiate the elements of the conflict into opposites with a phenomenological somatic inquiry, holding one aspect in one hand and the other in the other hand.
3. Gently trace your finger about twelve inches from the other's face in a figure eight around the eyes and the hands that are holding the opposites.
4. After one oscillation, rest and inquire about the current felt sense.
5. Continue several more times, allowing small shifts to settle.

Exercise 9.2: Oscillating Eye Movements to Deepen the Intersubjective Field

This exercise is helpful in creating a sense of connection and emotional containment with another while establishing the boundaries of the intersubjective field. It is a nonverbal visual eye movement in the form of a figure eight—you use your eyes and imagination to trace around your own boundaries of your body then around the boundaries of the other.

1. Rather than directly looking into the eyes of the other, widen your gaze to include the area around the person.
2. Allow your gaze to soften into the back of your eyes. Be aware of how energy can come out through your eyes to absorb the terror and horror of the other.
3. Now using your inner eye, imagine that you can weave a visual path around your own body, a path that allows you to scan the arousal in your body and slowly self-regulate. Go slowly—use the time you are wrapping the visual field around your body to ground, settle, relax, and soften.
4. Then allow your soft gaze to wrap around the second part of the figure eight—visually move around the body of the person you are working with. As you wrap the visual field around the body of the other, notice how the connection can be contained with the crossing of the two circles.
5. Attend to the intensity of the other. Allow this person to perceive your felt sense of their terror, rage, and confusion.
6. If you find yourself being drawn in to the other's boundaries too deeply, pause and take time to ground, center, and orient to your boundaries and the environment.

Exercise 9.3 Balancing on an Exercise Ball

A large exercise ball is useful to a body-centered somatic practitioner. It is helpful to take a few moments to sit on it and regulate the vestibular system between patients and to use it to support the vestibular system in patients. A somatic practitioner can help stabilize the vestibular system with small movements of the head or the natural movements people make to stabilize themselves on an uneven foundation, like an exercise ball. Before you invite a person to balance on a ball, explore this for yourself. Find out how you need to move, and how much support you need to balance. I like to stand behind someone who is using the ball to balance, offering support from the back.

1. First, invite the person to feel her pelvis on the ball, to sense how gravity pulls the pelvis to the ball and what it feels like to have contact with the perineum and gravity.

2. When a felt sense between the pelvis and the ball is established, invite the person to establish a felt sense of her feet on the ground and find the most stable posture as she feels her feet on the ground and her pelvis on the ball.
3. When and if she is ready, invite her to slowly move her feet and pelvis, oscillating between destabilization and restabilization. Do just a little bit at a time and continue to check in with the person to see the sensations she might feel in her body. This can stir up emotions, so take plenty of time to restore a sense of ground and center.
4. Once the person can regulate a sense of the ground, she can begin to discern her center core of strength and aliveness. This core moves up from the pelvis through the viscera, intestines, solar plexus, and chest, bringing vitality up through the body and moving it back down in a natural, pleasant rhythm.
5. Centering can be done with the imagination, so invite her to imagine the ground beneath her, then feel how her body connects with the image of the ground. The roots of trees or an embedded rock can provide a stabilizing image. The image can be oscillated with sensations until the sense of center emerges into awareness.

Exercise 10.1: Strengthening Transformation through Imaginal Perceptions

Transformation occurs when bodily-based experience is reconnected with the imaginal. A practice of transformation can enhance the neural connective of lived experience with the symbolic, clarifying meaning and add a sense of joy and completion.

1. Choose a book, poem, piece of music, or other work of art that resonates with you in the moment. Find a time and space for quiet contemplation and meditation, at least twenty minutes in length.
2. Read a passage aloud slowly, or if you have chosen a piece of music, painting, or other image, allow yourself to step into the work and simply observe the flow of sensory-based energy throughout your body.
3. Notice a particular phrase, and reread or listen even more closely. Notice any images that arise for you. Notice how your body responds to those images.
4. Assess the neural core of your response. Do the images feel safe, dangerous, or even life threatening? Bracket any images that feel life threatening or dangerous and return to the images that are safe, creative, and nurturing.
5. Begin to embody the images, sensations, and movements that feel safe, protective, and nurturing. Step into them and allow yourself to feel the restoration, calming, and vitality they offer.

6. Draw or journal your experience to share with another. Bring the images into the intersubjective field with a partner or small group for creative enhancement.

Exercise 11.1: Reflection on Images, Metaphors, and Archetypes that Emerge in Memories and Dreams

In a clinical setting, art making with paper and oil-based colors is relatively easy to integrate into short periods of time and can help clients communicate bodily-based experience. To work with clients in this way, it is helpful to maintain a dream journal, capturing the vivid aspects of your dream with oil crayons—as described in the last exercise.

1. Recall the colors, sensations, movements, emotions, symbols, and predominant images with oil crayons in a sketchbook before you try to recall the sequence of the story. These images will contain the embodied affect of the dream.
2. Draw and color any additional phenomena of the dream. As you color, notice the emotions that emerge.
3. Bracket any judgment of your ability to color or draw, this can distract you from the emerging meaning.
4. If the image has a historical significance, you might want to research what it has meant for others. Begin to connect the images with your daily experiences or memories from the past.

Exercise 11.2: Inviting Images to Speak the Embodied Truth

In this partnered exercise, embodied experience becomes images and spontaneous language. You will need paper and oil crayons—or other similar drawing implements to complete it.

1. Take a few moments to make yourself comfortable and sense into your body.
2. Bring somatic awareness to the sensations and movements in your body and invite any visual, auditory, or kinesthetic images to emerge.
3. Slowly oscillate your attention between sensations of comfort and expansion and those of discomfort and contraction. Attend to your sensations of expansion for a longer period of time and invite them to gestate into images.
4. If an image emerges, take some time to scribble it on paper with oil crayons. Let the colors inform you and the forms you make on the paper to emerge from your body. Note that an image can be generated by scribbling.
5. When the sensations have expressed themselves on paper, take a moment to orient to the present moment.

6. Now return to the image on the paper and describe what you see. It may not make sense at this time, but allow attention to sensations and images, and describe your experience.
7. Notice what happens in your body as you speak spontaneously about your inner sensations and symbolic images on the paper. Turn the paper in different directions to facilitate different perceptions of the same images.
8. Listen to your partner describe his or her image. It is not important to analyze the experience of the processing, only to witness, bringing interest and embodiment to the relationship.

Exercise 11.3: Written Somatic Reflection on Memories

Create a calm, meditative environment. This exercise can be done alone as preparation for a therapeutic session with a psychotherapist, counselor, or spiritual director.

1. Write down a memory you are interested in exploring. You may want to consider the following: When did this happen? Who was there to assist you, either spiritually or embodied? What was different after this experience? How has your memory changed over time? What is unfinished in your memory? When was it over? What strengths emerged out of this memory? What limitations occurred because of this experience? With each question, consult the sensations, movement, emotions, and images that arise from your body. Move slowly through the eight steps of embodied reflection (see page 178 of Chapter 11) to discern the responses to these questions as well as your own questions. As you write a brief description of each memory, track what you notice in your body, particularly if you have no sensations. This could indicate a deep state of hypoarousal and immobility with fear. Notice tension, gripping, and bracing. These reactions could predict the memory will contain a fair amount of hyperarousal. Other memories can restore vitality, joy, and congruency.
2. Choose one memory to share. Speak about it, taking time to observe how it feels in your body to talk about it. Explore nonverbal processing with another or a group. Observe the silent affective witness of the others; slowly take in the nonverbal caring from the group.
3. Each person should take turns sharing a memory and should identify for themselves the memories that need further exploration, regulation, and integration.

Exercise 11.4: The Phenomenological Encounter Process

In this exercise, you will explore your own subjective experience and develop the skill to perceive the invisible subjective experience of another— an important part of receptive somatic empathy. This exercise can help you assume a "beginners mind" with another; experience the dissociated inner subjective world of another; maintain the humility to be surprised by another; increase your skills to uncover your own troubling subjective feelings including fear, shame, and hatred; and enhance your ability to process difficult feelings with vulnerability in conflicted relationships. It is best conducted with a small group of peers where trust, transparency, and confidentiality are well established.

1. Reflect on a difficult or incomplete experience that occurred in relationship (either personally or professionally) during your ordinary day. Cues to identify unprocessed experiences are blaming another, a personal sense of shame or guilt, or obsessing over alternate ways you might have managed a situation.
2. In a journal, recall the encounter in present tense, moment-to-moment language—write about as if it is happening now from your perspective. Write a paragraph that includes an unfolding of the encounter in the moment with accompanying bodily-based sensations.
3. Now enter into *what you assume* is the bodily-based subjective experience from the perspective of the other person and describe the same encounter in writing. This is your current sense of the other's subjective experience—what happened, how it happened, and how it felt for the other.
4. Next describe differences and similarities in the two subjective descriptions, a process that can reveal something new in the relationship.
5. Describe your written reflection-in-action to your colleagues. Discuss what you learned about your own inner subjective world and that of the person you encountered. Your peer group does not offer opinions—their job is to listen and affirm the development of your somatic empathy.

    Note: The group reflection must be conducted with transparency, honesty, and confidentiality. Any fear of judgment, criticism, or competition disrupts the development of receptive somatic empathy. Listeners are asked to provide a receptive presence for the speaker to reveal and wonder without explaining, justifying, or withholding. This exercise can help the unseen transference, countertransference, and enactments to unwind from the body.

6. As a follow-up, consider bringing the fruits of your reflection to the person you wrote about in your dialogue. Your conversation may go something like this:

    Helper: "Mary, I was wondering about our conversation last week about your son. I imagined that I might not have felt how painful it is for you to not live with him."

Mary: "Well, I think you are trying, but yeah, I don't think you know how much I do love him!"

Helper: "Mary, I think you're right. I would really like to feel how much you do love him and what it is like for you when he says that he wants to live with his father."

In this moment, the helper can bring somatic empathy to the expression on Mary's face, her body posture, her eyes, gestures, and voice while attending to the sensations in her own body. The somatic empathy of the practitioner can awaken the shared perception of pain embedded in love, and then oscillate the two for a more complex integration of lived experience.

Index

Note: Page numbers in *italics* indicate figures.